Marketplace Best Practices

Transforming Commerce in the Platform Economy

By TOM MCFAD

MCFADYEN

D I G I T A L

ECOMMERCE + MARKETPLACES

Marketplace Best Practices
Transforming Commerce in the Platform Economy
by Tom McFadyen

Published by:

McFadyen Digital
8229 Boone Blvd. Suite 820,
Vienna, VA 22182
703.226.3800
info@mcfadyen.com
www.mcfadyen.com

ISBN 9798597910260

For the many clients who trusted McFadyen Digital as an advisor, implementer, and enabler of their marketplace transformation journey

Table of Contents

Preface

Disruptive innovation can hurt, if you are not the one doing the disrupting.

Clay Christensen, Academic & Author, The Innovator's Dilemma

Introduction

Over 50% of eCommerce happens on marketplaces—and not just on Amazon or Alibaba. Dozens of other marketplaces each sell over a billion dollars of gross merchandise value (GMV) annually, while thousands of additional product and service marketplaces are seeing rapid growth. Whether a company plans to operate their own marketplace, sell on somebody else's marketplace, or compete against other marketplaces, they need a marketplace strategy.

Two decades ago, eCommerce started disrupting brick-and-mortar retail. One decade ago, marketplaces started disrupting eCommerce and became a major driver of the retail apocalypse. B2B distributors have also lost tens of billions of dollars of annual sales to marketplaces.

eCommerce has not changed substantially in the quarter century since secure credit card processing was enabled via SSL (Secure Sockets Layer). For the first 15 years, most eCommerce operators could easily be more profitable than their brick-and-mortar counterparts. But the marketplace platform model has proven to be far more profitable and scalable than the old linear pipeline model of eCommerce.

Outsourcing much of the traditional eCommerce responsibility to third-party sellers enables asset-light marketplace operators to offer more, sell more, and learn more while generating higher margins. They scale more quickly, minimize expenses, increase agility, and create a more robust supply chain. Jeff Bezos used the "flywheel effect" phrase to describe the virtuous cycle of marketplaces that continue building upon their success as they gain more sellers, products, sales, data, and customer satisfaction.

The platform economy has enabled young marketplace companies that are just a decade old to displace century-old companies. For example, in about a decade the Airbnb marketplace has grown to offer far more lodging rooms than all US hotel chains combined (Marriott, Hilton, Hyatt, etc.). In the retail domain, compare Amazon to the fate of century-old retail stalwarts like Sears, Lord & Taylor, Hechts, etc.

This transformation is affecting both B2C and B2B organizations. If a major B2B brand is not selling their products on a marketplace, it is likely that somebody else is (either an official partner or a grey market seller). B2B distributors and manufacturers need a marketplace strategy for both offense and defense. A distributor that has to physically stock all goods it sells simply cannot scale as fast as one with a flexible network of third-party sellers. As marketplaces become the preferred customer shopping destination, many are selling private-label products and displacing name-brand manufacturers.

Marketplaces are enabling new business models beyond traditional B2C and B2B. C2C (Consumer-to-Consumer) and C2B (Consumer/Contributor-to-Business) marketplaces are enabling the "gig economy." In C2C marketplaces like Uber, TaskRabbit, and Etsy, individuals sell their services (or goods) to other consumers. C2B marketplaces like Fiverr and Shutterstock allow individuals sell to businesses.

Marketplaces are disrupting and creating new business models in the commerce value chain. This book helps the reader be the disruptor, not the disrupted.

Book Organization

This book was written to provide an understanding of the *what*, *who*, and *how* of marketplaces. Chapters are organized into three major segments:

What is a marketplace? (fundamentals, economics, models)

Who operates a marketplace? (case studies)

How to operate a marketplace? (platforms, people, partners, processes)

While the bulk of the content is in the *How* segment, to be successful it is important to understand the fundamentals of marketplaces (*what*) and learn from successful case studies (*who*) in order to make an impact.

Qualifications of the Author

Since founding McFadyen Digital over thirty years ago, Tom McFadyen has built the team to several hundred employees across North America, South America, and Asia. He is a frequent speaker at IRCE, NRF, and Shop.org, and he holds board and council positions at NRF, YPO, and the Oracle Commerce User Group.

This book is based on 15 years of experience designing and building dozens of enterprise-scale marketplaces that cumulatively generate billions of dollars of GMV. McFadyen Digital has supported many clients from initial strategy definition to marketplace design and implementation to long-term support and growth.

Our experience includes both B2C and B2B clients, as well as marketplaces for products and services. Many of the solutions we have built have scaled to over a million products or SKUs. We have built marketplaces from scratch, and we have leveraged commercial marketplace platforms as a starting point. Many of these marketplaces are internationalized, global solutions deployed to a multitude of countries, languages, currencies, payment processors, tax calculators, fulfilment systems, etc.

McFadyen Digital employs over a hundred marketplace experts, many of whom shared their hands-on experience in the writing of this book. Our challenge was not creating sufficient content, but instead trimming it down to fit into a reasonably sized business book. Many of the chapter topics—

Amazon, user experience, marketing, CRO, data, metrics—could fill a book by themselves.

What we are most proud of is that our clients have received awards for the great marketplace solutions that we have collaboratively designed and launched. Many clients have also presented their success stories at a dozen national and international conferences before thousands of attendees.

More information about McFadyen Digital is available at the end of the book and at www.mcfadyen.com. The website also contains many frequently updated white papers on the rapidly changing marketplace trends. For the latest marketplace updates, subscribe to our newsletter at www.mcfadyen.com/blog.

An annual report on the evolving marketplace platform vendor landscape is available in the "Marketplace Suite Spot" report. To read the most recent assessment of platform vendors visit http://www.marketplace-suite-spot.com/.

Section I: What is a Marketplace?

Chapter 1: Platform Economy

No matter who you are or what you do for a living, it's highly likely that platforms have already changed your life as an employee, a business leader, a professional, a consumer, or a citizen.

Geoffrey G. Parker, Marshall W. Van Alstyne, Sangeet Paul Choudary,

authors of *Platform Revolution*

Introduction

The most impactful companies of the past decade have been platforms: Airbnb, Alibaba, Alphabet (Google), Amazon, Apple, and many more that do not start with the letter "A."

Platform businesses have transformed entire industries: Amazon vs. retail, Airbnb vs. hotels, Apple vs. record companies, Uber vs. taxis, Instacart vs. grocers, DoorDash vs. restaurants, Craigslist vs. newspaper classifieds, etc. In just a decade, many of these newly formed platform companies unseated century-old incumbents as leaders in their categories.

Most unicorns (private start-up companies worth over $1 billion) are platforms. They are asset-light, so some can grow at 300% to 500% annually. On the other end of the spectrum, the seven most valuable public companies (Apple, Microsoft, Alphabet, Amazon, Facebook, Alibaba, and Tencent) are all platform businesses and also are growing rapidly. A decade ago only one of these public companies (Microsoft) was on the top ten list.

Marketplaces are a type of platform that promotes and enables transactions between multiple parties, such as a customer and a third-party seller. Marketplaces generally do not fulfill the products or services purchased. Marketplaces generally charge fees for enabling the transaction.

Many platforms are selling services (car rides, lodging, food delivery) not just products like traditional retailers. Services platforms have enabled an estimated 75 million American "gig workers" to earn a living without standard full-time employment. For example, roughly 1% of American household income comes from ridesharing platforms (Uber, Lyft, etc.), according to the Federal Reserve.

Platforms selling digital goods have also become very profitable. For example, the Apple App Store and the Google Play store respectively sell $60 billion and $30 billion in digital goods and earn roughly a 30% commission on each sale. That equals $20 billion and $10 billion in profit from enabling others to sell on their platform.

The **monetization** of some platforms may not be as visible as that of eCommerce marketplaces. For example, although most users of Facebook, Twitter, YouTube, LinkedIn, WhatsApp, etc. do not pay for those services, those platforms collect vast amounts of data and profit from very lucrative advertising revenue. The focus of this book is marketplaces which are platforms based on a clear system of payment (monetization) for goods or services.

Platforms have transformed how suppliers and consumers interact. A decade ago, before Uber, Airbnb, and DoorDash became popular, who would have felt comfortable getting into a stranger's car to go stay in another stranger's home, and then eating a meal prepared and delivered by other strangers?

1.1 The Platform Revolution

In 2016 the ground-breaking book *Platform Revolution: How Networked Markets are Transforming the Economy—And How to Make Them Work for You* defined the fundamentals of platform businesses and how they are transforming the world. The three authors, Geoffrey G. Parker, Marshall W. Van Alstyne, and Sangeet Paul Choudary, continue their thought leadership in association with the MIT Initiative on the Digital Economy (IDE). Further details on the concepts presented in this chapter are available in their book.

This book was a milestone in documenting how the platform economy is disrupting many legacy industries. Venture capital firms began focusing investments on platform business startups. The word *platform* started being used as a verb as business executives began asking how they can "platform their business." Phrases like "the platformization of ..." introduced new buzzwords. Investors often say, "Platforms beat products."

According to Parker, Van Alstyne, and Choudary, a platform includes these characteristics:

- It is a nexus of rules and architecture.
- It is open, allowing regulated participation.
- It actively promotes (positive) interactions among different partners in a multi-sided market.
- It scales much faster than a pipeline business because it does not necessarily bear the costs of external production.

Platforms are matchmakers that facilitate the exchange of goods, services, or social currency which enables value creation for all participants. This accelerates growth by leveraging the assets or services of others.

Andreessen Horowitz, one of the venture capital firms focused on platform businesses, offers this definition:

A Platform is a network of users and developers; the multi-sided feedback loop between those users, developers, and the platform itself creates a flywheel effect increasing value for each of those groups. It can also be thought of as a network that can be programmed, customized, and extended by outside users—it often meets needs and creates niches not defined by its original developers at the outset.

1.2 Pipeline v. Platform

It may be helpful to understand what a platform is not: a **pipeline**. Platform models eliminate many of the constraints of pipeline business models.

Traditional eCommerce businesses are pipeline businesses. Through a labor-intensive sequence of activities, they must source each product, negotiate contracts with each vendor, negotiate a price for each product, merchandise each product (write marketing text), acquire images (often their own photography), set prices, order inventory, hold inventory, fulfill orders, provide customer support, and receive returns. This linear pipeline shown below limits business agility, scalability, and profitability.

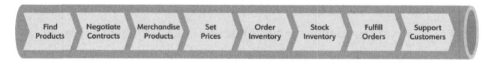

FIGURE 1.1 Example sequential events in a legacy eCommerce pipeline

Unlike traditional eCommerce businesses (pipelines), marketplace platforms do not need to source, merchandise, and physically hold and ship merchandise. Most aspects of traditional eCommerce activities are outsourced to third parties, which enables the marketplace to scale much faster. The third-party sellers operate independently and in parallel performing these activities.

In a platform, the value creation (a.k.a. production) happens outside the pipe. For example, lodging happens outside Airbnb, tweets are not produced by Twitter staff, videos are not produced by YouTube employees, most iOS apps are not created by Apple, and most products sold on Amazon are from third-party sellers.

A platform curates and facilitates instead of producing. This enables platforms to be asset light. For example, Airbnb simply connects people who need a room with people who can offer a room. They do not need to build hotels like Hyatt, Hilton, and Marriott. Uber and DoorDash do not need to buy cars. Pinterest does not need to hire photographers. Spotify does not need to produce music. OpenTable does not need to prepare meals.

Platform Revolution uses the term "inverted firm" to describe the benefits of the asset-light nature of platforms. The main approach for traditional pipeline firms to scale is to add more internal resources, like employees, machines, and capital. The main approach for platform firms to scale is to add more external resources, such as drivers, apartments for rent, and third-party sellers. Platform businesses can scale faster since they require far fewer employees and expensive assets than their pipeline competitors.

Orchestration is prioritized over production and requires less closed vertical integration within one firm. The focus on value creation shifts efforts to resources outside the firm. This is a transition from the trend of **disintermediation** and vertical integration to **reintermediation** and market aggregation.

Platforms enable interactions that exchange value units—goods, information, services, money, etc. This enables value creation outside the firm. As a platform grows, it adds more interactions between parties and broadens network connections.

Early competition for eCommerce success was won by the most efficient pipeline beating the less efficient pipeline. Now it is the platforms, like Amazon, beating the pipelines, like brick-and-mortar retail, due to better marginal economics and value produced by **network effects**. Quality control costs can also be reduced with community-driven **curation** (Amazon or Uber user ratings & reviews).

The platform shift can also be tracked in three stages of focus:

1. from resource control to resource orchestration

2. from internal optimization to external interaction

3. from focus on customer value to focus on ecosystem value.

1.3 Network Effect

The network effect is an important platform aspect that enables rapid scalability, efficiency, value creation, and competitive advantage.

A network can be a group of interconnected people (social network), a system of things (computers and printers), a collection of sellers and buyers, or other sets of relationships.

Platform Revolution uses a telephone network as an example and WhatsApp users are a modern equivalent. Two telephones only enable one connection, but five phones enable ten connections. A dozen phones enable 66 connections. The growth of connections is exponential, not linear. Imagine how many connections are possible between the billions of Facebook users.

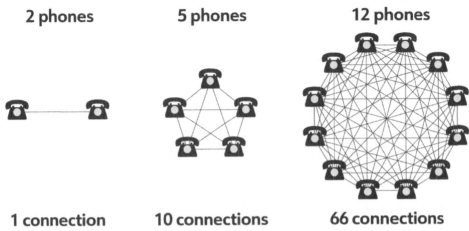

FIGURE 1.2 Telephone Example of Network Effects. Source: Platform Revolution.

A network effect occurs when a product or service becomes more valuable to its users as more people use it. As networks grow, this effect helps build a virtual moat around a platform business that makes it harder for competitors to enter their market. For example, the vast number of Airbnb consumers and hosts makes it difficult for a new entrant to compete in the lodging marketplace. Amazon's network of over a hundred FBA distribution centers provides a similar defensible moat.

The telephone, WhatsApp, and Facebook user examples are homogenous networks: all nodes are the same. Heterogeneous networks match different types of nodes. For example, eCommerce marketplaces have sellers and buyers. The full Facebook ecosystem includes users and advertisers (business customers). Uber has drivers and passengers. Heterogeneous networks are also called two-sided or multi-sided networks. Instacart is an example of a four-sided platform that connects consumers, grocers, personal shoppers/drivers, and **CPG** brands, like Coke and PepsiCo.

Successful platforms focus outside the firm (not internally) to scale the network effect. A solid community-building strategy is a valuable asset for growth. For example, Houzz focused on building a strong community with quality **user-generated content** before starting heavy monetization via home remodeling contractors and merchandise vendors. Successful heterogeneous platforms coordinate a harmonious ecosystem of different types of participants. Platforms must enable the ecosystem in which they operate.

Network connections can be unidirectional or bidirectional. For example, a LinkedIn connection is bidirectional (each person has equal access to the other), whereas a follower is unidirectional (different rights for each person). In some cases, a single user may fall on both sides of the equation, such as an Airbnb user could be both host and guest.

Heterogeneous networks and those with unidirectional relationships are presented with the chicken or egg question: Which should be the priority? Should a marketplace spend more energy finding sellers or finding buyers? The answer often varies by industry, stage of maturity, and other factors.

Generally, there is a critical mass inflection point at which the network effect kicks in and helps build a defensible market position. The network effect compounds the inverted firm efficiency as the platform user count grows. Rapid user-base expansion is also often referred to as going viral.

1.4 Flywheel Effect

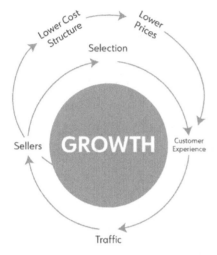

FIGURE 1.3 The Amazon
Virtuous Cycle Flywheel Effect

As the network effect builds, a platform will benefit from the virtuous cycle of the flywheel effect. Jim Collins coined the term "flywheel effect" in his 2001 book *Good to Great: Why Some Companies Make the Leap and Others Don't*. He explained the concept to Jeff Bezos, who built on the analogy at Amazon. As the marketplace flywheel momentum builds, it creates a virtuous cycle that increases the number of sellers, which increases the selection of products available, which improves customer experience, which drives more traffic, which drives more sellers, etc. Another beneficial factor in this cycle is reducing cost structures, which lowers prices, which improves the customer experience, etc.

This self-enhancing cycle is more efficient than the legacy pipeline model of investing in marketing, then investing in sales efforts, and then getting customers. Scaling the linear pipeline approach generally requires an investment proportional to the results. In other words, marketing and sales investments have to double sales. Platform business does not require this level of investment to scale.

The virtuous cycle can be expanded to include additional virtuous elements of the marketplace flywheel. Additional stages include data collection and the positive impacts on physical store assortment and foot traffic for omnichannel merchants.

FIGURE 1.4 The McFadyen Digital expansion of the marketplace flywheel virtuous cycle

The eight stages of the expanded marketplace flywheel summarize three benefits at each stage:

1. **More products**

    a. Existing categories

    b. Adjacent categories

    c. Fast catalog expansion by nimble third-party sellers

2. **More customers**

    a. Better organic SEO to drive traffic

    b. Larger brand footprint

    c. Greater customer mindshare

3. **More sales**

    a. Fewer sales lost to out-of-stock

    b. **Cross-sell** & **upsell** capabilities

    c. Better alignment with customer expectations

4. **More profits**

    a. Reduced or no inventory and logistics

    b. Free organic **SEO** instead of paid **SEM**

    c. First-party v. third-party mix optimized for **margin**

5. **More sellers**

    a. More interest from third-party vendors

    b.   Faster and easier vendor onboarding

    c.   Seller competition improves value for customers

6. **More data**

    a.   Gain insights from marketplace activity

    b.   Identify market trends before competitors

    c.   Automate seller management and UX based on data

7. **More store assortment**

    a.   Bring top sellers into physical stores

    b.   Move low margin products to the marketplace

    c.   Offer third-party products in-store via kiosk, QR codes, etc.

8. **More store foot traffic**

    a.   Buy online pick up in-store (**BOPIS**)

    b.   Buy online return in-store (**BORIS**)

    c.   Optimize in-store inventory

Platforms have access to large volumes of data which further accelerates the flywheel. There has also been a surge in the tools available to manage large volumes of data. With better tools, the data can be converted into insights and intelligence. Successful platforms build and manage a common data layer.

1.5 Are Platforms Too Powerful?

Is Amazon responsible for the retail apocalypse that has caused the decline or bankruptcy of hundreds of retailers? Is it unfair for Apple to charge $20 billion of fees to let applications be downloaded from their App Store? Should Twitter and Facebook be able to block the main communication channels of the US president? Did DoorDash and Uber Eats charge egregious fees to restaurants during the pandemic? Does it make sense for 43% of all venture capital raised to be spent on Facebook and Google Ads (source: Clearbanc 2020)? What are the risks of Alexa, Siri, and Google

Home listening in on so many conversations with their growing AI capabilities?

Should George Orwell's '1984' book have been titled '2020' with big tech as the omnipresent overlord?

There are many reasonable claims that platforms have become too powerful. Justifications include limiting competition, controlling narratives, restricting privacy, undue influence, and self-promotion.

Counterpoints can be posed for the platforms. Amazon's Small Business Report states they helped small businesses sell 3.4 billion items in 2020 including enabling a half million small sellers with FBA services. The Apple App store delivers $40 billion in net revenue to businesses, many of whom would not have other distribution channels (Google Play Store has the same 30% fee). Twitter and Facebook have enabled billions of people to connect and provide an avenue for free speech. Many more restaurants would have been shuttered during the pandemic had it not been for delivery service marketplaces.

It is difficult to say that these big tech firms are violating antitrust laws which require proof of causing consumers to pay higher prices. Most complaints from retailers are that they can't compete against Amazon's low prices. Amazon certainly has undercut competitors, but is this truly predatory pricing when most prices are set by third party sellers? Amazon may control a majority of US ecommerce sales, but they claim they represent less than 10% of US retail sales so they are therefore not a monopoly.

The case of Big Tech platforms versus the government will be unfolding over the coming years. In 2020 Capitol Hill called CEOs Jeff Bezos of Amazon, Tim Cook of Apple, Sundar Pichai of Google and Mark Zuckerberg of Facebook to testify on anti-competitive activities. China has begun an anti-monopoly probe into Alibaba whose marketplace controls the majority of Chinese ecommerce. The European Union has been proposing new regulations for big platforms.

While the top platform giants face government scrutiny, that should not dissuade other organizations from leveraging the platform model which helped them scale successfully.

Key Takeaways: Platform Economy

- Many start-ups, unicorns, and most of the largest fast-growing public companies leverage the platform model. Marketplaces are one form of platform.

- Most legacy businesses rely on a pipeline model of sequential activities performed within the company. Conversely, the platform model outsources many of these activities (production) to multiple third parties that work in parallel. The platform efficiently connects producers and consumers.

- The network effect is a critical element of the exponential growth of platforms. Much like telephones, the more nodes (e.g. sellers and buyers) on a network the more valuable it is.

- A platform is a combination of rules and an open infrastructure that enables value-creating interactions between external producers & consumers.

- Jim Collins and Jeff Bezos used the flywheel concept to show how continuous small improvements build momentum. This growth powers a competitive differentiator that builds a defensible moat around a busines.

Chapter 2: Marketplace Maturity Model (MMM)

If I have seen further than others, it is because I was standing on the shoulders of giants.

Sir Isaac Newton

Introduction

The Marketplace Maturity Model[SM] (MMM) is the industry standard for assessing and planning the capabilities of a marketplace. Like the Capability Maturity Model Integration (CMMI), the Marketplace Maturity Model consists of five stages of digital commerce. This objective framework guides marketplace operators through consistent iterative scaling.

MARKETPLACE MATURITY MODEL

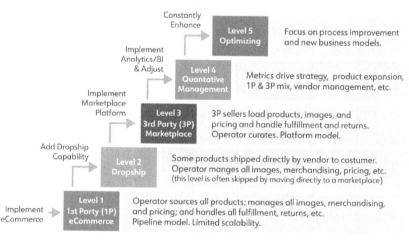

FIGURE 2.1 The Marketplace Maturity Model

The five stages of the marketplace maturity model are:

Stage 1: First-Party (1P) eCommerce

The site operator sources all products; manages all images, merchandising, pricing, etc.; and handles all fulfillment and returns. First-party eCommerce operates in a linear pipeline model which limits scalability and profitability.

Stage 2: Dropship

Some products are shipped directly from a third-party vendor to the customer. The site operator still has to manage all images, merchandising, pricing, etc. This phase is sometimes skipped, moving directly from Stage 1 to Stage 3.

Stage 3: Third-Party (3P) Marketplace

At this stage, the platform model focuses on connecting third-party sellers with buyers for a commission. Third-party sellers are added en masse. The sellers load products, images, merchandising, and pricing, and handle fulfillment and returns. The site operator can curate categories and products.

Stage 4: Quantitative Management

At this stage, the site manager has an operating and growing marketplace and uses metrics to drive strategy, product expansion, sourcing, store inventory, vendor management, etc.

Stage 5: Optimizing

The thriving marketplace runs with well-defined processes and metrics while the site operator focuses on process improvements by fine-tuning elements such as functionality enhancements, vendor promotions, financial automation, onboarding automation, etc.

The Marketplace Maturity Model is based on a decade of experience creating marketplace solutions plus detailed assessments of dozens of other marketplaces. This chapter will discuss the characteristics and challenges of each level and provide examples of these levels at work. Additionally, these levels will be examined in terms of strategy, technical considerations, and business models to highlight necessary enablement steps described in Chapter 28 Marketplace Enablement Steps (MES).

2.1 Maturity Level 1: First-Party eCommerce

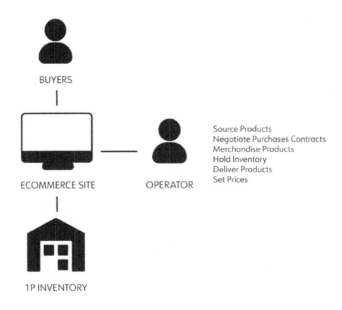

FIGURE 2.2 Maturity Level 1

Characteristics

Web eCommerce began in the mid-1990s (with the introduction of **SSL**) at Marketplace Maturity Level 1 with operators selling their own first-party (1P) goods. The vast majority of today's eCommerce sites still operate at Level 1.

In a 1P marketplace, the operator is responsible for sourcing all products and overseeing all aspects of the eCommerce business. This includes catalog merchandising, pricing, sourcing products, negotiating supplier contracts, warehousing, fulfillment, returns processing, customer support, carrying the financial cost of inventory, and many other activities.

Challenges

Of the current 1.3 million US eCommerce sites, 85% are only long tail (meaning a specialized niche catalog), and 50% ship less than 100 items per month. There are substantial capital and operating costs to expand to a catalog, so the investment must be justified by enlarging enough to attract sufficient customers. Many cannot afford to build (or outsource) the warehousing and fulfillment capabilities, nor carry the cost of large quantities of inventory.

In addition to the material costs, there are labor costs associated with scaling a Level 1 marketplace. Sourcing products, negotiating contracts, merchandising products, and related marketing can be very labor-intensive.

Examples

Louis Vuitton is the world's most valuable luxury brand and a major division of LVMH. Its products include leather goods, handbags, trunks, shoes, watches, jewelry, and accessories. And its profit margins generally rest north of 30%. The business model of Louis Vuitton fits well in the 1P eCommerce model. Exclusivity is a key element of their brand, and they do not want to dilute that image with lesser brands on their website.

NIKE, Inc., based near Beaverton, Oregon, is the world's leading designer, marketer, and distributor of authentic athletic footwear, apparel, equipment, and accessories for a wide variety of sports and fitness activities. Nike credits its Nike Customer Experience (NCX) platform as driving virtually 100% of growth in 2018. The cornerstone of the Triple Double Strategy is the Nike Consumer Experience (NCX), which includes Nike's own **direct-to-consumer** network, as well as a vastly streamlined slate of wholesale distribution partners. It is through the NCX that the company is feeding its 2X Innovation and 2X Speed initiatives.

Strategy

While most major retailers are already on their third-, fourth-, or fifth-generation eCommerce platform, many B2B organizations and some retail industries, such as grocery, have been slower to implement eCommerce and may be on their first- or second-generation platform. Those early-stage platform migrations or upgrades improved the first-party sales, but most have not yet added 3P marketplace capability.

Business strategy will drive eCommerce platform selection and the roadmap to technology implementation. Critical factors include the target market (e.g. apparel, hard goods, digital goods, perishables), catalog complexity (total items, many product-to-SKU variants, configurable products), B2C/B2B/B2B2C, subscriptions, unique requirements, budget, etc. Proper governance keeps the project on track in terms of scope, functionality, budget, and timeline.

A complete marketing strategy drives customer acquisition, so operators must first understand their target audience to design an engaging customer experience (CX). Once the customer journey is carefully mapped, digital marketing strategies (and sometimes physical or print) can be crafted and platforms can be selected for SEM/SEO, **marketing automation**, retargeting, and other functions.

Technical

Most eCommerce technology implementation projects follow an agile methodology with limited waterfall phases at the beginning and end. An architecture phase (also called Sprint 0) sets the overall architecture, the initial product backlog (requirements) configures development, and Q/A environments establish dev-ops automation, etc.

The main development work is typically performed in 2- to 3-week sprints which include requirement elaboration, development, functional Q/A, and a sprint demo. A waterfall-style Q/A phase will occur before launch and include end-to-end (E2E) testing, load & performance (L&P) testing & tuning, user acceptance testing (UAT), and PCI compliance testing.

Multiple systems are usually integrated into the eCommerce platform, including **enterprise resource planning** (ERP), **product information**

management (PIM) (usually only for complex catalogs), **order management system** (OMS), **customer relationship management** (CRM), **payment gateways**, analytics / business intelligence (BI), social channels, point of sale (POS), etc.

Business

The CX must combine an appealing **user experience** (UX) front end with business logic on the back end. The UX will include aesthetic aspects defined in a style guide with tools (guided navigation, search, page design, checkout flow, etc.) designed to maximize conversion rate and **average order value** (AOV).

B2C business logic includes promotions, coupons, personalization, wish lists/gift registries, buy online pick up in-store (BOPIS), and dozens of other features. B2B eCommerce is usually a superset of B2C with added features like an organizational model & delegated administration, purchase limits, credit terms, cost centers, custom catalogs per customer, custom pricing per customer, purchase lists (recurring wish lists), and more.

2.2 Maturity Level 2: Dropship

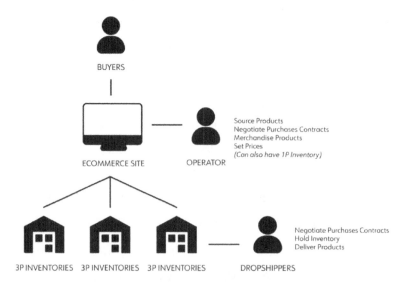

FIGURE 2.3 Maturity Level 2

Characteristics

Traditional drop shipping is a fulfillment method where a retailer does not stock the products it sells. Instead, when a site operator (B2C or B2B) sells a product, it purchases the item from a third party who then ships it directly to the customer. As a result, the merchant never sees or handles the product and does not need to purchase and hold that inventory. The site operator's online reputation relies heavily on the performance of the suppliers.

Some **dropship** vendors operate in a "white label" manner and will use packaging, invoices, bills of lading, and/or package inserts (e.g. catalogs) branded in the site operator's name.

Some eCommerce operators prefer to bundle or relabel products shipped from drop shippers and will use a practice of cross-docking. In this model, goods come in one dock at the operator's distribution center, are repackaged/relabeled/bundled, and sent out from another dock to the customer.

Challenges

Although dropship operations can increase product assortment and reduce inventory carrying costs, the processing overhead of establishing dropship vendors and loading their products limits the scalability of the dropship model. The site operator must still identify new vendors and products, negotiate costs and contracts, enter vendors and products into the ERP and/or PIM merchandise the products, set prices, and often handle customer support. Simply onboarding the new vendor may require one to two months, but in level 3 and higher marketplaces, all of those responsibilities are outsourced to the third-party seller.

The cross-dock technique adds the complexity of supply chain management (SCM) logistics, further shipping & labor costs, and increased risk of product damage.

Examples

W.W. Grainger is North America's leading broad line supplier of maintenance, repair, and operating products, with operations also in Europe, Asia, and Latin America. Grainger sells $6 billion worth of product online each year—more than half of its $10 billion total revenue.

Many of the 5 million products that Grainger sells are large, infrequently ordered, and require special shipping. These may include 1,000-gallon storage tanks or hazmat products. These products are ideal candidates for dropship delivery directly from one of the 10,000 manufacturers Grainger represents to the end customer.

Strategy

Since the effort of onboarding new dropship vendors and products can be onerous, it is important to choose the categories and vendors wisely. The cost to add vendors must be weighed against the profit potential. In maturity level 2 it is typically the operator selecting products, unlike level 3 when market forces (supply & demand) often drive product listings.

A strategy for **reverse logistics** (returns) must also be decided. If the shipment was white labeled as the operator's brand, will customers return to the operator's facilities or the drop shipper?

Technical

Some items are drop shipped because of their size, weight, or hazardous materials content. These factors affect shipping costs, shipping restrictions, and delivery timeframes, and may require scheduling a delivery time. Ideally, this business logic should be implemented on the website for real-time quoting. If the price of a drop shipped item will change frequently there may be a need to integrate pricing updates. The operator will have to adjust the price to their customer based on changes in the price from the drop shipper to the eCommerce operator.

Some third-party logistics providers can be integrated into an operator's eCommerce site. If cross-docking will be implemented there may be complex integrations into the OMS, WMS, and ERP.

Business

In the dropship model, it is typical to negotiate separate vendor contracts. Each vendor may have its own terms & conditions, product pricing, and shipping tables and costs. The website operator usually has to load the vendor and products into the ERP and PIM systems using a specific format. The operator then must merchandize the catalog with product descriptions and images and determine pricing. Customer satisfaction is dependent upon the delivery performance of the drop shipper, but that is rarely monitored by most operators.

2.3 Maturity Level 3: Third-Party Marketplace

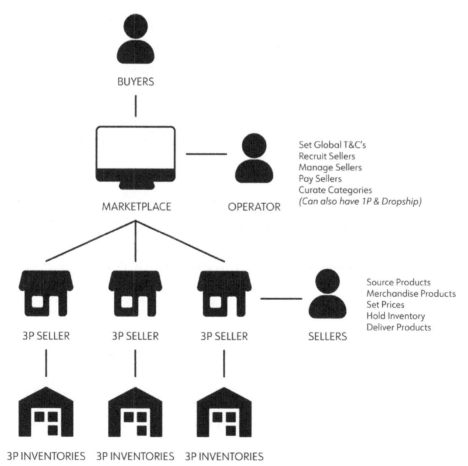

FIGURE 2.4 Maturity Level 3

Characteristics

Maturity level 3 is the typical target for most eCommerce operators implementing their first marketplace. A third-party marketplace leapfrogs the dropship level in terms of scalability and profitability. Most importantly, this level of maturity transforms the operator into a platform business. Marketplaces are platforms that enable third-party sellers to transact with buyers. As simple as that sentence is, there are critical strategy, technology, and business factors for success.

Platform businesses like Uber, Airbnb, and Fiverr have scaled quickly because the operator does not carry the costs of cars, hotels, or employees—the third parties do. The 3P marketplace operator sets terms and conditions for all sellers, recruits and manages sellers, pays sellers, and provides category and product curation. The third-party sellers find products, merchandise them, set prices, carry inventory, fulfill orders, and provide some customer support. The marketplace operator takes a commission typically ranging between 10% and 20% and dependent upon the category. New sellers can usually be onboarded in less than a week and new products within hours.

Marketplaces benefit from the network effect, much like social media and other networks. The more sellers and buyers, the more valuable the network. Some marketplaces, like eBay and PoshMark, carry no 1P inventory, but many (Walmart and Amazon) offer a combination of 1P and 3P products.

Examples

Urban Outfitters, Inc. is a lifestyle retail company offering omnichannel shopping with specialty brands like Urban Outfitters, Anthropologie, Free People, Terrain, and Bhldn. By improving customer experience, URBN prevented customers from navigating to competitor sites, like Amazon, and instead bolstered their revenue.

Carrefour is one of the largest hypermarket chains in the world, with 12,300 self-service shops in more than 30 countries, with Brazil as its second largest market. Instead of using marketplace sellers solely for adjacent product categories that complement the core business, Carrefour Brazil allows marketplace sellers to compete with its own products in core categories. In 2018, the company accelerated its marketplace strategy, adding 1,200 new sellers alongside more than 600,000 new active offers. This strategy has driven marketplace sales to account for 20% of their total eCommerce in Brazil.

Strategy

Transforming into a marketplace operator has great benefits but must also be done strategically. A common practice is to quickly launch a minimum viable product (MVP) marketplace to accelerate seller recruiting, marketing, and data collection. Generally, the more sellers and products, the more successful the marketplace.

Marketplace strategies can include offering an **endless aisle** or long-tail expanded catalog, minimizing stock-out conditions, testing new products, offering lower costs to your customers from competitive sellers, increasing cart size with cross-sell and up-sell items, offering third-party services, collecting data to identify 1P products or in-store inventory, improving site SEO, and many other approaches. The marketplace strategy will drive the selection of the categories and target sellers and the initial commission grid. Organizational planning should include headcount for marketplace manager, seller recruiters, seller support, and other staff.

Technical

For existing eCommerce organizations, the marketplace solution is usually integrated into the existing eCommerce platform. Otherwise, a new eCommerce platform (e.g. Magento, SAP CX/Hybris, and Oracle Commerce) may be implemented at the same time as the marketplace technology (e.g. Mirakl).

The catalog taxonomy is a critical foundation for the integration and must align with existing catalogs and future business strategy. Some integrations will be unique to marketplaces. For example, tax is calculated on the nexus of the third-party seller and the customer. For 1P, sales tax is based on the operator's nexus.

Business

Tactical business decisions and operations should follow the strategy. The user experience design is an example: for products with offers from multiple sellers, which seller will win the buy box? Lowest price, lowest price + shipping + tax, best seller rating, fastest shipping time, most inventory?

Seller terms & conditions should be clearly defined and accommodate various scenarios. Seller recruiting must be an active process, with support for seller onboarding.

2.4 Maturity Level 4: Quantitative Management

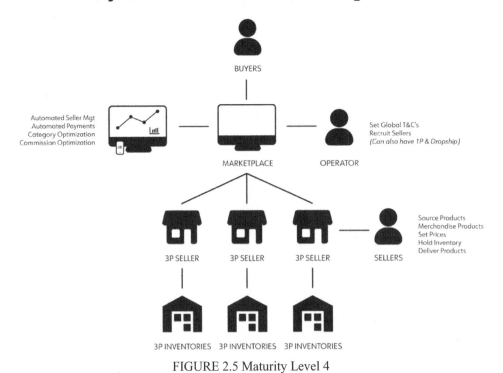

FIGURE 2.5 Maturity Level 4

Section I: WHAT

Characteristics

Marketplaces bring great scale, and with great scale, manual processes must be replaced with metrics-driven management (both manual and automatic). The processes used to manage ten thousand SKUs will not work for one hundred thousand SKUs or one million SKUs. Likewise, managing ten sellers is very different from managing one thousand sellers.

Without quantitative management and automation, the network effect of exponential value can also bring exponential complexity. Understanding and tracking the key performance indicators (KPIs) on marketplaces will provide guard rails for daily operations and set targets for optimization.

A simple marketplace example is the customer-generated star rating of drivers on Uber, homes on Airbnb, and workers on Fiverr. Those marketplace platforms automate the management of those sellers based on that data.

Automation of the seller management, payments, commissions, etc. reduces the headcount required to operate the marketplace and the speed with which optimizations can be made.

Many organizations collect data but do not take the next steps to understand what the data means, predict the effect of different changes, get recommendations on corrections, or ultimately to automate the changes.

DATA	INSIGHTS	PREDICTIVE	PRESCRIPTIVE	AUTOMATION
Here is what happened	Here is what it means	Here is what you could do	Here is what you should do	Here is what the system did

FIGURE 2.6

Examples

Albertsons Companies is an American grocery company with over 2,200 stores operating under twenty brands with 250,000 employees. The company is the second-largest supermarket chain in North America. Albertsons has launched an online marketplace that provides a venue for third-party vendors to sell directly to its customers. The Albertsons digital marketplace (www.MoreForU.com) offers more than forty thousand specialty food and non-food products. The virtual store focuses on natural, organic, ethnic, and alternative products, including hard-to-find items such as spices and condiments, specific flavors of coffee, and unique health and beauty aids. The Albertsons.com Marketplace will carry more than one hundred thousand products by early 2019.

Strategy

The simplified formula for eCommerce sales is:

Traffic x Conversion x AOV = Revenue

Substantial data is usually available in eCommerce platforms, external web analytics tools, back-end systems, and third-party systems like DMP. If needed, more data can be logged, but the challenge is usually converting data into meaningful insights and then into prescriptive recommendations (ideally automated).

At scale, metric-driven automation optimizes performance. For example, increasing seller commission by 1% if they exceed a 4.5-star customer rating will focus seller efforts on customer satisfaction. Automatically suspending sellers whose rating falls below three stars also improves customer experience. Data such as seller rating, inventory levels, price, shipping time, and the like can be used to determine which seller offer wins the buy box.

Technical

Data must be extracted, transformed, and loaded (ETL) into a reporting platform. An existing data warehouse (DW) and/or business intelligence (BI) tool can be used. There are also usually lightweight tools within eCommerce platforms for creating and viewing simple reports.

Vendor incentives and penalties, recommended products, buy box logic, incident escalation, and other logic can also be automated based on metrics. In more sophisticated systems, machine learning (ML) or artificial intelligence (AI) systems help process large volumes of data.

Other data interchange is also often automated in maturity level 4, such as seller onboarding, vendor payments, tax reporting, accounting reconciliation, and escrow management. Product curation can also be automated with image size constraints (minimum and maximum image dimensions), word restrictions (profanity or products like tobacco), trademark infringements, etc.

Business

The marketplace manager should be reviewing the performance of categories, products, return rates, sellers, and other metrics.

Insights on fast-moving 3P products could highlight potential sourcing for 1P products online, stocked in physical stores, or even private labeling. Likewise, insights on slow-moving or unprofitable 1P products could drive outsourcing them to 3P sellers.

2.5 Maturity Level 5: Optimizing

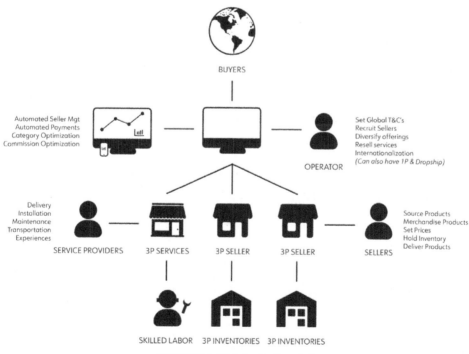

FIGURE 2.7 Maturity Level 5

Characteristics

"What's dangerous is to not evolve," states Jeff Bezos. Even as a dominant marketplace leader, Amazon is always testing and optimizing every aspect of its business.

For example, Amazon (and other product-only marketplaces) added a marketplace for services related to the products they sell. Likewise, IKEA acquired TaskRabbit, a services marketplace platform that connects gig economy workers with buyers looking for somebody to perform specific tasks (like assembling furniture).

Some marketplaces are a platform for more than just two parties (product buyers and sellers). For example, Instacart is a four-sided marketplace platform that enables transactions between grocery stores, customers, personal shoppers, and food brands promoting their products.

Examples

Best Buy is Canada's largest **omnichannel retailer**, with fifty million customers and over a quarter billion website visits per year. The scalability and insights from their marketplace have grown the business in many unexpected directions. For example, they have become the leading retailer of camping supplies and baby goods in Canada based on products from third-party sellers. The marketplace has been a very profitable business investment and is continuously being optimized.

Walmart Inc. is a $500 billion retailer, with nearly 250 million customers visiting more than 11,200 stores under fifty-five banners in twenty-seven countries. Walmart US launched its own marketplace in 2009 and also acquired Jet.com in 2016. Walmart reports a 37% gross profit margin on its marketplace operations and total online revenue of $12 billion in 2017, growing at 44%.

The Jet.com marketplace launched in July 2015, but when Walmart acquired it in August 2016, it had already achieved an astonishing $3.3 billion valuation after only one year in operation. At that time, Jet.com had

15 million product listings, 200 million unique visitors, and a $1.2 billion GMV run rate. Despite already being a half-trillion-dollar elephant, Walmart continues to dance by constantly optimizing their marketplace and other retail operations with insight from marketplace data.

Because Amazon is arguably the global marketplace leader, Chapter 9 Horizontal Business Case Study – Amazon is devoted to a broader exploration of the topic.

Strategy

The optimizing level combines constant incremental improvements with major innovative transformations. Often the data insights from the level 4 maturity uncover trends and new business opportunities.

Strategies can include changing the business model. Product marketplaces can add services marketplaces. Services marketplaces can add experiences marketplaces, as Airbnb did. Marketplaces can expand internationally. Two-party marketplaces can add third or fourth parties similar to Instacart. Online-only marketplaces may opt to open physical stores. Omnichannel retailers may add marketplace ordering in-store. Products may also be borrowed instead of sold, as per sharing economy models like Tulerie's peer-to-peer clothes sharing marketplace. Brick-and-mortar stores like Kohl's happily accept Amazon marketplace returns to drive foot traffic in-store. Amazon and Walmart offer seller fulfillment services. These types of strategies can accelerate growth of the marketplace while protecting its advantage over the competition.

There are also dozens of levers to adjust for incremental optimization. These are not as transformative but are critical to success in a competitive market. The predictive metrics of level 4 inform which levers to move and by how much.

Technical

The technical aspects of optimization vary depending on the level of transformation and the area of optimization. More disruptive transformations might involve a major rewrite or evolution of the marketplace platform.

Business

The business operations will change according to the optimization strategy. One option for optimization or faster scaling is to outsource some marketplace operations. This business process outsourcing (BPO) can include ongoing seller recruiting, seller management, catalog quality control, ongoing seller onboarding, seller support services, and customer support. There is an ongoing focus on people management at this level whether it is the function of sourcing candidate sellers, monitoring sellers in different segments, or associate training for the respective seller support services and customer support services.

Key Takeaways: Marketplace Maturity Model

- The Marketplace Maturity Model (MMM) is a prescriptive model to start and grow an online marketplace.

- The MMM consists of 5 maturity stages:

  - First-Party (1P) eCommerce

  - Dropship

  - Third-Party (3P) eCommerce

  - Quantitatively Managed

  - Optimizing

- Each maturity stage contains several enablement steps across strategic, technical, and business concerns.

- The MMM can help organizations start a new marketplace site or mature an existing property.

Chapter 3: B2C v. B2B v. C2C v. C2B

There's not a single business model, and there's not a single type of electronic content. There are really a lot of opportunities and a lot of options and we just have to discover all of them.

Tim O'Reilly – American Author

Introduction

Businesses typically identified themselves as selling business-to-business (B2B) or business-to-customer (B2C), but platforms have enabled new models like consumer-to-consumer (C2C) and consumer-to-business (C2B). Users are more comfortable engaging via new digital channels based on their positive experiences from the mass adoption of eCommerce and the proliferation of always-connected mobile devices.

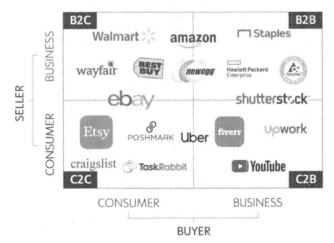

FIGURE 3.1 Examples of B2B, B2C, C2C, and C2B marketplaces

With the steady rise of people searching for products and services via eCommerce, businesses can now leverage content or sites they already have, create marketplaces around them, and allow people to do business with each other.

The table below shows typical characteristics of the four different business models. Of course, there are variations from these scenarios.

Factors	B2C	B2B	C2C	C2B
Sale Value (dollars)	Tens or Hundreds	Hundreds, thousands, or millions	Tens or Hundreds	Hundreds o thousands
Pricing	Fixed price	Fixed or negotiated	Negotiable market-based pricing	Negotiable
Sales Process Length	Minutes or Hours	Hours or days	Minutes or Hours	Hours or days
Decision makers involved	One or two	One	One, several or more	One or two
Buying process complexity	Relatively simple, typically credit card	Approval workflows, credit terms or other payment types	Simple, often P2P payment	Simple, typically credit card.
Delivery	One location	One or multiple locations	One location	One location
Buying process for providers	Multistep	More multistep	Single step	Multistep
Objective of Marketplace	Show a great variety of goods/ service Present the brands. Create condition for competition (more comfortable, reliable, and faster)	Suggest a solution for business Sell to big players Be the first in own niche	Present the good/ service Present own solution and UVP Create a community of customers	Low cost, Hassle free

Table 3.1 Typical Characteristics of B2C, B2B, C2C, and C2B Interactions

3.1 Business-to-Consumer (B2C)

B2C, or retail, is the most common marketplace model and allows businesses to sell to individual consumers. Large multi-vendor platforms also provide the customer with a single location for product selection and comparison shopping. Behemoths like Amazon, which sells hundreds of billions of dollars of third-party consumer products annually, and AliExpress, which averages over 732 million visits per month, have mastered the B2C model. Walmart, Wayfair, Newegg, Overstock, and hundreds of other marketplaces also sell B2C.

Retail ecommerce sales worldwide

2014 to 2021 by trillions of USD

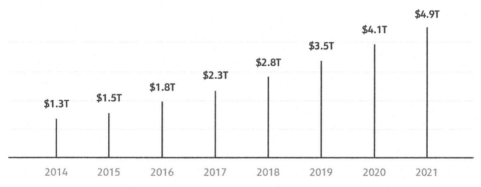

FIGURE 3.2 Source: Grand View Research & Statista

According to Grand View Research, the global B2C eCommerce market was at $3.5 trillion in 2019 and is expected to grow at CAGR of 7.9% from 2020 through 2027. Some of the key factors driving this growth are expanding internet penetration, rising disposable income, and global per capita income. The COVID pandemic has further aggravated the demand for online purchase through growing dependence on digital.

Key players in the global B2C marketplace include Amazon, Walmart, Alibaba Group, JD.com, Flipkart, and eBay. The global B2C market is relatively stable and highly competitive due to mergers and acquisitions. All the aforementioned companies continue to show tremendous growth and attract big investments. To expand their market share, B2C marketplaces are adopting strategies such as partnerships, business expansions, and new product developments.

Growth Drivers of B2C Marketplaces

Mobile apps lead the buyer easily to purchase. As people move away from physical workspaces to do more business on mobile devices, buyers appreciate the speed and convenience offered by an app. Additionally, when similar products are available on multiple platforms, buyers are more likely to purchase from the app already on their phone than the website they have to search for.

Big data enables better customer service. The challenge of eCommerce has always been providing a memorable customer experience without face-to-face interaction. Fortunately, AI and the resulting data collection have provided the solution. By tracking customer behaviors (searches, purchases, abandoned carts, etc.), businesses can understand the needs and preferences of individual customers and tailor campaigns to drive conversion rates.

3.2 Business-to-Business (B2B)

The B2B marketplace allows a business to sell products and services to another company that could use the product for its own operation or distribute to the end user. An example of a B2B marketplace platform would be a website selling computer components that a computer manufacturer will purchase to produce their own computer for the end consumer. B2B marketplaces foster a solid foundation for long term beneficial relationships between companies.

Some of the most recognizable B2B websites are Amazon Business and Alibaba, but niche examples include the following:

- **Healthcare** – Medinas, Vetcove, Zageno
- **Auto Parts** – PartCycle, CarParts.com

- **Manufacturing** – Asseta, Kinnek
- **Building Materials** – Brickhunter, GMEX
- **Real Estate** – Landscape Hub, Architizer
- **Fashion** – Joor, BOXFOX, Le New Black
- **Food** – FoodMaven, Full Harvest
- **Heavy Machinery** – BigRentz, IronPlanet
- **Freight** – Flexport, Uber Freight, uShip

Sales to or from governments are also often included in the B2B category but could technically be called B2G or G2B. Sometimes government equipment procurement happens on government-run marketplaces where companies offer their products and/or services. The government can also enable sales of goods like surplus farmer produce to businesses, sometimes subsidized for schools or non-profits.

With faster growth and larger market potential, the B2B eCommerce market is likely to grow at a higher rate when compared to B2C. McKinsey predicts that with the rising prosperity and participation of the emerging world, global flows of goods and services would more than double, reaching an estimated $54 trillion to $85 trillion by 2025.

As the B2B marketplace economy expands, operators will need to optimize the customer journey through powerful search capabilities, personalization (like product recommendations and retargeting), simplified purchase process (like one-click purchase), and efficient order processing and delivery. Maintaining the marketplace with current technologies and careful monitoring of KPIs and analytics will ensure the operator is aimed at growth.

The advantages of a B2B online marketplace include the following:

- Reach new customer segments and strengthen existing customer relationships.
- Identify and develop new revenue and distribution channels.
- Gain new data on product trends and B2B buyer expectations.

- Offer a wider range of products in a single location.
- Capture a share of D2C sales that might otherwise have gone to competitors.
- Build a high-quality supply chain by verifying and vetting suppliers online.
- Automate the sales process to provide better customer experience.
- Incorporate a unified multi-channel strategy across all touchpoints.

Growth Drivers of B2B Marketplaces

Millennials have arrived. Traditional B2B eCommerce now faces massive disruption as significant millennial talent enters the industry, many in decision making positions. A recent survey indicates B2B buyers are getting younger, and potentially 75% of B2B purchases could include a millennial decision-maker. For the generation that grew up with high-functioning tech at their fingertips, a smooth and efficient purchase process is more than an expectation—it is an assumption. Millennials now re-evaluate long-standing relationships and legacy processes in the B2B space.

Blazing fast order fulfillment is the standard. In the early days of online ordering, the catalog model for shipping was firmly established and product could be expected to arrive within a week at the earliest. By 2005, Amazon had established the 2-day shipping standard and forever raised the bar of customer expectation. Today, delays of even a few hours can mean the loss of sales, so B2B businesses looking to compete must invest in robust and reliable order fulfillment processes.

3.3 Consumer-to-Consumer (C2C)

While the transactions of other eCommerce models are generated by businesses, the C2C model, also called peer-to-peer (P2P), is a platform for private individuals to connect and transact. Sites like eBay and

Craigslist pioneered the online C2C marketplace in the mid-nineties, and this model has steadily expanded ever since.

SHARING ECONOMY

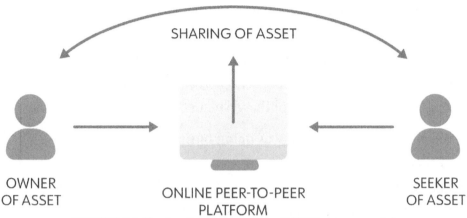

FIGURE 3.3 Sharing Economy subset of C2C business model

Most C2C product marketplaces involve the perpetual sale of a good. However, the sharing economy has seen the introduction of marketplaces to temporarily share the use of cars, clothing, and other items.

FIGURE 3.4 Sharing Economy

Today, C2C platforms cause significant disruption to traditional retail, rental, and professional services models. From transportation to accommodation, clothing to personal wealth management, shoppers no longer need to visit well-established brick and mortar players such as hotels, taxi companies, wardrobe rental businesses, or insurance companies. With a few clicks, interested parties can find a neighbor across town or a stranger across the country to fulfill their needs.

Growth Drivers of C2C Marketplaces

Trust is critical for a C2C marketplace. Individuals are drawn to explore C2C marketplaces by the ideas of supporting their neighbors and getting a great deal. However, safety becomes a significant concern when individuals are no longer protected by the laws that come with a business license. Successful C2C marketplaces protect the privacy of participants and provide a clear path for conflict resolution.

Transactions must be as easy as doing business on the large traditional platforms. Today's savvy shoppers appreciate saving a buck, but not at the expense of convenience. As the C2C landscape becomes increasingly competitive, better UX means faster growth.

Supply and demand must balance. Rather than studying sales patterns and manufacturing only the number of units that can be reasonably sold, C2C marketplaces must keep users engaged to ensure eCommerce continues to flow. Promotional codes and seasonal offers are simple ways to build customer loyalty.

3.4 Consumer-to-Business (C2B)

The consumer/contributor-to-business marketplace is the least common of all four models. By operating in the opposite direction of the traditional B2C model of retail sales, a C2B platform allows individual contributors to offer their goods and, more frequently, services to interested businesses for purchase or hire.

B2C MODEL

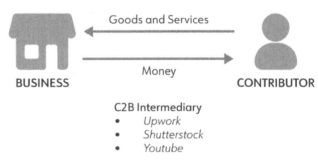

FIGURE 3.5 Traditional B2C vs C2B Model

And similar to C2C models, C2B marketplaces include 3 distinct participants: a consumer acting as the seller, a business acting as a buyer, and the intermediary business which owns the platform and ensures interactions are smooth and safe. Examples of popular C2B models would be iStock, which allows photographers to sell stock images to companies and collect royalties, or Fiverr, where freelancers can post their skills and services while businesses shop the various offerings in the way they would shop for office supplies.

Growth Drivers for C2B Marketplaces

The internet is bidirectional. Traditional media like TV and radio advertising travel one direction, and broadcast capability is typically limited to corporations who can afford the expense. Individuals selling goods or services historically have been limited by the marketing budget. However, today's internet offers a robust network of resources for anyone to deliver their message and connect with buyers.

Technology has become easy and affordable. As with any technology, everything from powerful computers to high-performing software was very expensive when first introduced to the market. But with time, new iterations, and lots of competition, prices have dropped drastically. Now the average consumer has easy access to the same top-notch tools as any corporation. In particular, content-based offerings like music or video are easy and inexpensive to produce, so platforms like YouTube have flourished.

3.5 Hybrid Marketplaces

Hybrid marketplaces most frequently combine B2B and B2C business models in a single location. In the way that Ford sells both family cars and fleet vehicles, many eCommerce sites provide services and products for individual users or business accounts. Amazon, of course, has taken the hybrid model significantly farther selling about $20 billion worth of B2B marketplace GMV. Beyond simply selling consumer goods to both private parties and businesses, Amazon also offers a host of business services like third-party selling and publishing.

FIGURE 3.6 Hybrid Marketplaces

Another type of hybrid marketplace that is gaining in popularity is the 3+ party marketplace, like Instacart. In this four-sided model, the marketplace hosts transactions between consumers, store owners, personal shoppers, and the brands directly.

Section I: WHAT

Growth Drivers of Hybrid Marketplaces

One marketplace is easier than two. In the public arena, marketing and communications can focus on a single brand, though distinct business and consumer audiences necessitate customized strategies. But the simplicity of hybrid marketplaces is most notable in the technical and back end operations. Site management, upgrades, changes, and even integrations all happen in a single location. All products are housed in one database with all warehousing and logistics chains operating on a unified system.

Business models are transforming faster. With the rising diversity of attractive customer segments and increased market volatility, the business models are aging faster than ever. This has necessitated business model innovation as a driver for generating value-creating growth. The hybrid marketplace businesses showcase the innovation at the business model level. These are either created by reinventing the customer-value proposition, which fundamentally disrupts the industry, or even finding adjacent businesses or markets to create a new core business model.

Business and consumer shoppers get the same easy buying experience. The internet has provided powerful tools for shoppers to research options and make buying decisions independent of in-person salesmen. And because online consumer shopping has been made so simple, business shoppers want the same experience. Having a single marketplace platform for all kinds of shoppers allows everyone to have the same pleasant experience regardless of the context in which they will use that purchased item.

Data and collaboration tools are highly available. Tracking the how, when, and why of customers using a marketplace can provide new prospects for innovative products, services, and corresponding business models. The opportunities created by that data study will provide better shopper experiences, identify new revenue sources, and draw more customers in.

Key Takeaways: B2C v. B2B v. C2C v. C2B

- While the first wave of marketplace growth was led by B2C and C2C, the next wave of growth will come from B2B and hybrid business models.

- As the gig economy and sharing economy gain popularity, opportunities in C2C and C2B models will increase.

- As millennials familiar with the B2C marketplace experience step into the business world, better user experiences will be expected of B2B marketplaces.

- Trust plays a critical role across all the types of marketplaces but especially for C2C and C2B models.

- More innovative marketplaces will be created in the future as business models change rapidly enabled by evolving technology and advanced collaboration tools.

Chapter 4: Marketplace Features

4.1 Operator Features
4.2 Seller Features
4.3 Customer Features
4.4 Other Characteristics

---

*Any damn fool can make something complex; it takes a
genius to make something simple.*

Pete Seeger, Product Director at DocuSign

Introduction

Marketplace sellers want to sell more.

Marketplace customers want to easily find and buy more.

Marketplace operators want to connect sellers and customers for more
sales.

While some marketplace features enable a single constituent group, others
apply to more than one type of user. Many customer-facing features, like
customer login and customer account, are native to the eCommerce engine
used in the marketplace, but this chapter will address only those features
which are unique to marketplaces.

Chapter 15 General Architecture describes the overall marketplace
architecture and its interaction with the customer-facing eCommerce
platform. Chapter 26 Advanced Technical Features is devoted to
discussion of services outside the scope of the foundational features found
here.

Following is a high-level summary of the features and characteristics,
grouped by marketplace operator, seller, and customer. Other
characteristics are noted in the fourth section.

OPERATOR FEATURES

Marketplace Set Up

- Commission Management
- Branding
- Pricing Management
- Emails & Notifications
- Internationalization
- Tracking and Reporting

Product & Catalog Management

- Data Integrity & Accuracy
- Product Deduplication
- Inventory Optimization
- Smart Data Update
- Multi-Source Inventory
- Auto Cross-sell/Upsell
- Automated Approvals
- Multiple Sellers Product Checkout

SELLER FEATURES

Vendor Management

- Onboarding
- Vendor Profile
- Vendor Connect
- Vendor Dashboards
- Vendor Shipping Options

Orders, Shipping & Returns

- Order Management
- Shipping Management
- Returns Management
- Returns Workflow

- Integrations

Accounting & Vendor Payouts

- Automatic Payment Splits
- Vendor Financial Statements
- Vendor Returns
- Multiple Payment Provider Support
- Scheduled Payouts & Options

CUSTOMER FEATURES

Mobile Experience

- PWA-Ready
- Responsive Mobile Experience
- Social Media Integration
- Push Notifications
- Enhanced Browsing, Cart & Checkout
- Multiple offer review
- Combined 1P + 3P cart
- Multiple shipments

OTHER CHARACTERISTICS

Extensive APIs

- Vendor API
- Integration API
- Orders API
- Products API
- Inventory API
- Headless API

Performance & Scalability

- Scalability
- Resilient Architecture

- Speed Optimization
- Reliability & Security

Governance & Administration

- BI & Analytics
- Admin Moderation
- Admin Dashboard
- Multi-storefront Capability
- Automated Supervision

Integration Capabilities

- Integration Tools
- Realtime Data Exchange
- Integration Flexibility
- Decoupled Architecture
- Native Integrations

4.1 Operator Features

Marketplace Set Up

Commission Management – By default, most of the marketplace platforms let the store administrator add commissions and fees at their end to be charged on the sale of the products. This is how the marketplace primarily earns its revenue.

- Global Commission usually has the lowest priority in terms of applicability. It is applied when no other type of commission is enabled for the product being sold.

- Advanced Commission allows the marketplace operator to set fixed or percentage-based commission according to seller assigned categories, store category, and seller products. Advanced commissions usually take precedence over global commissions.

Branding – The branding features of the marketplace platform work both at an operator level and seller level to help them differentiate their brand and products. This also covers campaign features and customer relationship management.

- Custom Email Templates save time on creating email from scratch and can be used in retargeting and upsell campaigns, or even triggered transactional emails.

- Custom Domains give the marketplace operator the option to use a white-label marketplace solution with its own domain name. From there, further subdomains can be created.

Pricing Management – Pricing features of a marketplace platform allow the operator to maximize profits by controlling the prices at the optimum level. These include settings around global markups, discounts, and multi-currency pricing.

- Global Mark-up Settings allow the operator to set a mark-up for all sellers. It is recommended to use a tiered approach to markup instead of a fixed percentage.

- Advanced Mark-up Settings allow the operator to set mark-up levels based on individual sellers, SKU, categories, and products.

- Global Discount allows the application of discounts on all products.

- Advanced Discounts apply to a vendor, product, or category level.

- Multi-currency Pricing lets a global marketplace offer prices in foreign currencies and apply real-time foreign exchange rates.

Emails & Notifications – Communication and messaging to the customer are powered by data flowing through the CRM and backend systems.

- Global Disable Notification enables the operator to either enable or disable all email notifications.

- Advanced Disable Notification gives the operator the ability to enable or disable email notifications by seller, product, category, and many other parameters.

- Customized Notification Templates facilitates the creation of custom email templates for customer messaging and communication.

Internationalization – These features support content and information presentation in multiple languages. This is helpful for marketplaces that have a global presence and handle cross border shipping and delivery. For internationalization to happen seamlessly, backend systems, like PIM and ERP, should also be enabled for multilingualism.

- Language Switch allows the end user to switch between different languages while browsing the online marketplace. For the marketplace operator, that means easier expansion into new geographies.

- Multiple Language Support allows the operator and sellers to import catalog information in multiple languages.

Tracking & Reporting – This helps the operator to efficiently handle the operations and track activity.

- Real-time Activity Tracking provides data about sales, refunds, customer complaints, and shopping cart abandonment.

- Advanced Reporting provides deeper data, such as sales reports in a graphical representation. These types of reports can be generated based on order status, category, date, or even a specified vendor.

Product and Catalog Management

Data Integrity & Accuracy is the set of rules that governs consistent accuracy of the product catalog.

Product Deduplication removes duplicate product listings for optimal merchandising.

Inventory Optimization notifies the operator and vendor when inventory levels fall below thresholds that are predefined by the vendor.

Smart Data Update imports values only for product records that have changed while ignoring records that have not. This feature also deletes discontinued items.

Multi-Source Inventory synchronizes vendor product data from multiple sources, geographies, and systems.

Auto Cross-sell/Upsell allows the operator to set rules-based assignments for upsells, cross-sells, and related product suggestions to create a richer experience for customers.

Automated Approvals optimize the process of price and inventory updates by vendors.

Multiple Sellers Product Checkout allows customers to purchase from multiple sellers in a single transaction.

4.2 Seller Features

Vendor Management

Onboarding – One of the most challenging tasks that a marketplace needs to perform is efficiently bringing in new vendors and helping them understand the processes and culture.

- Onboarding Workflow should have the functionality to send out vendor invitations both individually and in bulk by uploading the .csv files. As part of the account signup and approval process, administrative approval should trigger the system to automatically create a vendor account, issue temporary login credentials, and email the new vendor a link to the vendor portal.

- Vendor Registration allows for a registration link to be embedded in emails and on the site. It also gives the operator the option to track vendor registration email open rates.

Vendor Profile – This set of features focuses on enabling more autonomy for the vendor to help them market and sell their products more effectively.

- Vendor Self-Service Portals allow the sellers to manage their account settings, integration preferences, and shipping configurations. It also allows them to manage products and shipments, process customer orders, access reports, etc.

- Vendor Microsites display their products only. These operate on either dedicated URLs or subdomains and have vendor information like ratings, reviews, logo, and other configurable info.

- Advanced Vendor Profiles enable vendors to use custom fields.

- Vendor Promos & Coupons let sellers create and manage their coupons, promo codes, free shipping, and other types of promotions and specials.

Vendor Connect – These features allow sellers to connect with a larger audience set.

- Vendor Connect allows the vendors to connect their existing online stores directly to the marketplace. Once connected, it facilitates automatic orders and product sync, eliminating the need for manual updates.

- Vendor Chat enables live chat between the marketplace operator and the vendor.

Vendor Dashboards – A dashboard displays information from multiple reports on a single screen, giving administrators a quick overview of various KPIs.

- Basic Dashboards provide information on vendor income (daily, weekly, monthly), vendor payouts, pending balances, and recent order activity.

- Advance Dashboards can filter the reported information by category, order status, dates, etc. Charts and graphs provide additional insights at a glance.

Vendor Shipping Options – Here vendors can select global shipping methods and carriers. They can also choose between flat rates, tiered rates, and live rates and set up auto-generated packing slips and shipping labels.

Orders, Shipping & Returns

Order Management – These critical features allow the marketplace platform to integrate with the vendor's systems for quick and accurate order fulfillment.

- Live Order Updates keep both operators and vendors up to date on incoming orders. Notifications can be customized for workflows, rules, and late order alerts.

- Auto-Accept Purchase Orders are automatically created and dispatched to vendors based on specified rules and order status.

- Aggregated Order Invoices allow the operator to aggregate invoices by vendor and process according to customized protocols.

- Automated Order Workflow defines the parameters for a fully automated sales order lifecycle.

Shipping Management – This set of features allows vendors to define their shipping options and keeps the operator, vendors, and customers informed of shipping rates and statuses.

- Shipping Fees identify the cost of shipping based on live rates, flat rates, table rates, zone rates, small parcel, etc.

- Third-Party Shipping Integration allows operator and vendor software to communicate with 3P specialist tools.

- Cross Border is native support for quoting rates and shipping outside the vendor's region.

- Shipment Tracking notifies the operator, vendor, and customer of shipment status, proactively identifies delivery issues, and sends additional notifications when needed.

Returns Management – These are the features that govern returns, reverse logistics, gatekeeping, etc. The operator typically contracts a specialist to oversee these activities.

Returns Workflow – This workflow includes returns management, returns pickup and transportation, warehouse returns, return merchandise authorization (RMA), and return to vendor.

Integrations – The returns workflow needs to be integrated with WMS and TMS (transaction management system) and needs to have business intelligence embedded to deal with reverse logistics challenges.

Accounting & Vendor Payouts

Automatic Payment Splits divide the payouts automatically when a customer purchases from multiple vendors in a single transaction.

Vendor Financial Statements list all the commissions and fees.

Vendor Returns integrate with the RMA system to automatically apply refunds and financial adjustments to vendor accounts.

Multiple Payment Provider Support allows for major payment methods, providers, and gateways worldwide.

Scheduled Payouts & Options control the schedule of paying aggregated customer payments to individual vendors.

4.3 Customer Features

Many of the customer features are seen on the eCommerce front-end, but the marketplace platform must provide functionality to enable the user experience.

Mobile Experience

PWA-Ready ensures the marketplace is search-engine optimized and will function well on any device and browser.

Responsive Mobile Experience includes features like full-screen mode, offline-mode, and push notifications without the need to develop native apps for iOS and Android.

Social Media Integration with platforms like Pinterest, Instagram, Facebook, Twitter, and Tumblr will result in a better CX.

Push Notifications allow the platform to retarget customers like a native mobile app.

Enhanced Browsing, Cart, and Checkout

Multiple offers are often shown on a single product. One offer usually wins the buy box based on specific criteria, such as lowest total cost (unit cost plus shipping). Sometimes shipping time, seller inventory, and/or seller rating are used to prioritize how offers are shown to customers.

Combined 1P and 3P cart allows the shopping cart to show first-party inventory and third-party goods with relevant details like shipping times and costs.

Multiple shipments split a single shopping cart into multiple orders if products come from first-party goods and/or one or more sellers.

4.4 Other Characteristics

Following are features and characteristics which serve more than one constituent group on the marketplace.

Extensive APIs

Vendor API enables the marketplace platform to fully integrate with the vendor's order management system (OMS), ERP, PIM, shipping and accounting, etc.

Integration API does not serve a single specific function but allows full integration with all third-party systems, components, and services.

Order API facilitates sending and receiving order notifications, data, and statuses through the OMS.

Products API integrates with the vendor PIM to maintain accurate product data.

Inventory API allows for inventory updates in real-time or according to a predefined schedule.

Headless API leverages the benefits of headless architecture by integrating with the marketplace frontend.

Performance & Scalability

Scalability refers to the ability of a platform to accommodate increases in vendors and SKUs as the marketplace grows. The operator should choose a platform that allows for ample expansion and plan ahead for migration to larger platforms as needed.

Architecture Resiliency is the ability of a platform to function through large volume fluctuations such as seasonal spikes in traffic and transactions.

Speed Optimization ensures optimal CX, increases conversion, and reduces shopping cart abandonment.

Reliability & Security refer to platform infrastructure which provides optimal uptime, resiliency, and performance to ensure that customers' financial and personal data is protected with the highest level of web security.

Governance & Administration

BI & Analytics should provide insights into the performance of the marketplace and the preferences of customers.

Admin Moderation allows the operator to moderate product data and seller-to-customer communication and provides better overall control over the marketplace.

Admin Dashboard provides actionable data and insights regarding sales, orders, and processes to aid the operator in making informed decisions about the marketplace.

Multi-Storefront Capability enables easy creation and operation of multiple store views, storefronts, and websites based on the same product and vendor catalog backend.

Automated Supervision gives the operator the means to supervise overall vendor actions with configurable vendor access.

Integration Capabilities

Integration Tools allow the marketplace platform to interface with vendors' ERP, accounting, PIM, WMS, 3PL, and back-office systems natively. APIs are the most common tool.

Real-Time Data Exchange maintains and updates accurate data for all parties. The operator controls scheduling or real-time data communications with all parties.

Integration Flexibility easily handles integrations with major vendors as well as small vendors. This option should facilitate global integration rules for all or perform custom integrations per vendor.

Decoupled Architecture aids API functionality, provides for complete headless commerce capabilities, and helps in scaling and adding features.

Native Integrations will simplify APIs with vendor systems.

Key Takeaways: Marketplace Features

- Marketplace features can be considered based on the audience they serve—operator, vendor, or customer.

- Other characteristics of marketplaces include high functioning APIs to ensure better CX and faster, more accurate order management with less effort on the part of the operator and vendors.

- Advanced technical features are covered in Chapter 26.

Chapter 5: Marketplace Financial Model

Intellectual capital drives financial capital and growth.

Andrew Yang, American Entrepreneur

Introduction

Marketplaces operate on a different financial model than traditional first-party eCommerce and retail.

The simplified math of first-party eCommerce and retail is to buy a product for $A, sell it for $B, and earn a gross profit of $B - $A.

The simplified math of most marketplaces is to enable third-party sellers to set their own price at $X, charge the seller a commission of Y%, and earn a gross profit of $X * Y%.

This simplification does not include many other factors that affect net margin. However, the profitable growth of many marketplaces compared to the low (or negative) margins of eCommerce and retail has proven the financial benefits of the marketplace model.

This chapter will start by explaining the types of revenue and the types of expenses in a marketplace. Those elements will then be organized in a sample financial model in the third section followed by a discussion about optimizing the financial return.

The following graphic provides a conceptual equation for marketplace financial ROI. The up arrows show revenue sources (fees, ads, other) that should be maximized, while the down arrows indicate expenses (CapEx and OpEx) that should be minimized.

Optimize each element of marketplace ROI Equation

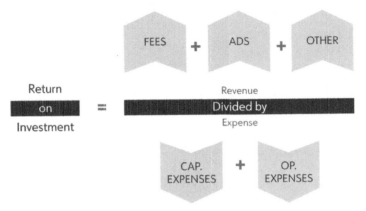

FIGURE 5.1

This is not correct math; for example, one-time CapEx and recurring OpEx costs are not simply added together to calculate ROI. The intent is to indicate which elements should be maximized and which should be minimized. Samples of the types of revenue and expense in each category are shown below.

Optimize each element of marketplace ROI Equation

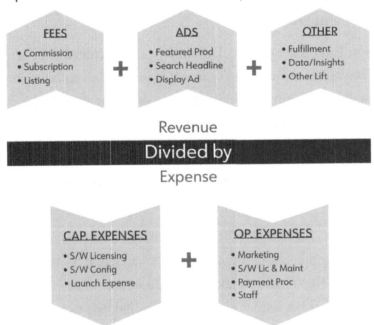

FIGURE 5.2

Although marketplaces want to increase both GMV and revenue, it is important to understand the difference between these terms. Gross Merchandise Value is the total sales price of a third party good to a customer. The revenue to the marketplace is usually calculated as just the commission fee percentage of the sale. For example, a marketplace sale of a $100 item with a 20% commission fee would result in $20 of revenue to the marketplace operator. Other sources of marketplace revenue are explained in the following section.

5.1 Types of Revenue

Marketplace revenue typically comes from three main categories: fees, advertising, or other. The most common types of fees are commission, membership, and **listing fees**.

- Commission is the most common and often the largest marketplace revenue source. Vendors are charged only when they complete a sale. The commission rate can vary based on category, seller rating, and other factors, and many marketplaces choose to charge lower fees initially to entice new vendors. Commissions are often in the 10%–20% range but can vary greatly.

- Membership charges sellers (and sometimes users) a sign-up fee or a recurring fee to gain access to the marketplace platform while individual transactions might be charged lower or no commission fees. Launching a marketplace based on this financial model frequently requires strong branding and marketing at the outset, so the operator may consider waiving membership fees in order to build the initial user base. Tiers of membership (e.g. premium seller) may also be offered for higher fees with additional features and benefits.

- Listing fees are charged for each new product or service posted by a vendor. Commonly used for C2C markets like eBay, Etsy, and traditional classifieds, listing fees can provide the marketplace operator a steady, if small, source of revenue. While the vendor benefits from paying only for the items listed, the operator must maintain and refresh a large catalog of goods to drive traffic and sales. Some marketplaces choose to combine a minimal listing fee with a nominal commission to maximize revenue.

- Lead fees, in contrast to listing fees, are charged to those responding to posts. In this scenario, the buyer usually posts a request on the platform and the service providers pay for the ability to bid (or vice versa). Vendors may also pay a small membership fee. In this model, the operator is faced with the risk that customers and service providers may take future work off the platform once the relationship is established (platform leakage).

Advertising on a marketplace platform is a fast-growing opportunity. Amazon collects tens of billions of dollars of advertising revenue annually from marketplace sellers.

- Featured listings and ads can be a valuable source of revenue for the operator. Vendors who pay for listing or advertising can move their posted products and services to the top of the search results, guaranteeing increased visibility and engagement. Operators can increase their fees, as the user base increases or by offering additional services like retargeting.

- Featured brands can promote a collection of products from one seller in a product portfolio.

- Search Headlines are a type of ad that allows marketplace sellers to promote their offers with ads appearing at the top of the customer search result page.

- Display Ads are another medium that allows sellers to show sponsored ads using product targeting, remarketing, and audience interests.

- Offsite Ads appear on web properties other than the marketplace via channel advertising.

There are a wide variety of other mechanisms to monetize marketplaces.

- Paid tools and features give vendors better reporting, analytics, and deeper insights into the behaviors of their offerings, as well as greater flexibility and customization in the way they use the platform. Quality tools and features can attract new vendors.

- Technical support for basic functions and systems failures must be provided free of charge if marketplaces expect vendors and customers to use their platform. However, operators frequently charge for technical expertise like API integration. Users who lack the knowledge or resources to manage their own implementation, integrations, or customizations, may consider the platform's technical fees to be a more cost-effective option than hiring outsourced help.

- Commercial services, like customer support and financial services, serve a twofold purpose. For the small or inexperienced vendor, having an experienced professional handle some of the backside operations frees up resources for selling and shipping. For the operator, helping vendors with these tasks generates revenue while ensuring quality customer experiences.

- Logistics and fulfillment services, like FBA, have proven to deliver massive revenue for the large marketplaces that are able to invest heavily in warehousing and shipping capabilities. When the operator controls the supply chain, the marketplace as a whole can better guarantee shipping timelines for the customer. Additionally, vendors who manage their own fulfillment must adhere to the same standards or be penalized. Overall, the operator is able to collect logistics fees and meet or exceed customer expectations.

- API Calls, or monetized APIs, most frequently apply to advertising and product sales data. As a marketplace grows in popularity, more valuable data is collected about customers, orders, products, offers, etc. Sellers and advertisers can mine this data for intelligence that helps them effectively target users with offers, on-site advertising, and off-site retargeting. Some marketplace operators include such seller and advertiser insights as part of their core functionality, some offer it as part of an add-on service, and others offer direct API access. Especially when a marketplace reaches a consistent enterprise level of sales, operators should consider an API monetization strategy as a potential profit center.

- Usage-based licenses and paid apps are similar to memberships offered at various levels and are common for marketplaces offering digital content. Users pay upfront for a certain quantity of content or digital storage within a defined period of time. For example, Shutterstock users pay a monthly fee which allows them to download a specified number of images. Additional images are charged at a per image rate.

5.2 Types of Expenses

Like any business, marketplaces incur capital expenses (one-time up-front investments that depreciate over time) and operating expenses (recurring costs of doing business). But beyond the usual office furniture and employee wages, marketplaces have specific expenses unique to the platform economy.

Capital expenses (CapEx) of a marketplace are the up-front purchases of hardware, software, and professional services required to make the platform a reality.

- This includes software licensing, initial configuration and integration, and consulting costs associated with the setup effort.

The cost of design and code development and can fall anywhere between a few thousand dollars and millions of dollars depending on the platform and requirements. Certain launch expenses and later enhancements might also qualify as CapEx. Most computing hardware is now licensed as a recurring cloud service and is considered an OpEx expense, but there might be some up-front hardware purchases, such as an on-premise firewall.

- Logistics, fulfillment, and shipping can also incur capital expenses if the operator chooses to build a warehouse or purchase items like warehouse automation systems or delivery trucks.

Operating expenses (OpEx) for marketplaces include software maintenance, support services, staff salaries, and other recurring expenses.

- With the growing popularity of SaaS platforms and cloud computing, some or all hardware and software expenses may shift from capital to operating expenses. A SaaS solution may save up-front money and time with reasonably good functionality but may not be the ideal solution for a business that has unique requirements or wants a unique user experience. See chapter 16 for a discussion of factors when deciding to build, buy, or rent a marketplace platform.

- Some expenses may vary with the total value of sales. For example, credit card processing fees may range from 1% to 4% based on the value of the transaction. Also, some SaaS software platforms charge a revenue share or "success fee" in a similar percentage range.

- If a marketplace offers seller fulfillment services (like Amazon FBA), the operator must account for set-up, picking and packing, receiving and intake, storage, shipping, and management fees. Fulfillment cost per item will vary on the type of item, size and weight, delivery speed, location, and volume of sales.

- Marketing spend will vary based on goals and channels. For instance, investments in SEO usually show long-term effectiveness, while SEM or PPC investments often drive stronger ROI for seasonal and short-term goals. By contrast, if the goal is to build brand awareness and strengthen customer retention, then additional OpEx investments in email and social media may make financial sense.

- Website maintenance and security expenses are sometimes unplanned but are critical considerations that ensure the online marketplace runs efficiently and reliably. A well-maintained marketplace website is likely to load faster, rank better, and bring in more sales. The three primary website maintenance OpEx costs are hosting fees, tool fees, and personnel salaries.

5.3 Financial Model

A marketplace financial model can be built with an understanding of the sources of revenue and expense. Other important inputs and assumptions for the model will include the number of buyers and sellers, churn rate, website traffic, conversion rate, average order value, etc.

The following financial model shows sample data for a medium-size enterprise - not a startup nor a $300 billion Amazon marketplace. For simplicity, it does not include first-party revenue or expenses nor any marketplace operator fulfillment services.

Commission rates usually vary based on the category of goods sold. This model uses one average commission rate.

This financial model is simplified to fit on the small pages of a book. Contact McFadyen Digital for a more robust financial model in a spreadsheet format with built-in formulas.

Tables 5.1 and 5.2 respectively show a simplified description of the revenue side and the expense and margin side of a marketplace financial model.

Sample Marketplace Financial Model

REVENUE	Launch Year	Year 2	Year 3	Year 4	Year 5	Subtotal
Customers (MAU)	20,000	50,000	200,000	500,000	1,000,000	
Conversion Rate	3.0%	3.3%	3.6%	4.0%	4.3%	
Avg orders per month	1.5	1.7	1.9	2.2	2.5	
Monthly orders	900	2,805	13,680	44,000	107,500	
Annual orders	10,800	33,660	164,160	528,000	1,290,000	2,026,620
Average Order Value	$125	$150	$175	$195	$225	
Annual GMV	$1,350,000	$5,049,000	$28,728,000	$102,960,000	$290,250,000	$428,337,000
Commission Rate	15%	17%	20%	20%	20%	
Annual commission Revenue	$202,500	$858,330	$5,745,600	$20,592,000	$58,050,000	$85,448,430
Sellers	50	200	500	1,000	2,000	
Seller annual membership fee	$250	$300	$400	$450	$500	
Annual membership Revenue	$12,500	$60,000	$200,000	$450,000	$1,000,000	$1,722,500
Ads bought per seller per year (avg)	2,000	5,000	10,000	12,000	15,000	
Ads served (clicked) per year	100,000	1,000,000	5,000,000	12,000,000	30,000,000	$48,100,000
Cost per ad (CPC)	$0.40	$0.50	$0.60	$0.65	$0.65	
CPC or impression ad revenue	$40,000	$500,000	$3,000,000	$7,800,000	$19,500,000	$30,840,000
Other ad revenue	$0	$20,000	$1,000,000	$4,000,000	$8,000,000	$13,020,000
Advertising revenue	$40,000	$520,000	$4,000,000	$11,800,000	$27,500,000	$43,860,000
Total Revenue (Comsn, Subscr, Ads)	$255,000	$1,438,330	$9,945,600	$32,842,000	$86,550,000	$131,030,930

TABLE 5.1

EXPENSES	Launch Year	Year 2	Year 3	Year 4	Year 5	Subtotal
Marketplace Software	$200,000	$0	$0	$0	$0	
Marketplace Implem/Enhancement	$300,000	$100,000	$100,000	$100,000	$100,000	
Marketplace Software Subscr / Maint		$50,000	$50,000	$50,000	$50,000	
Subtotal Platform Costs	$500,000	$150,000	$150,000	$150,000	$150,000	$1,100,000
Marketplace Staff	3	5	8	10	14	
Cost per staff member	$75,000	$77,000	$79,000	$81,000	$83,000	
Subtotal Staff costs	$225,000	$385,000	$632,000	$810,000	$1,162,000	$3,214,000
Marketing: SEM & Other Ads	$360,000	$400,000	$500,000	$500,000	$500,000	
Marketings: Social, email, other	$360,000	$400,000	$500,000	$750,000	$1,000,000	
Subtotal Marketing	$720,000	$800,000	$1,000,000	$1,250,000	$1,500,000	$5,270,000
Payment Processing Fee (2% of GMV)	$27,000	$100,980	$574,560	$2,059,200	$5,805,000	$8,566,740
Total Expenses	$1,472,000	$1,435,980	$2,356,560	$4,269,200	$8,617,000	$18,150,740

PROFIT	Launch Year	Year 2	Year 3	Year 4	Year 5	Subtotal
Annual Profit	-$1,217,000	$2,350	$7,589,040	$28,572,800	$77,933,000	
Cumulative Profit	-$1,217,000	-$1,214,650	$6,374,390	$34,947,190	$112,880,190	
Cumulative ROI	-83%	-42%	121%	367%	622%	

TABLE 5.2

5.4 Optimization

One advantage of the platform economy is that marketplaces generate huge volumes of valuable data. As sellers and products are added and transactions are processed and the user base grows, the platform can log myriad data for fine-tuning business performance. Dashboards can visualize the data to show trends, opportunities for improvement, and other insights. The data can also be used to automate certain activities like suspending underperforming sellers and promoting fast-moving profitable products.

Chapter 21 describes some Key Performance Indicators (KPIs) for marketplaces. Level 4 of the marketplace maturity model in chapter 2 describes quantitative management.

The engine diagram at the start of Chapter 21 provides a good analogy for tuning a marketplace. Many levers can be pulled and the results should appear on a dashboard. Seller-facing levers include the commission rate, advertising rates, the strictness of curation (i.e. how tightly categories and products are filtered), and the investment in seller recruiting. Customer-facing levers include search engine marketing (SEM) spend, email and social marketing, payment options, the user experience, and B2B sales staff if applicable. The dashboard can indicate changes to gross merchandise value, monthly active users, conversion rates, average order value, seller count, churn rate, customer acquisition costs, seller acquisition costs, customer satisfaction, and many other metrics.

Some best practices from past experience can be applied as a starting point for optimization. For example, selecting a strategy of breadth vs. depth in category expansion within a specific industry. However, as a marketplace matures optimization is often performed with real-world tests, either A/B split tests or multivariate tests. Often sensitivity testing is performed to quantify the changes in KPIs based on different levels of input changes. For example, by what percent would total advertising revenue increase (or decrease) with a 5%, 10%, 15%, or 20% increase in ad fees?

Marketplaces that also offer first-party product sales should evaluate 1P and 3P performance and intelligently move product sales between the different sources depending on margin, velocity, storage expense, etc. Omnichannel operators may decide to bring profitable 3P marketplace products into their brick-and-mortar stores or migrate slow moving store products to 3P sellers. Marketplace data can also indicate products that could profitably be sold as private label brands (e.g. Amazon Basics batteries).

Analysts should review reports and dashboards regularly to glean optimization insights. For example, comparing product categories for total GMV and margin contribution can indicate focus areas for profitable growth.

Automations like dynamic pricing can also improve margin. For example, Uber charges surge pricing during periods of high demand and shares some of the added revenue with drivers to incentivize more of them to serve customers.

Different monetization models experience different risks and opportunities for optimization. For example, personal services marketplaces like UpWork and Fiverr are susceptible to leakage where a buyer and seller begin transacting directly outside the marketplace after their first transaction. To minimize leakage, it may make sense to minimize or eliminate commissions (per-transaction fees) but increase membership, listing, or lead fees.

Incentive systems based on customer reviews encourage vendors to provide quality customer service, which in turn translates to more traffic. Incentives may include decreasing the vendor's commission or moving their listings higher in the search rankings.

Regular price testing of fees and commissions charged to both vendors and customers ensures platform prices are competitive and acceptable to users and leads to long term stability of the marketplace.

Key Takeaways: Marketplace Financial Model

- First-party eCommerce buys for $A, sells for $B, and earns a gross margin of $B-$A. Marketplaces let 3P sellers set a price of $X, charges them Y%, and earns a gross margin of $X*Y%.

- The core marketplace revenue sources are fees (commissions, subscriptions, listings, etc.), ads (featured product, search headline, display ad, etc), and other (fulfillment, tools, and other lift).

- The core marketplace expenses can be grouped into CapEx (software licensing, system configuration, launch expenses, etc.) and OpEx (marketing, software subscriptions & maintenance, payment processing fees, and staff).

- A marketplace financial model combines the revenue and expenses with other parameters like seller count, catalog size, customer traffic, conversion rate, average order value, and commission rate.

- Offering advertising services to 3P sellers is becoming a very profitable element of many successful marketplaces.

- The data generated by the platform itself is valuable to evaluate, tune, and optimize the performance of the marketplace.

SECTION II: Who is Operating a Marketplace?

Chapter 6: Marketplace History

Every once in a while, a new technology, an old problem,
and a big idea turn into an innovation.

Dean Kamen, American Engineer, Inventor, and Businessman

Introduction

Although most marketplace digital transformation occurred in the last decade, commerce and marketplaces have been evolving for thousands of years. The history of eCommerce itself is more than fifty years old and continues to evolve on the back of new technologies and the sheer number of businesses entering the online market each year. Due to its vast reach and popularity, the internet has completely changed the way the world does business. How did commerce begin and how has it evolved over the centuries to our modern global marketplaces?

6.1 Pre-Industrial Revolution (Before 1800)

Bazaars originated in Persia as early as 3000 B.C. and gradually spread to the rest of the middle east and later to Europe. Between 550 and 350 B.C., Greek stallholders started to form groups according to the type of goods carried — fish-sellers were in one place, clothing in another, etc. During this time governments began to oversee weights, measures, and transactional integrity. By 100 B.C., Trajan's Market in Rome was a vast expanse of buildings with shops on four levels and one of the earliest examples of a permanent retail shopfront.

In the twelfth century, England was home to some 2000 markets in towns and villages across the countryside. By law, local lords were granted charters from the king to protect the town's trading privileges and charge the merchants an annual fee. Both charters and competition increased in the thirteenth century. Towns and villages became known for the quality of produce, efficiency of market regulation, and amenities provided.

Across Europe, the Middle East, and Mesoamerica, the fifteenth century saw the rise of organization and quality products, as well as visitors who traveled longer distances to shop. As competition increased during the sixteenth century, some locations became associated with particular types of products, such as Indian tea. Customer trust in the quality of goods from specific places could be considered the earliest form of product branding.

Extensive overseas exploration throughout the seventeenth century brought about major economic changes and paved the way for commercial and industrial revolution. As European powers focused on shipping and colonization along the western Atlantic coast, economic activity increased across Portugal, Spain, France, the Netherlands, and England, while declining in Italy and Turkey. And the Americans who gained independence through revolution set out to create their own manufacturing and marketplaces.

6.2 Industrial Revolution and Physical Marketplaces (1800–1960)

As the early 1800s ushered European and American societies from agricultural to industrial economies, small family-oriented stores gained popularity. But gradual transitions to city living created new factories, new jobs, urban development, and new standards of living. Consumers sought a broader selection of product and department stores like Macy's (1858), Bloomingdales (1861), and Sears (1886) answered the call in New York City and Chicago.

In 1859, The Great Atlantic & Pacific Tea Company started as a coffee and tea seller before evolving into the grocery markets known as A&P. While Sears, Roebuck and Co. was officially founded in 1893, the company dates its history back to 1886 when Richard W. Sears, a railroad agent in Minnesota, received a box of errant watches and then sold them to other agents. In 1915, Vincent Astor spent nearly $1 million to build and open Astor Market at 95th Street and Broadway on the Upper West Side of Manhattan. Essentially an open-air market harkening back to the ancient bazaar, the precursor to modern shopping malls was ultimately unable to compete with the convenience of a neighborhood grocery store and closed within 2 years.

In 1916, Piggly Wiggly, the first self-service grocery store was opened by entrepreneur Clarence Saunders. The self-service model pioneered modern retail with varieties of food and goods and gave birth to modern supermarkets. The first outdoor mall in the US, called Country Club Plaza, was opened in 1922 by the J.C. Nichols Company of Kansas City. The first indoor mall, called Southdale, opened in Edina, Minnesota in 1956. By the end of 1960, more than 4500 malls covered America and accounted for over 14% of total retail.

Department stores had become a fixture of the American landscape as the growing middle class enjoyed a new level of wealth. Disposable income, social interaction, and window-shopping made shopping malls indispensable. But consumers also sought cost-effective products alongside the one-stop-shop convenience.

To meet the need, 1962 saw the opening of Walmart, Target, and Kmart— and a new era in customer experience. While the early department stores provided personalized customer attention, the new big box stores focused on self-service and efficiency. The large assortment of products and discount pricing under a single roof made the big box stores highly attractive to consumers.

6.3 Early Digital Marketplaces (1960 – 1995)

Financial innovation of the 50s set the stage for our current long-distance transactions. Diner's club offered the first credit card in 1950, while Bank of America launched the first bank-owned credit card in 1958. In 1960, structured transmission of data between organizations via electronic data interchange (EDI) opened up a new world of possibility in retail. But it was ARPANET that passed the first digital message through the new internet in 1969. Around the same time, CompuServe was founded as a processing and time-sharing service and remained a major connectivity and computing service throughout the 1980s. It reached its peak in the early 90s before facing major competition from AOL.

Basic systems of electronic commerce began to emerge in the 1970s and used new technologies like electronic funds transfer (EFT) and electronic data interchange (EDI), but mostly for B2B transactions. Broader use of credit cards and the introduction of ATMs further prepared consumers for the future of online shopping. Some of the groundbreaking innovations of this era include 1970's Unix computer operating system at Bell Labs; the creation of email in 1972 by Ray Tomlinson; and the founding of Telenet, the first internet service provider, in 1974.

The second half of the decade delivered innovation that would lead the world into a new modern age. Vint Cerf and Bob Kahn became known as the fathers of the internet when, in 1974, they designed the popular TCP/IP protocol suite. In 1975, Bill Gates and Paul Allen founded Microsoft to develop and sell BASIC interpreters for the Altair 8800. Microsoft rose to dominate the personal computer market with MS-DOS in the mid-1980s, followed by Windows a few years later. Competitors Steve Jobs, Steve Wozniak, and Ronald Wayne founded Apple in 1976 to develop and sell Wozniak's Apple I personal computer. Sales of its computers, including the Apple II, grew quickly. In the UK, Michael Aldrich pioneered online shopping in 1979 when he connected a modified domestic television via a telephone to a transaction processing computer.

Forward-thinking technology innovators were willing to start small and work hard to grow fast, so the '80s ushered in Adobe Systems (1982), Dell (1984), McFadyen Digital (1987), and Chinese telecom giant Huawei (1987). But in 1989, it was Sir Tim Berners-Lee, an English engineer and computer scientist, who changed our lives forever and carried us into the Information Age when he invented the World Wide Web.

The World Wide Web was opened to the general public in August 1991, and companies like America Online made good use of it by introducing its own email addresses, a Windows version, and access to the rest of the Internet for its users.

The US National Science Foundation (NSF) lifted its ban on commercial use of the Internet in 1991. Within a few years, a number of commercial eCommerce platforms were launched, including Art Technology Group (ATG), InterShop, Broadvision, and Vignette. Other technology firsts in the early 90s included the first-ever SMS sent on a Vodafone GSM network (1992), the first internet browser Mosaic (1993), and Newton, Apple's first PDA (1993). Although the Newton was not commercially successful, it provided lessons for the future successes of Apple's iPod, iPhone, and iPad.

In 1994, Netscape's SSL was developed to secure communications between a client and server on the web, enable widespread use of credit cards online, and start the rapid growth of eCommerce. Also in 1994, Jerry Yang and David Filo founded Yahoo, the first searchable index of web pages. This forever changed the way people looked for information on the web and paved the way for many big search engines.

In 1995, tech-savvy self-taught computer designer Pierre Omidyar founded AuctionWeb, later rebranded as eBay, in his San Jose, CA living room. The site was created to bring buyers and sellers together in an honest and open marketplace and would eventually inspire many other C2C marketplaces.

6.4 The Dotcom Era & Bubble (1995–2002)

The 90s was a period of rapid technological advances with the birth of the internet, email, online marketing, and overall commercialization of the internet. These advancements generated the greatest expansion the stock market had ever seen, followed by its epic crash. Some of today's eCommerce giants got their start in the late 90s, including the following:

- Amazon (1995) – Marketed as "Earth's Biggest Bookstore," Jeff Bezos expanded his catalog to carry over 2 million titles after only two years. Amazon managed to survive the dotcom bust by expanding further to include music, electronics, apparel, furniture, and many other categories. In 1999, Amazon's 3P GMV represented only 3% of Amazon's retail sales—now it's about 60%.

- Craigslist (1995) – Craig Newmark began the service as an email distribution list to friends featuring local events in the San Francisco Bay Area. It took shape as a web-based service in 1996 and expanded into many other classified categories.

- Alexa (1996) – A firm best known for web traffic and internet analytics, Alexa was named after the Library of Alexandria in Ancient Egypt. Amazon purchased the company in 1999 for $250 million in stock.

- Netflix (1997) – Reed Hastings and Marc Randolph of Scotts Valley, California initially rented DVDs by mail but evolved into the leading movie streaming platform.

- PayPal (1998) – This global eCommerce payment platform introduced the average consumer to the idea of secure online payments and money transfers as an electronic alternative to traditional paper methods.

- Google (1998) – Larry Page and Sergey Brin were Ph.D. students at Stanford University when they launched their search engine platform with funding from several investors, including Jeff Bezos.

- Priceline (1998) – This travel-related website helped providers offload unsold inventory by allowing users to name their own prices on hotels, car rentals, and airfares.

- Alibaba (1999) – In his apartment, Jack Ma founded China's answer to eBay and Amazon as a B2B marketplace connecting Chinese manufacturers with buyers in the west.

- Baidu (2000) – Launched in a Beijing hotel room by internet entrepreneurs, Baidu is now the second-largest search engine platform on the planet with a revenue of $14.9 billion.

The dot-com bubble burst on March 10, 2000, after the Nasdaq index peaked at 5048, nearly double the prior year. Leading high-tech firms like Dell and Cisco placed huge sell orders on their stocks, sparking immediate panic selling among investors. Over 10% of stock market value was lost within a matter of weeks. Investment capital dried up and with it the funding of cash-strapped dot-com companies. Dotcom firms with valuations and market caps of hundreds of millions of dollars became worthless almost overnight. By end of 2001, over a trillion dollars of investment capital had evaporated. Pets.com was an example of the irrational exuberance when it went bust after only two years despite a $300 million investment and an infamous sock puppet mascot.

But those who survived the bubble went on to thrive despite the technical and financial carnage. In 2001 alone, Wikipedia and Skype launched, and Apple released the first iPod. The iTunes marketplace followed in 2003.

6.5 eCommerce Mass Adoption (2002–2010)

Having learned from the dotcom crash, those technology companies that survived the 90s used the first decade of the new century to grow and develop strategically. In 2002, eBay acquired PayPal for $1.5 billion, and Amazon launched Amazon Web Services (AWS). Another big expansion year for Amazon was 2005 when it launched the Amazon Prime membership program with free 2-day shipping and allowed users to post ratings and reviews. Sears and Walmart both joined the B2C marketplace world in 2009. Walmart now has over 60,000 sellers offering over 50 million items.

Google also used the decade to grow and expand. In 2006, Google Checkout, an online payment service, launched in both the US and UK. Google introduced the Android operating system and the HTC Dream device in 2008, designed primarily for touchscreen mobile devices such as smartphones and tablets. In 2007, Apple launched the iPhone, the world's first multi-touch smartphone.

MySpace, the first major social network, launched in 2003 and peaked in 2008 with over 75 million unique users. But competitor Facebook launched in 2004, initially limited to Harvard students. After expanding to the general public, the platform quickly outpaced MySpace and now boasts about 3 billion active users monthly. 1-800-Flowers.com became the first retailer to launch a transactional eCommerce storefront on the Facebook platform in 2009.

Other social platforms launched in the following years. LinkedIn (2003) became the first networking platform for professionals, YouTube (2005) popularized video sharing, Twitter (2006) launched the first microblogging site, and Instagram (2010) created a way to capture our lives in photos. Marketplaces erupted, including Etsy (2005) for craft-style sellers, Farfetch (2007) for designer clothing, and Airbnb (2008) for lodging.

Online commerce became more trusted in 2004 when the Payment Card Industry (PCI) Data Security Standards Council (DSS) was formed to ensure online business met various security and compliance requirements. The CANSPAM act was signed into law in 2007, establishing the first US national standards for the sending of commercial e-mail to be enforced by the FTC.

6.6 Marketplace Mass Adoption (2011–Present)

As consumers grew accustomed to online shopping, technology and advertising worked in tandem to drive sales. In 2007, Varien launched Magento's open-source eCommerce platform and would be acquired by Adobe for $1.68 billion only ten years later. In 2011, Philippe Corrot and Adrien Nussenbaum, of SplitGames fame, created Mirakl as an online platform solution for marketplace operators.

Cyber Monday sales reached a new milestone at $1 billion on November 26, 2012. Amazon's stock prices hit record highs in 2013 and have only grown since. In the same year, digital spend surpassed newspaper for the first time and TV spend the following year. Technological advancements in 2015, like Apple Pay and Amazon's voice-activated Echo, made online shopping easier than ever before, and consumers responded by completing a record $1 billion in mobile sales on Black Friday 2016.

The COVID-19 outbreak took 2020 by storm with far-reaching health and economic implications for the entire world. The novel virus has been a tragedy of human life but a boon for online retailers and marketplaces as millions worldwide were forced to stay indoors and shop from home. According to the US Department of Commerce, US eCommerce grew from 7% to 17% between 2010 and 2020. However, eCommerce grew from 17% to 27% in just the first 10 weeks of the pandemic.

Key Takeaways: Marketplace History

- In-person commerce has been evolving for 5,000 years, but digital enablement only began in the 1960s.

- Before the industrial era, commerce was primarily based on subsistent living, that is, providing for immediate family.

- The industrial revolution concentrated population in cities and improved buying power which enabled more physical marketplaces. The growth of cities also led to the success of department stores and big box retail.

- The development and growth of eCommerce and online marketplaces were driven by the internet, SSL, affordable broadband, **PCI DSS**, and other rapid technological advances.

- The current stage of marketplace and eCommerce growth is being led by enhanced cloud computing power, big data capabilities, smartphone proliferation, and **social commerce**.

- The platform revolution gained traction about a decade ago and has either transformed or killed many traditional businesses.

Chapter 7: Marketplaces of Today & Tomorrow

7.1 Top marketplaces around the world
7.2 Marketplace Trends
7.3 Types of Marketplaces

What we need to do is always lean into the future; when the world changes around you and when it changes against you – what used to be a tailwind is now a headwind – you have to lean into that and figure out what to do because complaining isn't a strategy.

Jeff Bezos, CEO, Amazon

Introduction

Today's online marketplaces account for more than 50% of global eCommerce and contribute about $2 trillion of GMV to the global economy. These revenue numbers have enabled fifty-five of the top 100 marketplaces to raise a combined $43 billion in investor funding. Digital marketplaces are a major factor driving the retail apocalypse and the disruption of many B2B businesses. Even the services industries are being transformed by online platforms like Uber, Fiverr, TaskRabbit, and others.

This chapter will review the top marketplaces in the world, some trends across marketplaces, and different types of marketplaces.

7.1 Top Marketplaces Around the World

Launched in 2003, Chinese eCommerce platform Taobao is owned by Alibaba and is its largest sales and revenue contributor. Developing areas now account for the bulk of growth, and in 2019 it boasted a mobile user base of more than 700 million.

Similarly, Chinese B2C marketplace Tmall spun off from Taobao with over 500 million active users and sales of over $472 billion GMV. On Singles Day, November 11, 2020, the platform set a new record with $74 billion in sales in one day.

Rank	Marketplace	GMV (Billions)	Country
1.	Taobao (Alibaba)	$538	China
2.	Tmall (Alibaba)	$472	China
3.	Amazon	$339	USA
4.	JD.com	$295	China
5.	eBay	$90	USA

TABLE 7.1 Global ranking of marketplaces based on GMV

Another Chinese marketplace, JD.com, holds the number four spot and is a major competitor to Tmall. Known for investing in new tech and AI, JD.com owns the largest drone delivery system in the world.

Americans hold the third and fifth positions with Amazon and eBay respectively. While Amazon.com became the most valuable company in 2019, ahead of Microsoft, Apple, and Google, eBay grew to 182 million users and over 1.3 billion listings in the same period.

The main difference between Amazon and eBay lies in the fact that Amazon focuses on B2C and B2B retail, while eBay is mostly a C2C and B2C auction site. Also, Amazon is a hybrid marketplace selling its own first-party goods and third-party products, while eBay is a pure-play marketplace that only enables third-party transactions but does not stock any goods.

The top 100 online marketplaces around the world sold more than $2 trillion worth of gross merchandise. Sales from the major players like Amazon, Alibaba, and eBay accounted for over 58% of global online sales in 2019. As compared to 2018, the gross merchandise sales grew by over 22%.

Marketplaces in the Asian Pacific region are among the world's fastest growing for three primary reasons: the expanding middle class, increasing mobile and internet penetration, and improvements to logistics and infrastructure.

FIGURE 7.1 Locations of Top 100 marketplaces around the world
Source: Digital Commerce 360

Even though the US has a sizeable number of marketplaces in the top 100, it is still the second largest online marketplace in the world. Limiting sales to the US reduces global sales challenges of language, currency, taxation, and shipping.

Europe and UK also offer excellent marketplace business opportunities. Close proximity and solid European infrastructure simplify payment and shipping within these markets.

Similarly, the Latin American eCommerce market is growing quickly, with some of the major markets like Brazil and Argentina showing 20%

year-over-year growth. Consumers there also show a preference for international brands, making Latin America a lucrative opportunity for many marketplace operators.

Rank	Marketplace	GMV (Billions)
1.	Amazon	$339
2.	eBay	$90
3.	Walmart	$49
4.	Wish	$10
5.	Houzz	$9

TABLE 7.2 Top 5 US Marketplaces based on GMV from 3P sales only

Amazon remains the dominant US force, selling about $300 billion worth of products. After adding marketplaces in Singapore and the United Arab Emirates, Amazon now runs sixteen marketplaces worldwide. However, the platform still faces the challenges of continuously discovering new products and growing competition from the likes of Walmart, Target, Google Shopping, and Shopify.

Walmart remains a stalwart brick-and-mortar retailer, but invested over $5 billion in eCommerce, technology, and supply chain in 2019 and grew its online sales by over 40%. Despite reducing its real estate investments, grocery remains the major revenue driver at 55% of overall sales. This may be credited to new shopping options, in-store and touchless pickup available at more than 5,000 US store locations for omnichannel shopping and home delivery.

As of 2019, Wish is the fourth largest eCommerce marketplace by sales. Rather than relying on a search bar format, its platform provides a personalized shopping experience for each buyer using modern browsing technologies. It is a pure-play platform where Wish does not stock products but only acts as an intermediary to facilitate transactions between sellers and consumers. The platform has gained significant investor attention recently and received series H funding, taking the company valuation over $11 billion.

Growing with a sharp upward trajectory in its early days, Houzz has leveled off but shows no signs of slowing down. Its current valuation stands at $4 billion with over 40 million unique users monthly and 2.3 million active home renovation and design professionals. Houzz invested in localized platforms in over a dozen countries and has created a revenue stream through product advertising and premium listings for local home professionals and service providers. Houzz is a great example of the flywheel effect of attracting more users with user-generated content (UGC).

7.2 Marketplace Trends

A 2020 Digital Commerce 360 study found that the top 100 global marketplaces sold $1.7 trillion worth of products. According to Coresight Research, global marketplace revenue (commissions on GMV) is projected to reach $40 billion by 2022. Of that revenue, 57% is projected to be in the US.

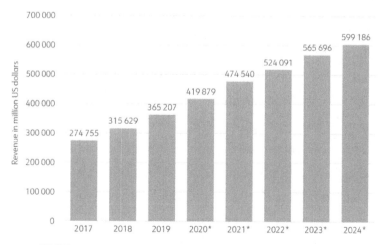

FIGURE 7.2 Retail eCommerce sales in the United States
Source: https://www.statista.com/statistics/272391/us-retail-e-commerce-sales-forecast/

With such extensive revenues available, marketplaces hoping to compete will be required to follow the pattern of history and innovation. Operating ahead of the technological curve and creating greater convenience for the shopper will become paramount as the global platform economy expands.

Through common experience with marketplace giants like Amazon, modern consumers have come to expect a personalized, channel-agnostic shopping journey. Shoppers are also becoming accustomed to a wide selection of products at lower prices, forcing traditional retailers to develop new strategies to remain competitive. Some have chosen to embrace the marketplace model, while others sell only through their own website. The following trends will define marketplace operations in the coming years.

Frictionless Customer Journey – Friction is anything that impedes the consumer's path to purchase, and Amazon has mastered removal of all obstacles. Moving forward, marketplace operators will strive to provide the high-quality experience that consumers expect while looking for innovative ways to provide value and convenience.

Ratings and Reviews – A recent survey indicates that over 97% of consumers look at reviews and ratings before making a final purchase. Particularly for small marketplaces and niche products, ratings and reviews will become increasingly important for closing sales.

Marketplace Loyalty – Many consumers are loyal to the brands that demonstrate quality and value. As marketplaces expand their catalogs with unknown brands, building loyalty to the marketplace becomes paramount. If the consumer trusts the value of the marketplace and its offering, they will be more likely to purchase unknown brands based on their confidence in the marketplace. With that marketplace loyalty firmly in place, the buyer can base purchase decisions on price, delivery options, or payment options rather than mere brand name.

Multi-Channel Selling – Consumers purchase from a vast selection of online locations. Many vendors currently shy away from multi-channel selling due to the complexity, but in the future, selling on the company's own website, in retail locations, on at least one marketplace, and through social media will become imperative to remain competitive. Several existing eCommerce platforms simplify the process of integrating all channels, and the technology sector will continue to develop new and better solutions as demand increases.

Embrace Amazon – Amazon works constantly to provide brands the tools they need to market themselves better. As a result, some smaller brands have abandoned their own eCommerce site to direct traffic to their Amazon brand page. With its top-shelf branding capabilities, customer analytics suite, and policing of unauthorized sellers, Amazon provides tremendous value to brands.

Advertising Growth – As the battle for online customers heats up, paid ads will gain popularity on major marketplaces, social media platforms, and search engines. When paid advertising takes the lead, the first item of organic results appears at the middle or bottom of the first page. Despite the cost of paid advertising, a short-term boost in sales can still reduce the cost per sale. Amazon's annual advertising revenues in 2019 touched roughly $14.1 billion, up 39% from $10.1 billion in 2018. These staggering figures land Amazon in third place behind Google and Facebook.

Second-hand Goods and reCommerce – As Millennials mature into the generation with the strongest spending power, sustainability has become a driving force in the modern economy. Purchasing used products is now considered by many as both environmentally and socially responsible. As sales increase, so will the number of B2C and C2C reCommerce platforms.

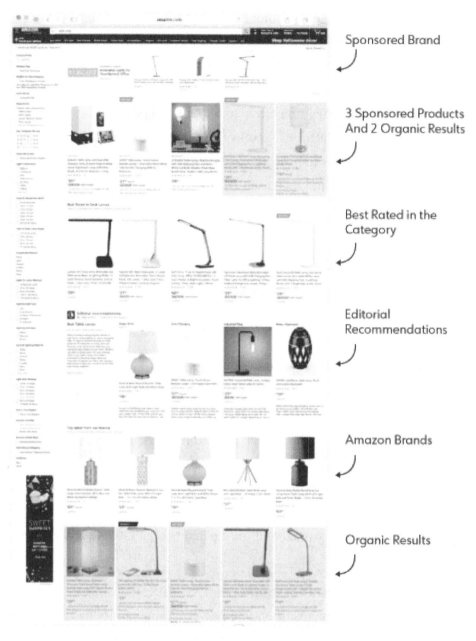

FIGURE 7.3 Growth in Advertising

Niche Marketplaces – Historically, small retail stores have struggled to compete with the giants, and eCommerce marketplaces are no different. But while they cannot boast the massive selection and efficient order processing systems of sites like Amazon and Walmart, niche marketplaces will continue to serve a valuable purpose in the platform economy. Particularly in personal CPG like fashion, jewelry, and health, socially conscious shoppers and those of discriminating taste are inclined to look beyond the major players to find small marketplaces that position themselves as experts in the desired segment. Already, 11% of online American shoppers have purchased products from Chinese marketplaces and this trend is likely to grow.

Blockchain – The transaction security of blockchain creates significant implications for marketplaces. Blockchain-based marketplaces (also called decentralized marketplaces) are more like peer-to-peer networks that directly connect consumers and sellers, negating the need for any intermediaries. Additionally, as mobile phones become the primary channel for eCommerce transactions, marketplace operators looking to reduce checkout time and increase customer satisfaction now offer eWallet options (like Google Pay and Apple Pay), which are made more secure by blockchain technology. Some marketplaces have even begun to accept Bitcoin as a payment method.

Social Commerce – Traditionally, marketplaces purchased paid advertising on social media to drive traffic to their platform. However, many of the larger social media sites have recently developed their own marketplaces allowing users to purchase within the social media platform. Early adopter Instagram has made its paid advertising transactional, enabling users to shop and checkout without leaving the app. Similarly, Facebook Marketplace allows private parties to buy and sell items locally or shop eCommerce. According to a 2019 Facebook survey, close to 40% of online shoppers start their shopping journey with a chat message, so it will come as no surprise when messaging tools like WhatsApp, Facebook Messenger, and Snapchat become transactional. In China, apps like WeChat are already integrating more transactional capabilities.

Marketplace Proliferation – To compete with mega-platforms like Amazon, more large retail and big box stores will follow the lead of Walmart and Target to create their own marketplaces.

Platforms for platform businesses – With seven of the top ten global companies operating a platform business model, it is no surprise to now see platforms to "platform your business." Marketplace pioneer Mirakl provides enterprise organizations easy integration of an existing eCommerce platform and unlimited scale. Cutting edge APIs allow the operator system and vendors to automate operations like seller onboarding, catalog integration and management, communication with customers, etc.

Shopify is a cloud-based commerce platform designed to help small and medium-sized businesses set up and manage their stores across multiple channels, including physical stores, social media, web, mobile, marketplaces, and even **pop-up shops**. The platform offers merchants a suite of services like marketing, customer engagement, payments, and shipping tools to simplify the process of running an online store. For as little as $29 per month, Shopify's fast and inexpensive solution currently powers over 800,000 businesses in approximately 175 countries around the world.

VTEX is another provider of cloud-based eCommerce and omnichannel solutions. It is based on a single code multi-tenant, scalable, and extensible eCommerce platform. For businesses, this translates into faster development, reduced operational cost, and increased revenue. It has the community support of partners and developers for its end-to-end omnichannel solution, which consists of several modules and hundreds of extensions. The key modules are eCommerce, Marketplace, Order Management System, **Content Management System**, Logistics and Inventory, Pricing and Campaign Management, and a Database Service that serves as a Customer Data and Product Information.

Before 2015, a business looking to build a custom marketplace platform budgeted a seven- to eight-figure investment ($3–$15 million). Now with the advent of platforms to platform your business, a 6-figure investment ($10K - $900K) can be expected.

Broader discussion of this topic can be found in Chapter 16: Build, Buy, or Rent a Platform?

Mobile and Progressive Web Apps (PWA) – Statista predicts mobile eCommerce sales will hit $3.5 billion in 2021, with much of the growth being led by PWAs. For the first time, smartphones have edged out PCs as the most popular device for carrying out eCommerce transactions. While the gap between online and offline will continue to grow, consumers will gravitate to the avenues and channels that offer the easiest purchase journey.

PWAS OFFER THE BEST OF BOTH WORLDS

	PWA	Responsive Web	Native App
Full Screen Presentation	Yes	No	Yes
Offline Content Viewing	Yes	No	Yes
Push Notifications	Yes	No	Yes
Offline Checkout	Yes	No	Yes
Search Engine Friendly	Yes	Yes	No
Content Aggregation	Yes	Yes	No
No Download Required	Yes	Yes	No
Cross-Device Responsiveness	Yes	Yes	No
No Updates-Required	Yes	Yes	No
Direct-Link to Content	Yes	Yes	No
Bypass App Store Approval Process	Yes	Yes	No

TABLE 7.3 PWA Statistics

While mobile websites and responsive designs are relatively commonplace and easy to execute, they lack certain user experience aspects seen in native apps. And where native apps provide a fantastic user experience, they generally have a higher barrier to entry. PWAs combine the best of both worlds by taking advantage of the latest web technologies to bridge the gap between native mobile app and responsive website.

Voice Commerce & Chatbots – Apple's Siri, Google Assistant, and Alexa are driving a new wave of online shoppers who prefer the hands-free convenience of voice-enabled transactions. Another AI technology emerging in eCommerce is chatbots, which provide users with highly accurate and timely responses to their questions. Many marketplaces now use chatbots for 24/7 customer support to solve issues around user accounts, payments, and order delays.

Drone Delivery – Moving quickly from concept to reality, drone delivery is likely to become mainstream in the next few years. Similar to the way eWallets and one-touch purchase accelerate the buying process, the drone delivery expedites the last mile delivery and gives a boost to the user experience. For example, Amazon's Prime Air uses drones to autonomously fly individual packages to customers in certain major cities within 30 minutes of ordering. JD.com, China's eCommerce giant, has also made effective use of its drone fleet to reach customers in the most remote areas.

7.3 Types of Marketplaces

Horizontal Marketplace

Aiming for a broad audience, a horizontal marketplace offers consumers one-stop-shop convenience. The most obvious example is Amazon, which started as a vertical-specific eCommerce website focused on just books but quickly expanded its catalog to cover an array of market segments at scale.

FIGURE 7.4 Horizontal Marketplaces

Advantages of a Horizontal Marketplace:

- Horizontal marketplace business provides excellent coverage of products and services.

- Versatility of the catalog allows greater diversification opportunities.

- Market reach is maximized by having something for everyone.

- A larger catalog and larger audience dictate a larger operational scale.

Disadvantages of a Horizontal Marketplace:

- Focusing on every vertical means you are an expert in none.

- The complexities of managing multiple product categories simultaneously require advanced marketing strategies.

- Market share can be easily lost to a niche marketplace which specializes in a single category or industry.

Vertical Marketplace

In opposition to a horizontal marketplace, the vertical marketplace concentrates on a narrow target market with the goal of conquering a single industry. The idea is to create optimal purchase conditions for a small set of buyers. As a result, consumers view the platform as a specialist who provides greater value to them.

FIGURE 7.5 Vertical Marketplaces

Some of the examples of vertical marketplaces are Wayfair, a B2C marketplace selling furniture and home goods, and Etsy, a C2C marketplace for handmade items and craft supplies. Similarly, Newegg focuses on consumer electronics and computer equipment, while Vivino sells only wine. Each of these platforms is considered a go-to marketplace in their industry.

Advantages of a Vertical Marketplace:

- Focus on a single category minimizes the complexity and variables of managing the catalog.

- Marketing budgets and resources are substantially reduced.

- Domination of a vertical comes more quickly when the operator focuses on excellence in a single space as opposed to every space.

- Customer loyalty and advocacy are the benefits of specializing in a single vertical and doing it well.

Disadvantages of a Vertical Marketplace:

- If the product or category goes out of trend or becomes obsolete, the marketplace could easily fold.

- The opportunity costs are high as there is very little flexibility to enter new products and categories.

- Continual market research is required to monitor market trends and stay ahead of the competition.

Digital Goods Marketplace

Similar to a vertical marketplace in that the focus is solely on non-physical products, digital goods marketplaces can offer a vast selection of electronic content, including video and photo, e-books, music, and more. An online marketplace is a natural fit for sellers of digital goods.

FIGURE 7.6 Digital Goods Marketplace

An early prominent marketplace in this space was the iTunes store. Initially conceptualized as a simple music player for Apple's own iPod devices, the app evolved into a sophisticated multi-media content manager and eCommerce platform. Similarly, because Kindle devices enabled users to browse, buy, download, and read e-books, newspapers, magazines, and other digital media, the acquired company is a natural complement to Amazon's large catalog of digital content. Other major players are Shutterstock, which maintains a massive catalog of photography, footage, music, and editing tools, and Udemy, which offers online classes across several categories.

Advantages of a Digital Goods marketplace:

- The lack of production cost gives digital goods nearly limitless margin.

- There are no warehousing or shipping costs.

- The marketplace is truly borderless.

Disadvantages of a Digital Goods marketplace:

- Piracy, unlawful replication and resale of digital content, will always be a challenge for digital goods platforms.

- Similar to the Loss Prevention department of major retailers, monitoring for revenue leakage and unlicensed product use can become an overhead cost for digital goods platforms.

Niche Marketplaces

Where vertical marketplaces focus on a single industry, niche marketplaces narrow their focus to excel in a single, specific category. To succeed in the global marketplace without directly competing against marketplace leaders, many small and innovative businesses leverage the internet marketplace business model to quickly build a large user base and high recognition.

FIGURE 7.7 Niche Marketplaces

Some of the noteworthy examples of niche marketplaces are Houzz, an online community about architecture, interior design and decorating, landscape design, and home improvement; StubHub, for exchange and resale of tickets for sports, concerts, theatre, and other live entertainment events; StockX, providing resale of sneakers, clothing, trading cards, and collectibles; and Threadless, an online **crowdsourcing** of T-shirt designs that allows the artist to sell their designs.

Advantages of a Niche Marketplace:

- Marketing becomes clear and direct as there is only one audience pain point to identify and only one solution.

- Depending on the product catalog, there could be little or no physical product, warehousing, or shipping.

- The singular focus on a very small product or industry naturally lends itself to becoming a subject matter expert.

Disadvantages of a Niche Marketplace:

- To compete with industry giants who may dabble in the niche industry, smaller marketplaces must provide a smooth customer journey and outstanding customer service.

- If a product or category of singular focus goes out of trend or becomes obsolete, the marketplace could easily fold.

Services Marketplace

Catering to both the gig economy and consumer desire for services **on-demand**, services marketplaces facilitate the discovery, evaluation, and purchase of services. The services marketplaces have increased dramatically in recent years, and many, like Uber, Fiverr, and Airbnb, have met with astonishing success.

FIGURE 7.8 Services Marketplaces

Service marketplaces typically cater to a specific vertical or niche, such as Uber's on-demand transportation and Airbnb's lodging and tourism experiences. Similarly, Fiverr connects freelancers with new clients, while DoorDash delivers food orders that diners have placed online with local restaurants.

Advantages of a Services Marketplace:

- No physical product means there are no inventory, warehousing, or shipping costs.

- Rather than negotiating contracts for individual products, the operator has only to establish standardized rules of participation. Service providers can choose to participate according to the rules or opt out.

Disadvantages of a Services Marketplace:

- The operator must monitor the quality of services to ensure consumers are getting value.

- Because the delivery of service requires direct interaction between buyer and seller, the operator must have safety and privacy protocols in place.

- Once the seller and buyer have worked together, they may choose to take additional business offline.

Because services marketplaces are the fastest growing segment of the platform economy, Chapter 8: Services Marketplaces is devoted to a broader exploration of the topic.

Key Takeaways: Marketplaces of Today & Tomorrow

- China leads the pack with three of the top five marketplaces around the world.

- Amazon has not had the same level of success in China as elsewhere but is still positioned better than TaoBao, JD, and Tmall. With 15 marketplaces worldwide, Amazon is a truly global marketplace.

- The key trends driving the growth of the marketplaces in the US are niche marketplaces, social commerce, increased advertising spend, and third-party logistics.

- Some of the key buyer expectations from a marketplace include frictionless buyer journey, ratings and reviews, and overall trustworthiness of the marketplace operator.

- When selling on a fiercely competitive marketplace, merchants need better visibility and multi-channel capability.

Chapter 8: Services Marketplaces

Every once in a while, a new technology, an old problem,
and a big idea turn into an innovation.

Dean Kamen, Segway Inventor

Introduction

The last 10 years have witnessed an explosion of services becoming available online, with hospitality industries leading the charge. In the space of only a few years, services marketplaces like Uber, Airbnb, DoorDash, Instacart, and others have captured tens of billions of dollars in transactions and moved a new segment of our lives online. Many have tried to replicate the success of Uber ($14 billion in transactions in 2019) and Airbnb (nearly $4 billion in revenue in 2019), but few have succeeded. In the US, service industries account for $9.7 trillion (70% of the consumer GDP), but only 7% of those transactions are digitally enabled. It is expected that by 2021 close to 50% of the US workforce will be either freelancers or self-employed. With 125 million Americans currently working in

ON-DEMAND SERVICE INDUSTRY STATISTICS

49%

Forecasted growth rate of global on-demand services marketplaces 2017-2021

Revenue Estimates

2017 — $213.35B
2019 — $317.89B
2021 — $435.41B

FIGURE 8.1

services industries, this segment of the economy is ready for digital takeover.

But why are so few services sourced digitally? Some might argue that for thousands of years, services have existed and succeeded without the internet. For this reason, many small businesses offering services have never considered online selling as a focus for their business. In fact, for most services, particularly those in the home, a good word from a friend is better than the most expensive advertising campaign. In addition, the varying attributes for different types of services and the different aspects of service that individual customers value mean there is no standard format for making a services marketplace excel.

8.1 Early Services Marketplaces

In 1995 Craig Newmark started the "Craig's List" email newsletter to inform friends of social events that might interest software developers in the San Francisco area. Members quickly began using the email list to share job openings and other non-event posts. By 1996, users were requesting internet access and the website was born.

Having expanded to include postings in community events, services, housing, private sale, employment, and discussion forums, Craigslist is now one of the top 20 sites in America, generating over $1 billion in revenue. Every month the platform serves 50 million unique visitors, 20 billion pageviews, 80 million new offers (classifieds), and 2 million jobs. Craigslist has been a leading siphon of traditional newspaper classifieds revenue, which declined from its height of $20 billion in 2000 to less than $5 billion in 2012. And to demonstrate the leverage of a popular marketplace, all of this was accomplished with a staff of only 50 employees.

Over the years, Craigslist has had problems with spam, controversy that suggested their personal ads were encouraging sex trafficking, and even a bank robber who crowdsourced his getaway. But on the whole, Craigslist has been popular because of its versatility. The fast-growth days of Craigslist are now in the past. As Andrew Parker of Spark Capital highlighted in 2010, various niche marketplace start-ups, like Airbnb, StubHub, Etsy, have begun "unbundling Craigslist." On the following page, Figure 8.2 shows a few of the marketplaces that tackled specific capabilities of Craigslist in 2010. Only five years later, more than eighty vertical marketplaces carved out parts of Craigslist. Today that competing marketplaces would be difficult to count.

FIGURE 8.2: Spark Capital 2010: Unbundling Craigslist into multiple vertical marketplaces

Groupon is another services marketplace pioneer. In fact, they were the fastest firm to be valued at over a billion dollars (within 16 months of formation). Within 24 months of formation, services were offered in 250 cities across North America, Europe, Asia, and Latin America serving 35 million registered users.

8.2 Services-only Marketplaces

There are a wide variety of services marketplaces including travel, lodging, concierge, health & beauty, experiences, installation, repair, dining, delivery, professional services, education, entertainment, car wash services, and many others. And among the multiple marketplaces for parking, Time Magazine named SpotHero to its list of The 50 Most Genius Companies of 2018.

Angie's List is a well-known services marketplace that started in 1995 offering home maintenance related services that were validated with crowd-sourced reviews. For many years Angie's List collected fees from both sellers (service providers) and buyers (homeowners) but dropped the subscription fee element in 2016. Millions of users paid subscription fees to access the 10+ million seller ratings which helped identify qualified service professionals.

TaskRabbit is an example of a services marketplace that matches freelance labor with local demand. Tens of thousands of vetted taskers offer a wide array of services like cleaning, moving, delivery, and handyman work. Taskers have performed over 350,000 hours of services which includes 10,000 hours waiting in line for clients.

Initially, TaskRabbit used an eBay style bidding process for engaging taskers with clients. In 2014 they improved the conversion rate by allowing taskers to set rates and schedules. The first to respond to a new job won the work and TaskRabbit receives a 15% commission on services sold. In 2017 TaskRabbit was acquired by IKEA and soon added an IKEA furniture assembly service.

8.3 Product + Services Marketplaces

Cross-selling related services can be a great expansion tactic for a product marketplace (or basic product eCommerce). Examples of add-on services for products include delivery, installation or assembly, configuration of complex products, cooking, or experiences (e.g. guided trips). For certain products, Amazon offers optional installation services that are rendered by a third-party service provider through the Amazon services marketplace.

Service professionals selling through Amazon pay no fees for signup or subscription, but they are charged a commission fee ranging from 15% to 20%. Trade licenses (e.g. electrician, plumber, HVAC) are required for relevant services. In some cases, customers can also purchase recurring services on a subscription plan.

8.4 Digital Services & Products Marketplaces

Many services can be procured and delivered digitally. For example, Udemy is a marketplace that remotely connects 50 million students with 50 thousand instructors. Within a few months of bootstrapping their platform (before raising any investment), Udemy had ten thousand students accessing a couple of thousand courses from a thousand instructors. Top instructors earn over a million dollars per year.

Fiverr is a marketplace for freelance professional services (starting at $5), who perform a variety of work thousands of miles away from the buyer. Within two years of launching in 2010, the platform hosted over a million gigs. Today Fiverr hosts more than a million transactions each month and close to $10 trillion in transactions each year. Some of the most popular services on Fiverr include logo design, resume and cover letter writing, whiteboard animation, video creation, content writing, mobile app development, and website testing. Fiverr.com has grown to be one of the top 100 websites in the US and in the top 200 globally but now competes with many other digital services marketplaces like UpWork (formerly Elance), Freelancer.com, and Toptal.

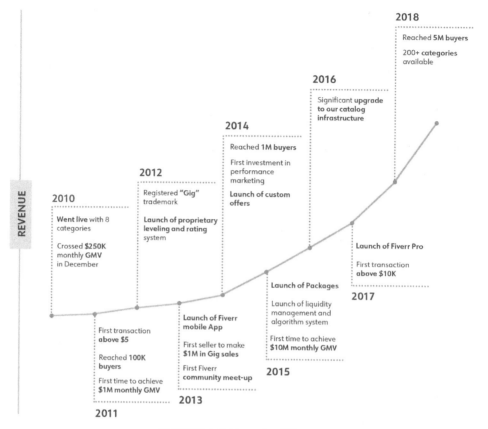

FIGURE 8.3 Growth of Fiverr
Source: Fiverr Prospectus

Some digital services marketplaces are more narrowly focused. For example, OneHourTranslation.com has 25,000 remote human translators in 100+ countries working on 120 languages serving 80,000 business customers. Human translation usually often more accurate and desirable than machine translation, such as Google Translate.

Because digital services are frequently performed by independent contractors and sold to businesses, a digital services platform is sometimes classified as C2B.

8.5 Managed and Regulated Services Marketplaces

While home services industries, like handymen and landscapers, have benefited greatly from basic review and referral platforms, there is still room to grow. Professional services providers are beginning to recognize the benefits of the marketplace model. But some services require additional vetting of the providers. Today more than a quarter of the US workforce needs some form of occupational license.

To meet that need, Angie's List, Houzz, and Amazon have developed processes for validating licensing of service providers such as electricians. Uber Freight, Convoy, and NEXT Trucking are marketplaces serving the $700 billion US trucking industry by connecting businesses with licensed commercial truck drivers. Cosmetology licensing varies by state, but the Glamsquad marketplace requires that all beauty pros be licensed in the use of Barbicide cleaning products.

Figure 8.4 on the next page shows four major generations of service marketplaces, from the spotty coverage of early service provider platforms to the end-to-end customer experience modern consumers have come to expect.

The Listings Era – The very first iteration of the services marketplace simply involved bringing listing platforms online, primarily unmanaged horizontal marketplaces. It was an impersonal, transactional service where the onus was on the user to assess providers, contact them, arrange times to meet, and transact.

The Unbundled Craigslist Era – In this generation, horizontal marketplaces zeroed in on a specific sub-vertical in an effort to compete with Craigslist anything-for-anyone format. For example, Care.com focused on childcare and provided tech value-add, structured information, and better customer experience.

The "Uber for X" Era – Beginning in 2010, a new wave of on-demand services came into prominence on the heels of technological breakthroughs around smartphones and mobile apps. The widespread mobile adoption helped create full-stack experiences for individual services. Every platform sought the meteoric rise of Uber, but few were so successful.

EVOLUTION OF SERVICES MARKETPLACES

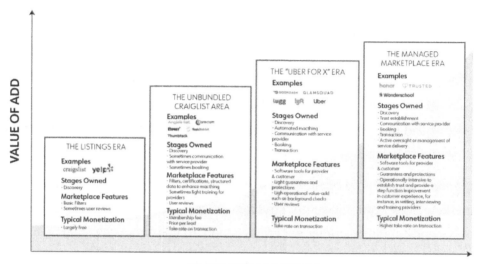

FIGURE 8.4: Andreessen Horowitz view of services marketplace evolution
Source: https://a16z.com/2018/11/27/services-marketplaces-service-economy-evolution-whats-next/

The Managed Marketplace Era - Over time, services marketplaces evolved so that they could better tackle services that were more complex, higher priced, and required greater trust. Instead of just enabling consumers to discover and build trust with the end service provider, these marketplaces went a step further to create trust for the platform.

Figure 8.5 below shows how services marketplaces have evolved in terms of both the complexity of services represented and the level of responsibility the marketplace brand takes on to guarantee customer satisfaction.

SERVICE MARKETPLACES:
EVOLUTION OF THE REVOLUTION

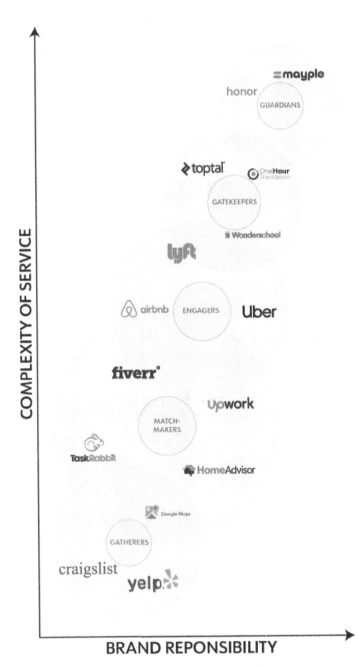

FIGURE 8.5 Source: Mayple

Gatherers are marketplace listing services, like Craigslist and Yelp, which function mainly as a directory.

Matchmakers go a step further to customize the list of the services provided with better filters and reviews, such as TaskRabbit and Fiverr.

Engagers, like Uber and Airbnb, provide an even higher level of service and engagement while assuming higher responsibility toward the service they provide.

Gatekeepers set a high standard for their industry by screening providers and assuring quality. For example, brands like Wonderschool provide high-end services based on a judicious screening process, one that is very complicated and expensive to execute independently.

Guardians take gatekeeping to the next level offering fully managed services marketplaces everyone can trust. This works better in a B2B scenario where relationship is held to the highest of standards, so these marketplaces tend to operate in complex and fragmented industries where trust is crucial but hard to attain.

8.6 Features of a Services Marketplace

Because offerings of a services marketplace are significantly different from traditional retail products, building and operating such a marketplace requires additional capabilities beyond those of a products marketplace.

Seller Management – Much like in a product marketplace, sellers must be onboarded and managed. Aside from standard seller information, seller profiles should include types of service rendered, qualifying certifications or licensing, and experience. Customer opinions of services tend to vary far more than they do for products, so it is important to maintain objective metrics for seller performance management and their ratings and reviews.

Organization of Catalogue of Services – While a catalog of physical goods may include fields for product color, size, or type, a catalog of services will include attributes that define and categorize by need, time frame, or level of expertise. Having the right options will show customers that the operator truly understands the industry, providers, and consumers.

Geolocation Strategy – Physical services, unlike digital services, typically have a geographic region in which they can be rendered. A map view which sorts providers and services by proximity to a specified zip code may be the best interface for finding a local service provider.

Vouchers and Coupons – To entice new and returning users, vouchers or coupons for services can be digitally transmitted to customers and then presented at the time of services to receive the agreed-upon price. The voucher lifecycle typically includes various stages like Requested, Pending Validation, Accepted, Cancelled, Consumed, etc. The service provider is then paid after the service has been rendered.

Availability Schedule – The availability of services is usually constrained by schedules. In marketplaces, schedules are maintained by the sellers (e.g. Instacart shoppers deciding when they are working). A calendar interface allows sellers to manage their schedules and communicate changes with buyers.

Messaging – To protect privacy and reduce revenue leakage (conducting business outside the platform), the marketplace should provide a messaging platform for the service provider and the buyer to conduct their business. This platform enables secure and tracked communication between the buyer and seller to ensure expectations are met and disputes are quickly resolved.

Proof of Service Delivery – In a product marketplace, package tracking serves to confirm delivery of physical product before sellers are paid. In a services marketplace, the buyer must complete the process, such as an Uber rider submitting a review or an UpWork client releasing funds. The service provider also needs a resource for reminding the buyer to take this last step so that providers can be paid in a timely manner.

8.7 Success of Services Marketplaces

To make these types of marketplaces successful, operators will have to achieve three primary goals.

- Court the suppliers and demonstrate thorough understanding of their industry, process, and goals. Amazon has the luxury of requiring its vendors to obey specific rules or they are not allowed to sell on the marketplace. However, service providers can only work within regulated guidelines. Marketplace operators must provide an environment that allows service providers to qualify and customize the projects on which they bid.

- Provide a frictionless customer journey. Savvy consumers who are used to the ease and convenience of Amazon-style shopping will expect similar simplicity in finding and selecting service providers.

- Continue to improve technology. All marketplaces will be required to employ the most current technologies to remain competitive. Services marketplaces will be no different.

Key Takeaways: Services Marketplaces

- Services marketplaces are likely to grow significantly in the coming decade as the on-demand culture dictates ease of shopping for everything from plumbers to legal services.

- Services marketplace operators must demonstrate depth of knowledge of the given service vertical to attract quality service providers and win the trust of new consumers.

- Safety of service providers and consumers alike will always trump a good price or fast delivery, so operators must vet providers carefully and offer privacy safeguards.

Chapter 9: Horizontal Business Case Study – Amazon

Your margin is my opportunity.

Jeff Bezos, Amazon CEO

Introduction

As the name suggests, a horizontal marketplace is a general marketplace offering a wide variety of products and services. These eCommerce sites cater to the needs of more than one industry in a diversified market. Horizontal marketplaces position themselves as a one-stop-shop with the fundamental value proposition being convenience. With massive product assortments, these sites use economies of scale to offer better prices to their customers. In the beginning, many marketplaces were happy being horizontal; the primary idea was that adding categories just added more bits and bytes and not physical real estate, so why not sell everything? This has changed with the onslaught of vertically focused marketplaces. The most famous horizontal marketplace is, of course, Amazon, which sells electronics, books, furniture, food, grocery, apparel, toys, software, music, gadgets, and a whole lot more.

9.1 About Amazon

Amazon has averaged a compound annual growth rate of 52% for the last two decades. In the last decade, the Amazon Marketplace has seen a 100% increase in sales from its third-party sellers. Gross merchandise value

(GMV), that is total sales on all Amazon websites, grew to $335 billion in 2019, a YOY growth of 21%.

1In the 25 years since Amazon opened shop, it has become America's online retailer and a household name. Each year it further cements its leadership position across markets and categories by sourcing new products, developing service offerings, and enlarging its customer base.

Having built a trillion-dollar business empire, Jeff Bezos's leadership is the stuff of legends. At Amazon, every decision made, or problem solved—from brainstorming to hiring—is based on fourteen driving *Amazon Leadership Principles*.

4. **Customer Obsession** – Start with the customer and work their way backward.

5. **Ownership** – Think like an owner looking for long-term value instead of short-term gain.

6. **Invent & Simplify** – Innovation is often misunderstood, so leaders and teams should bring new ideas and look for ways to simplify.

7. **Are Right, a Lot** – While data drives many decisions, leaders should also have strong judgments and good instincts, and they should be right most of the time.

8. **Learn and be Curious** – Never stop learning, being curious, or improving yourself.

9. **Hire and Develop the Best** – Raise the bar with each new hire, recognize exceptional talent, and treat them as an organizational resource rather than a team star employee.

10. **Insist on the Highest Standards** – Expect teams to deliver at their highest levels to provide high-quality products and services. Problems should get fixed within a team, not sent down the line.

11. **Think Big** – Leaders and employees inspire others to think big, look for better ways to serve the customer, and search for that next big idea.

12. **Bias for Action** – Most decisions can be reversed without major costs and extensive studies, so take calculated risks to increase speed.

13. **Frugality** – Constraints breed invention, self-sufficiency, and resourcefulness, so changes should not grow the headcount, add expenses, or expand the budget.

14. **Earn Trust** – Leaders should be transparent, honest, respectful, and self-critical while holding themselves and teams to the highest standards.

15. **Dive Deep** – Everyone, leaders included, should be hands-on, operating at all levels, and staying connected to the last mile.

16. **Have Backbone; Disagree and Commit** – When necessary, leaders should challenge decisions respectfully, even if it is uncomfortable. But once a decision is made, commit to it 100%.

17. **Deliver Results** – Stay focused, never settle, deliver high-quality results on time.

9.2 Market Landscape

In the last three years, over 3 million new sellers have joined the Amazon marketplace worldwide—that is nearly 3000 new sellers daily. The US marketplace added 1 million sellers, India added 400,000, and the UK added 300,000. In total, Amazon hosts 8 million global sellers, 2.7 million of whom are based in the US. Amazon operates 16 marketplaces in the US, Canada, UK, Germany, France, Italy, Spain, India, Japan, Australia, China, Brazil, Mexico, Turkey, UAE, and Singapore, and ships to over 100 countries.

Amazon Marketplace sales stand at $200 billion, which is a 25% growth from 2016. Currently, marketplace sales contribute over 60% of the total Amazon sales worldwide. Over 66% of the top sellers use Amazon's FBA program, for which Amazon charges both fulfillment and storage fees.

Amazon has over 90 million Prime subscribers in the US. Due to discounts, exclusive offers, and ease of shopping and shipping, Prime subscribers spend an average of $1,400 per year on Amazon, while non-Prime customers spend about $600.

The electronics category was the most popular product category in the US, with 44% of shoppers making purchases. Other top performing categories include clothing, shoes & jewelry (43%), Home & Kitchen (39%), beauty & personal care (36%), books (33%), cell phones & accessories (28%), movies & TV (25%), pet supplies (20%), sporting goods & outdoors (17%), grocery & gourmet food (15%), automotive parts & accessories (13%), and baby products (9%).

According to a 2019 Amazon study, small and medium businesses (SMB) sold more than 4000 items per minute on Amazon. Amazon's 2020 SMB report states that more than half of Amazon's sales come from 3P sellers,

3,400,000,000	SMB products sold / yr (6,500/min)
$7,000,000,000	SMB B2B sales / yr
$3,100,000,000	SMB export sales / yr
$160,000	Average SMB seller sales / yr
3,700	SMB's sell > $1 mil / yr
450,000	SMB sellers use FBA
$1,000,000,000	Loaned to SMBs
$320,000,000	Earned by Kindle authors / yr
82,000	Drivers @ 1,000 delivery partners
>200,000,000	Alexa devices (100,000 types)
100,000	Alexa skills
>2,000,000,000	Alexa interactions / wk

FIGURE 9.1 2020 Amazon Small Business USA Sellers
Source: Amazon

but this report represents only SMB sellers inside the US. According to Marketplace Pulse, 42% of Amazon sellers are based in China.

Jungle Scout recently reported that around 86% of the sellers on Amazon are profitable, close to 67% become profitable within the first year of operation, and over 92% said that they want to continue selling on Amazon. On the flip side, 53% of the marketplace sellers are concerned that Amazon products compete with their products. Close to 50% are also worried that Amazon has full visibility into seller operations and product analytics.

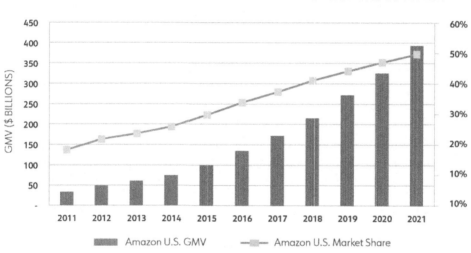

FIGURE 9.2 Amazon Market Share
Source: Company Reports, US Census Bureau, eMarketer, Needham & Company, LLC

Amazon crossed the $1 trillion market valuation milestone in September 2018 while its B2B Amazon Business unit crossed the $10 billion GMV mark—just 3 years after it began. As Amazon's stellar business growth and capacity for reinvention took the global spotlight, it became a compelling example of an ambidextrous organization. Amazon's tightly integrated senior team strives to improve its existing business while creating an organizational space to invent future businesses at the same time. As Amazon founder Jeff Bezos puts it, "We want to be a large company that's also an invention machine. We want to combine the extraordinary customer-serving capabilities that are enabled by size with the speed of movement, skill, and risk-acceptance mentality normally associated with entrepreneurial start-ups."

9.3 Marketplace Strategy & Revenue Model

Jeff Bezos adopted the Flywheel strategy first introduced by Jim Collins in his book *Good to Great*. Amazon carefully considered how it might maximize customer experience for greatest growth and landed on three primary aspects: lower prices, broader selection, and excellent delivery.

Had Amazon attempted to expand its catalog with only 1P products, the company would not have reached its current size for many decades. Instead, Amazon opened the marketplace to 3P sellers and showed its customers what broad selection looks like. Then Amazon made the bold move of minimizing dividends to shareholders and investing its profits into warehousing and shipping infrastructure. Amazon's marketplace virtuous cycle is designed to drive traffic to its platform and third-party sellers.

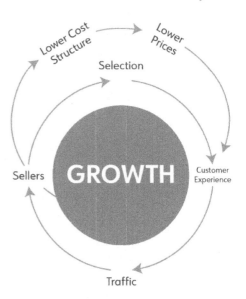

FIGURE 9.3 Flywheel Concept

The result has astonished the world of eCommerce. As Amazon increases the selection of products, sales increase, which enables Amazon to bring down costs, source more products, provide better customer experience, and increase sales. Like a flywheel, the system itself speeds up growth and expansion.

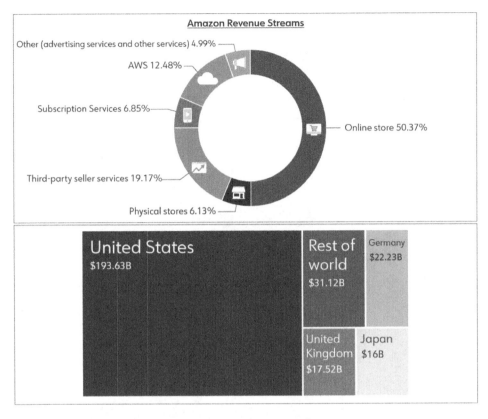

FIGURE 9.4 Amazon Revenue Streams
Source: Amazon/ https://fourweekmba.com/amazon-case-study/

Even though Amazon started as a vertical eCommerce player in books, the company's diversification efforts over the last twenty-five years have exponentially fed its market growth as it gains momentum. Its 2019 revenues stood at $280 billion with net profit at $11.5 billion. The majority of this came from online stores, with physical stores, AWS, subscription services, 3P seller services, and advertising revenue following in that order.

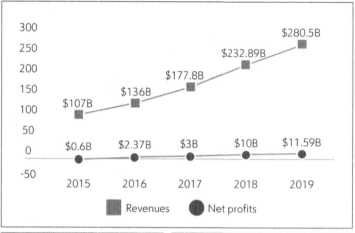

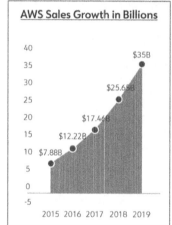

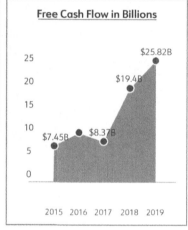

FIGURE 9.5 Amazon Business Model
Source: Amazon/ https://fourweekmba.com/amazon-case-study/

Amazon's net profits have grown at a rate of 21% year on year while, during the same year, its net profit has seen 15% year on year growth. Over the 5-year period, AWS has seen a phenomenal growth of over 350% in gross sales. AWS is responsible for the major cash flows for Amazon. In 2019 Amazon's free cash flow stood at $25.82 billion.

With tentacles in so many industries and markets, defining Amazon's core business can be difficult. The fastest growing segments within the Amazon kingdom are AWS and subscription services like Prime membership, Prime Video, and Amazon Music. Subscription revenue has seen phenomenal YOY growth of 37% and stands at $4.7 billion in revenue currently. Given the flywheel effect, Amazon's long-term investments in this arena are starting to make sense.

Amazon Web Services **(AWS)** is described by many as Amazon's cash king. It currently holds a 33% market share, more than double the share of its closest competitor, Microsoft Azure. AWS realized YOY growth of 37% and brought in annual revenue of $40 billion for 2019, covering the bulk of Amazon's operating income. As AWS becomes the infrastructure for thousands of startups and SaaS companies, it is a classic example of a platform business increasing in value as more users join.

AMAZON CONTINUES ITS REIGN ATOP THE CLOUD MARKET
Worldwide market share of leading cloud infrastrcuture service providers in Q2 2019′

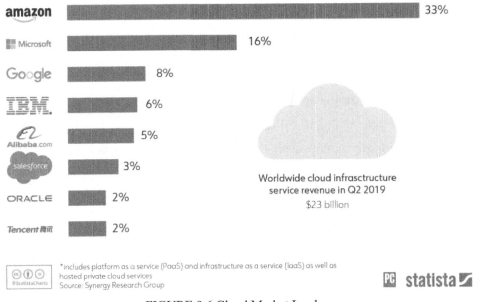

FIGURE 9.6 Cloud Market Leaders

Because **Prime Video** is bundled with Prime membership, pinning down precise revenue numbers is difficult. However, as more viewers move from the cable model to streaming services, Amazon's investment in streaming services and studio production appears wise. Amazon Studio spends billions of dollars each year to finance original content, and the payoff was 47 Emmy nominations and 15 Emmy awards in 2019. Analysts predict that Amazon will earn as much as $3.6 billion in 2020 from its video services.

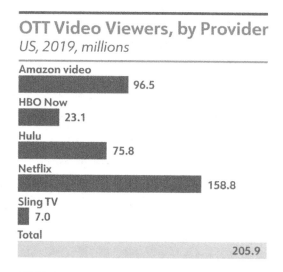

FIGURE 9.7 OTT Video Viewers by Provider
Source: https://www.emarketer.com/chart/220561/us-over-the-top-ott-video-service-viewers-by-provider-2018-millions

Amazon Advertising is another division showing stellar growth. It closed the last fiscal year with $10 billion in revenue and 37% YOY growth. Top competitor Google monopolizes the search market but shows only half the advertising growth.

FIGURE 9.8 Top 5 companies in Digital Advertising Revenue

Interestingly, Amazon has built an advertising empire on the back of its online retail, yet few have noticed it. For many years, Amazon resisted ad sales for fear it could impair the customer journey. However, the organic nature of paid ads appearing as best sellers or recommendations when the customer searches for products enhances the customer experience. Other factors that have bolstered the performance of Amazon Advertising are the platforms 50% penetration into US households, a slant toward more affluent customers, and deep data on customer purchasing behavior. From an advertiser's point of view, Amazon's higher conversion rate makes the investment more valuable than Google Ads.

Amazon began its career in the hardware products business with Kindle, Fire, and Echo devices. On the back of these successes, Amazon launched as many as 14 hardware products in September 2019, all powered by Alexa. In the last Christmas season, Amazon sold over 100 million Alexa gadgets for a stunning 70% share of the smart speaker market in the US. While many feel Apple's Siri and Google's Assistant function better, the attractive price point of Alexa devices is currently winning consumer dollars. Given Amazon's penchant for R&D, it is safe to expect Alexa's performance to improve soon.

9.4 Amazon Innovations

While the flywheel has helped Amazon gain momentum among partners, sellers, and buyers, the company itself is driven by innovation. Amazon continually examines current challenges and looks ahead for ways to outpace the competition.

FBA (Fulfillment by Amazon) – Amazon understood fast, reliable delivery to be a key to customer satisfaction, but saw that the logistics were a challenge for many of its smaller 3P sellers. FBA relieves those sellers of the burden by warehousing their products and shipping them in Amazon-branded packaging. Customers get lightning-fast delivery, sellers save on costs and complexities involved with maintaining physical stock, and Amazon has gained a revenue source.

Amazon Prime – Amazon was doing brisk business in the first part of the twenty-first century, but consumers still appreciated the convenience of walking into a brick-and-mortar store and walking out with product. The marketplace needed to sweeten the deal to gain consumer loyalty. In February 2005, Amazon launched the first and largest online loyalty program in the world. Currently, 112 million US consumers and another 48 million global consumers pay an annual membership fee of $119. The program began with free two-day delivery on any item and eventually offered one-day and same-day delivery. Today, Amazon Prime members receive free streaming content, expedited and reduced-cost shipping on specified items, Prime Day bonuses, and many other benefits.

Amazon in Grocery Space – Amazon knows there are many inherent challenges with selling fresh groceries (meat, dairy, produce) on its traditional marketplace platform. Consumers want to see and touch those products before purchase and safely shipping delicate items like eggs and bananas would be far from cost-effective. So how can Amazon become the consumer go-to for CPG when shoppers can easily pick up those household items when they visit the grocery store for fresh items? In 2017 Amazon loudly declared its intention to compete when it acquired Whole Foods for a whopping $13.7 billion. Amazon's long-term plans for the chain are unclear, but it has been a good opportunity for the online giant to learn about the grocery industry. Additionally, offering special in-store discounts to Prime members has served to boost Prime membership.

Amazon Go – Its purchase of Whole Foods in 2017 taught Amazon a critical lesson. The only effective way to truly compete with the convenience of a local brick-and-mortar store is to open right next door— so Amazon did in 2018. But in standard Amazon fashion, the Amazon Go stores stunned the world with a new level of convenience. Using the Amazon Go app, shoppers simply swipe their phones on the way in, pick up the items they want, and leave. Using a mix of computer vision, sensor fusion, and AI, the app charges the primary credit card on the customer's Amazon account, so registers and checkout lines are unnecessary. There are currently 26 Amazon Go stores selling groceries in four major cities across the US, with plans for as many as 2000.

Research and Development — Nineteenth-century banker J.P. Morgan once said, "The first step towards getting somewhere is to decide that you are not going to stay where you are." Amazon embodies this sentiment as it spends more on R&D than any other company in corporate America. The company's dissatisfaction with remaining in one place drives the desire to stay ahead of the game. A quick look at the R&D spends at Amazon underlines this fact.

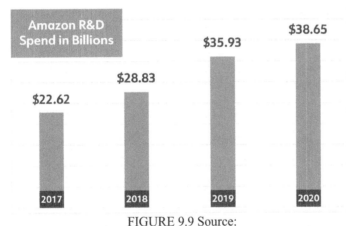

FIGURE 9.9 Source:
https://www.macrotrends.net/stocks/charts/AMZN/amazon/research-development-expenses

Amazon R&D expenses for the quarter ending June 30, 2020, were $10.38 billion, a 14.59% YOY increase. During the fiscal year ending June 30, 2020, the company spent $38.652 billion, a 21.46% YOY increase, on cloud computing through Amazon Web Services (AWS), improvements to Alexa, and support for Amazon Go stores.

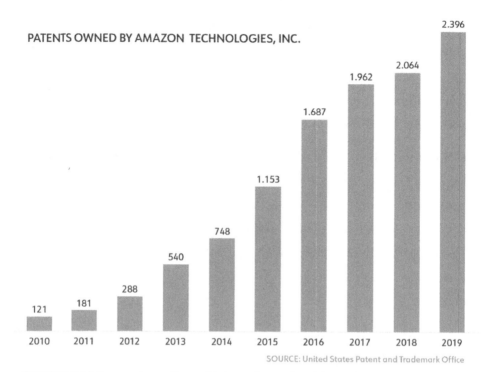

FIGURE 9.10 Source: https://www.bizjournals.com/washington/news/2019/12/13/the-most-interesting-amazon-patents-of-2019-from.html

This relentless focus on R&D also reflects in the number of patents Amazon holds. In 2019, the company filed for 2396 patents. While it cannot compete with the likes of Microsoft and Samsung on sheer numbers, it has made a steady climb over the last decade.

9.5 Business Impact

Started twenty-six years ago as an online book retailer, Amazon is today one of the most valuable companies in the world, with a market cap reaching $1 trillion in 2020. Its annual revenue for 2020 is projected to hit $320 billion, thanks to constant innovation, relentless customer focus, and tireless work toward its long-term vision. As a result, Amazon is not simply a retailer. It is an online advertising giant, a book publisher, a film producer, a hardware manufacturer, a logistics service provider, a marketing platform, a delivery network, and a payment service. Some might say Amazon has had a positive macro effect on the economy, employment, and small business.

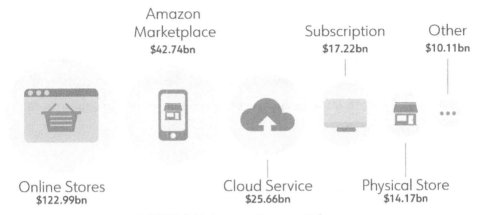

FIGURE 9.11 Amazon Revenue Drivers

Economic Growth – Amazon started with books but became a store for everything over a period. Ultra-fast doorstep delivery led consumers worldwide to embrace Amazon with open wallets. A recent eMarketer study indicates Amazon accounts for about 4% of the retail sales and close to 40% of eCommerce sales in the US for 2019. From a purely economic standpoint increased consumer spending contributes to the GDP, and Amazon's rub-off effect has led to people buying more on other eCommerce portals as well.

Keeping Inflation in Check – Amazon has massively disrupted retail and expedited the demise of market players that were already struggling. Amazon's lack of overhead from physical stores allows the platform to undercut the competition on pricing while operating on a thinner margin. Lower prices across categories drive inflation down. And thanks to its scale, Amazon also can make investments at a negative rate of return because it can cross-subsidize. Economist Dr. Ed Yardeni says, "Amazon arguably has done as much as the Chinese to kill jobs and keep a lid on inflation by enabling fast and easy price discovery for anyone with a cell phone."

Employment Creation – At the time of this writing, Amazon has 750,000 full-time and part-time employees worldwide. Although this sounds like a substantial number, it pales in comparison to retailers operating brick-and-mortar storefronts. For example, Walmart has 2.2 million employees. But apart from Amazon's direct employees, it supports a huge ecosystem of contractors, suppliers, and delivery personnel. This indirect creation of jobs means Amazon directly supports the economies of the countries in which Amazon operates.

AMAZON'S EMPLOYEES WORLDWIDE

Total number of staff employed

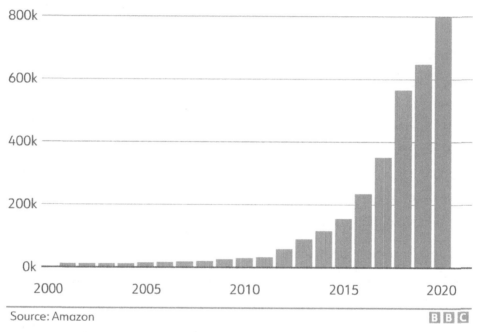

Source: Amazon

FIGURE 9.12

Helping SMBs – According to Amazon, over 900,000 jobs were created outside the company because of Amazon's third-party marketplace. Logistics have long been a pain point for many a small business, hindering their ability to scale. With Amazon, they have access to world class logistics infrastructure, increased market reach, and rapid scale.

As is common when a single entity demonstrates such vast superiority over the competition, a growing chorus now complains of unfair trade practices and cries for the breakup of Amazon.

The Accusations

- **Amazon holds a monopoly** – Merriam-Webster defines monopoly as "exclusive ownership through legal privilege, command of supply, or concerted action." Truth be told, Amazon has taken concerted action to own many product categories.

- **Operator or retailer?** – One of the biggest criticisms of Amazon is the conflict of interest created by being both a marketplace operator and a retailer on its own platform. By identifying best-selling products and offering its own branded version, Amazon directly competes with its vendors.

- **Fixing the race** – Amazon is accused of burying the listings of merchants who are selling the same product for a lesser price outside the platform. Also, merchants who do not advertise with Amazon run the risk of their listings pushing to later pages.

- **Stifling competition** – It is impossible to say how many companies have folded because they were unable to compete with Amazon's aggressive pricing. Old-guard enterprises like Toys R Us and Sears have been on the ropes for decades, but Amazon delivered the final blow. Similarly, in every category and geography that Amazon enters, players of all sizes struggle to compete with the behemoth's, vast catalog, logistics efficiency, and rock-bottom prices.

- **Unfair labor practices** – A growing body of evidence suggests Amazon's relentless drive for efficiency comes at the cost of its frontline workforce, creating a contentious relationship between employer and employee. Workers have leveraged the COVID-19 pandemic to gain ground on their longstanding demands, including raises and paid time off.

- **Data privacy issues** – Amazon's privacy problems may not compete with those of Facebook and Google, but they still bear discussion. Amazon's claim that employees and contractors are studying recordings from the Echo and Alexa voice assistants to improve device accuracy does not negate the serious privacy concerns of strangers listening to the lives of millions of private citizens.

The Defense

- **Megalith, not monopoly** – Despite its unprecedented growth and market domination, Amazon does not warrant the attention of the US Department of Justice for monopolization. According to section 2 of the Sherman Act, monopoly power is concerning when it raises prices and decreases innovation, two points which certainly do not apply to Amazon. Further, the Supreme Court has ruled that simply possessing monopoly power does not violate antitrust law where that power is the product of superior skill, foresight, or industry, all areas where Amazon excels.

- **A split does not guarantee competition** – While breaking Amazon into pieces may give some of the larger vendors an opportunity to grow, there is no guarantee that any of the competitors would survive and thrive without the attention delivered by the Amazon banner. Rather, those former Amazon companies would become powerful and direct competition to the smaller vendors while the disbanded Amazon efficiency would drive an increase in prices. In the end, consumers would suffer the most.

- **A Consumer paradise** – The fact is that Amazon has built a retail paradise. Consumers can find almost any product for a reasonable price, have it delivered to their doorstep, and return it for any reason, frequently free of charge. Amazon's unwavering focus on customer experience (speed, selection, and convenience), has created a ripple effect of consumer benefit across eCommerce and other industries.

- **Driving business growth** – Amazon's self-stated purpose is to provide its vendors with the opportunity to sell throughout the world by leveling the playing field and reducing barriers to entry. The 60% of all Amazon sales which are made by its vendors are a testament to the company's enormous capital expenditure in the fulfillment and distribution network which directly benefits the sellers. In addition, Amazon spends billions of dollars each year to help merchants drive traffic using marketing programs and technological infrastructure.

- **Encouraging innovation and competition** – Among large tech companies, Amazon has the third-largest R&D budget. Kroger, Target, and Walmart have all increased their spending on R&D and have begun to use robotics and other innovative technologies to stay in the game.

Key Takeaways:

Horizontal Business Case Study — Amazon

- Unlike other companies in the trillion-dollar club, Amazon has built an empire by harnessing the flywheel effect to create a virtuous cycle of growth.

- Amazon has demonstrated to the world that long-term vision and persistence can pay off handsomely.

- The symbiotic relationship between Amazon and its 3P sellers helps Amazon's exponential growth and supports millions of small businesses.

- Despite its massive size, Amazon moves nimbly and fosters innovation as evidenced by FBA, Amazon Prime, and the advertising business.

- Amazon stays true to itself and relevant to the times through its 14 leadership principles, the most significant of which is customer obsession.

- Among Amazon's other businesses outside the 3P marketplace, AWS contributes most significantly to the operating income.

Chapter 10: Grocery Business Case Study – Instacart

American households spend over a hundred hours every single year shopping for groceries. That's time they could spend with their families, with their friends, doing the things that they love.

Apoorva Mehta, Founder CEO - Instacart

Introduction

The COVID-19 pandemic saw online grocery transform from a niche service used mostly by the upper class to a vital societal need, almost overnight. For many shoppers, the pandemic created the push they needed to shop for groceries online. This new normal could potentially be the most significant shift for an industry that has struggled to go digital. According to Orian Research, the global online grocery market is likely to grow at a CAGR of 23.7% between 2020 to 2025. On the other hand, challenges remain. Research by TABS Analytics shows that less than 30% of Americans shop online for groceries. Over 99% continue to shop at brick-and-mortar stores, while 44% never buy groceries online. Despite significant investments from Amazon and Walmart, online grocery growth has been slow in the US compared to other parts of the world, mainly South Korea, China, and the United Kingdom. The development and success of third-party delivery services, such as Instacart, Shipt, and FreshDirect, provides a fresh perspective on how to win in online grocery using the marketplace model.

10.1 About Instacart

Online grocery shopping is set to hit $100 billion in sales by 2025, according to a Nielsen study sponsored by the Food Marketing Institute, and Instacart is leading the charge. Founded in 2012, Instacart is a four-sided marketplace available to 80% of US households and 70% of Canadian households. Their current partnerships include Sam's Club, Costco, Kroger, Safeway, Target, Albertsons, Publix, CVS, and more.

With an electrical engineering degree and two years of experience as a supply chain engineer at Amazon, Mehta Apoorva set about creating twenty companies in only two years—all of which failed. But in 2012, Apoorva and partners Max Mullen and Brandon Leonardo hit on a winning idea. With $2.3 million in seed money, the trio built a mobile app to bring grocery stores, CPG brands, personal shoppers, and consumers together.

10.2 Market Landscape

Grocery shopping has always been an in-store experience for consumers who want to carefully examine and choose fresh products. However, 2020 and COVID-19 forced a dramatic shift in the grocery industry. As government regulation and fear of illness swept the world, consumers decided a small delivery fee was worth the price of safety if they knew a vetted personal shopper could be trusted to select quality fresh foods. Instacart was ready.

In truth, the concept of grocery delivery has been around for decades, but the expense and complex logistics of safely delivering fresh foods made the concept cost prohibitive. Webvan attempted a full-scale dive into online grocery shopping during the dotcom bubble and lasted only three years thanks to the dotcom crash and massive capital expenditures involved with building warehouses and maintaining inventory.

The buy online, pick up in-store model (BOPIS) has gained popularity among many big box chains over the last few years. But for true home delivery of groceries, Instacart leads the pack. Available in nearly every medium and large city around the US and Canada, customers can choose from select partner stores in their area, pay a small delivery fee, and expect their grocery delivery in a few hours. Delivery fees vary based on size of order, peak shopping hours, and the customer's chosen membership level.

Shipt, owned by Target, has a similar operating model and pricing structure but is currently limited to the Southeast and a few select states. Unlike Shipt and Instacart, Peapod is a true online grocery store warehousing most of its own inventory. All orders can be delivered at competitive delivery charges or picked up in-store.

In select major cities, Amazon Prime membership includes Prime Now home delivery service. Available only for products in stock at a nearby Amazon warehouse or Whole Foods market, two-hour delivery is free while one-hour delivery costs about $10. Google Shopping is an extremely limited player in the grocery game, offering only dry goods, like cereal and canned goods, for home delivery. The platform does however offer far more than just dry food items and includes partnerships with a wide variety of stores like Kohl's, Costco, and PetSmart. Delivery fees and times vary depending on items ordered, the retailer, and the location.

10.3 Revenue Model

With the explosion of the modern gig economy, marketplaces like Uber and DoorDash have seen meteoric growth. Instacart has made significant use of the gig worker concept to simplify the grocery home delivery problem. Consumers pay for items they want at the store they want, Instacart dispatches a personal shopper, the groceries are delivered. But what makes Instacart unique is its speed and efficiency. Some orders can be delivered in as little as an hour.

FIGURE 10.1 Instacart 3-step Home Delivery Service

Without warehouses or inventory, Instacart does not need source products or maintain a catalog. They also save dramatically on full-time employee costs, delivery trucks, and property taxes. Revenue obviously comes from delivery and membership fees, but the fourth side of the marketplace is also a revenue source. CPG brands can choose to advertise on the platform. Like a Google or Amazon search, advertising on Instacart pushes sponsored products to the top when customers start searching. As many as 30% of all purchases on Instacart include advertised items, so the model has proven effective.

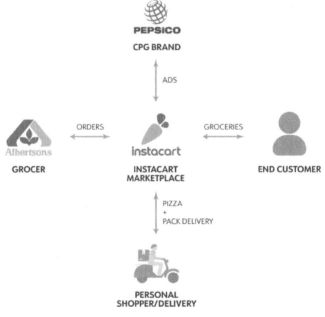

FIGURE 10.2 Instacart as a four-sided marketplace

10.4 Challenges

Despite experiencing rapid growth and leading the grocery delivery market, Instacart has faced some significant challenges and critical attention. Overall, there is a sense of skepticism about its prospects as analysts predict rough weather ahead.

Employee Relations — Foremost among the difficulties has been the charge from the personal shoppers that the company treats its employees poorly. With complaints of everything from not receiving benefits to having to pay for their own personal protection equipment like masks and gloves, the part-time workforce has been unhappy with the company's actions. It is important to note that these issues are not unique to Instacart but encompass the entire gig economy. As the gig model has gained in popularity, legislators have jumped into the fray with attempts to regulate the industry, though no one has solved the issues completely.

Vendor Relations — While grocery vendors have not tried to sue Instacart as the shoppers have, many are re-evaluating their relationship with the company. Instacart has been tight-lipped about exact contract terms with vendors, but grocery stores may be losing as much as 3% on each order total. They may gain some customer loyalty over time, but they cannot confirm because they do not receive analytics. Instacart collects plenty of customer data that it does not share with the vendors. In addition to the unknown return on a very real expense, many grocery chains discovered in the recent pandemic that they could offer BOPIS without the help of an outside vendor. Instacart's value to the grocery stores may very well be eroding.

Customer Relations — In every business, there will be unhappy customers. However, customers who are tech-savvy enough to buy groceries online are sure to post their dissatisfaction on social media. In some cases, customers have disparaged the personal shopper, Instacart, and the grocer for a variety of reasons. Common grievances include

Instacart marking up prices as much as 15%, poor service quality from personal shoppers, or even shoppers who delivered large orders in multiple trips because their vehicle is too small to carry the full load. Additionally, some customers have engaged in tip baiting, in which they enter a large tip at the time of order but remove the tip after receiving delivery.

10.5 Business Impact

While online grocery has gained steadily in recent years, the market exploded with the COVID situation, closing a record $4 billion in sales during March 2020 and $5.3 billion in April. At the current pace, the grocery eCommerce hit $20 billion in the next two years. Some sources estimate that total US online food and beverage sales could grow to $32 billion by the end of 2021.

Instacart's rapid growth can be marked by several notable milestones. In its first year of operation, the company saw 35% revenue growth each month in selected markets. By 2014 Instacart was present in fifteen US cities and closed $100 million in sales. Receiving more funding in 2015, Instacart was valued at $2 billion. In that same year, the company signed a five-year exclusive partnership with Whole Foods, allowing Instacart to directly reach a more affluent audience. Even though Whole Foods was acquired by Amazon in 2017, thereby invalidating the five-year contract, Instacart continued to expand across the US and Canada.

$337M+	$75M+	$154M+	$55M+
in California	in Illinois	in New York	in Washington

FIGURE 10.3 Instacart's role in retail employment

The Instacart Effect, a study conducted by Dr. Robert Kulick of NERA Economic Consulting, shows the impact of Instacart's presence in California, New York, Illinois, and Washington in 2019. According to Dr.

Kulick, Instacart added 23,000 retail grocery jobs and accounted for $620 million worth of grocery purchases in these four markets.

These days Instacart has an extensive list of partner stores, all of whom are desperate to compete with Amazon. In the US, Instacart now has a partnership with over 350 stores across 4000 cities.

FIGURE 10.4 Instacart partners

Naturally, the pandemic has significantly accelerated the growth of online grocery. Instacart has seen over 500% increase in order value in 2020, and app downloads increased by 218% in March. Additionally, Instacart notes that consumers are ordering more product and with greater frequency. Currently, 44% of orders include more than 15 items (versus 38% in 2016), and the average shopper now places an order about once every three weeks.

While Instacart has struggled with public opinion in the past, the evidence proves the grocery delivery model resonates well with a growing consumer base. And despite stiff competition, Instacart appears to be well-positioned to maintain its front runner position in the online grocery market.

Key Takeaways:

Grocery Business Case Study — Instacart

- Grocery eCommerce had considerable momentum before 2020, but the COVID pandemic has positioned the market to reach $20 billion in the next two years.

- With a market valuation at $18 billion (as of October 2020), Instacart looks to take advantage of the explosive surge in online grocery demand.

- Instacart has adopted a true platform model with zero investment in warehouses and transportation. Its only assets are its shoppers.

- Instacart's four-sided marketplace encourages interaction between customers, shoppers, grocery stores, and brands.

- Instacart is now accessible to 80% of American households because of its wide variety of merchant partnerships.

- Through its innovative business model, Instacart has also helped the local job markets.

- While its growth has been nothing less than phenomenal, the two key challenges it faces are worker backlash and growing competition from big guns who have a brick-and-mortar advantage.

Chapter 11: Services Business Case Study – Uber

Ultimately, progress and innovation win.

Travis Kalanick – Former CEO, Uber

Introduction

Ride-hailing has proven to be a perfect use case for the marketplace model. Before Uber and Lyft's breakout growth, the taxi ecosystem was inefficient. For instance, in California (where both Lyft and Uber were born), people could book a taxi over the phone or on the internet. Still, the drivers were dispatched based on the queue position, resulting in a longer wait time for customers. Adoption of the marketplace model helped match supply and demand efficiently. The ride-hailing market is set to grow at 15% CAGR from 2020 to 2025, catering to the consumer's need for quick, convenient, and cost-effective transportation. The major drivers for this growth are the growing need for personal mobility due to urbanization combined with the fall in car ownership. Uber's success story presents an ideal template on how to win in this sector.

11.1 About Uber

In 2007, Travis Kalanick was looking for a way to reduce the cost of direct transportation and realized a cost-sharing model would be affordable. In March of 2009, Kalanick and his friend Garrett Camp invested their own $200K as seed funding for UberCab, a cab company based in France. By May 2010, the company launched operations in San

Francisco and by the end of 2020 were operating in 785 metropolitan areas across 83 countries. Uber drivers serve 110 million worldwide riders, and the company is currently valued at $74 billion with annual revenues of over $11 billion.

Uber's dramatic growth can be attributed to a variety of ride-hailing services, like UberX for private drivers, UberPool for carpooling, and in some countries, options to hire bikes and minivans. Operating on a similar model, Uber Eats delivers food orders from local restaurants. By catering to the varying needs and budget constraints of diverse populations, Uber demonstrates a thoughtful strategy of acting as a market-disrupting trendsetter with user-friendly technology for the sharing economy.

11.2 Market Landscape

Hailing a cab on a city street has not changed in more than 100 years, and millions of riders worldwide have mastered the system of being in the right place at the right time to wave an arm and jump in the back seat. And yet Uber managed to revolutionize the taxi industry in the space of just a few years. Suddenly taxi companies and rental car services find themselves taking the back seat to Uber.

So, what has helped Uber transform itself from being a late entrant in the taxi market to be the leader in the sector? From the start, Uber set out to move riders from simple participants in the existing public transit system to owners of their own transportation experience. With the creation of a self-regulating global network, Uber removed schedule, expanded access, and provided reliable choices.

Uber's business model is primarily driven by three key elements—drivers, riders, and price. Drivers are the backbone of the Uber system. Uber supplies its drivers the flexibility to work whenever they want, earn supplemental income, and be their own boss.

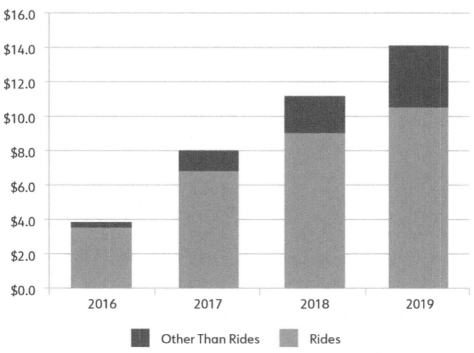

FIGURE 11.1 Uber vs Taxi vs Car Rental, Source:
https://www.nakedcapitalism.com/2020/02/hubert-horan-can-uber-ever-deliver-part-twenty-two-profits-and-cash-flow-keep-deteriorating-as-ubers-gaap-losses-hit-8-5-billion.html

Riders are the drivers of the Uber system. The cost of owning a vehicle in a major city is on the rise, so the fast pickup, low cost, convenience, and safety of an Uber ride makes the decision against purchasing a car easy.

Fare estimates; flexible payment options; and transparent fares vary based on car type, distance, and time of day are all contributing factors to the success of Uber.

11.3 Revenue Model

Like traditional taxi and rental car services, Uber's revenue model is based on fares received from customers. However, like other marketplace business models, Uber has found a variety of other revenue sources.

Commission – As the principal revenue source, Uber keeps 20% of the fare charged to the rider and the remaining 80% goes to the driver.

Vehicle type – To capture every segment of society, Uber offers a more economical ride in a modest vehicle or a higher-priced ride to those opting for a luxurious car.

Cancellation fee – Riders are charged for canceling a ride but can apply that fee to their next ride.

Leasing – To generate revenue from drivers who do not own a car already, Uber supplies a lease option at a minimum rate.

Alternative rides – Uber has adapted to the needs of its riders by providing alternative ride options like Uber for Kids, Uber Pet, Uber Moto, Uber Works, and electric scooter rides.

New business segments – Uber Eats delivers prepaid food orders from local restaurants.

Brand partnership/advertising – Uber now sells ad space on the side of its vehicles as they rack up miles on busy city streets.

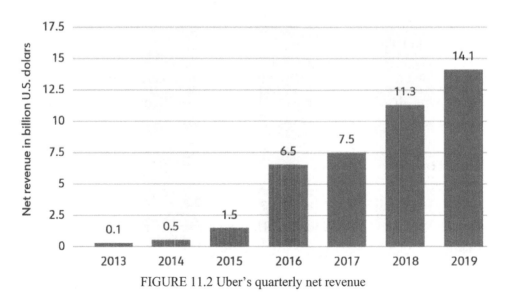

Global net revenue of Uber from 2013 to 2019
(in billion U.S. dollars)

FIGURE 11.2 Uber's quarterly net revenue

Image Source: Statista

Pricing – Uber's prices begin with a base rate and are then calculated according to the distance and estimated time of the route and the demand for rides at that time and place. Uber also employs several pricing strategies to generate maximum revenue and at the same time offer fair rates.

- Upfront pricing shows the rider an exact price before booking a trip. If the trip changes mid-journey (either route or drop location) the upfront price is also adjusted to reflect actual time and distance traveled. However, many riders have said that the fact they can see a firm price before riding has encouraged them to use Uber.

- Route-based pricing is based on demand for rides in that area. Pricing may be lowered on certain routes at certain times to attracts more riders or expand the market into new areas of the city.

- Surge and dynamic pricing are affected by the number of riders compared to the number of available drivers. When there are more riders, prices surge to encourage drivers to give rides, thus restoring balance to the system. When there are fewer riders, prices lower to encourage drivers to take a break.

11.4 Challenges

Uber has been widely accepted by riders who were tired of public transit or expensive vehicle ownership, leading to a valuation of $74 billion in ten short years. However, Uber's path to growth has been fraught with challenges.

Cash burn – To capture a larger ride share and attract drivers, Uber is paying out more money than it brings in. Uber loses 25¢ on every dollar it brings in and an average of $1.20 on every ride. As a result, the company has yet to make a profit and is burning investor money to overcome losses.

Low unemployment rate – In most markets, Uber suffers high turnover and struggles to retain well-trained drivers. And in economies with low unemployment rates, attracting new drivers is even more difficult.

Disgruntled drivers – The company has been forced to reduce driver incentives and wages to keep rider fares low. Most Uber drivers now earn only $10 to $12 per hour and many have switched to other rideshare services.

Competition in both domestic and global markets – When Uber first launched, it was one of a kind. Now several other players are offering competitive fares and Uber has been forced to roll out promotional incentives to attract riders. The rise of the sharing economy has led to many businesses copying Uber's business model.

Major Uber Competitors by Market & Last-Round Valuations

FIGURE 11.3

Poor customer loyalty – According to Vox, 34% of people in the US who use ride-hailing services use both Lyft and Uber. That figure is up more than fifty points from two years ago.

Stringent regulatory compliance – In most markets that Uber entered, established taxi and car rental companies were regulated by government transportation policies. Because those policies did not apply to Uber, the company was able to operate at significantly lower employee costs and offer subsequently lower fares to riders. Those suffering competitors took their case to the regulators, and in some cases to court, so that Uber is now subject to those same government regulations.

Prop 22: Contractor v. Employee – Many companies operating in the gig economy now face labor laws and conflict around the treatment of drivers as independent contractors rather than employees. Recently California voters carried Uber and Lyft to an overwhelming victory by approving Proposition 22, a ballot measure that lets companies like Uber, Lyft, and DoorDash treat its driver as independent contractors. Labor groups and state lawmakers were involved in a hard-fought battle with ride-hailing and delivery start-ups. The companies spent a staggering $200 million to fund their campaign which saw them win in California. At the time of this writing, this story is still unraveling as the labor groups and lawmakers continue the fight in other states to bring down Prop 22.

11.5 Business Impact

Uber employed strategies to their cost and revenue models which had never been considered in the taxi industry previously. As a result, Uber quickly disrupted the taxi industry and captured the market lead.

Cutting transaction costs – The taxi industry traditionally carried heavy overhead costs of owning, maintaining, and parking its vehicles—costs that were passed onto the riders. Uber eliminates these fees.

Minimizing driver-related costs – In the Uber model, drivers do not require a permit to operate as a transportation service provider. Also, other overhead costs like commercial insurance and business licensing do not apply to Uber drivers.

Increased productivity of assets and employment rates – The sharing economy works on the principle of turning unused or under-used assets into resources that are productive or profitable. The platform allows car owners whose vehicles were sitting idle to log on, drive for Uber, and make money for themselves and the company.

Use of cutting-edge technology – The smartphone app was the single largest game-changer in the industry. The convenience of GPS technology helps to match drivers and riders, track and monitor trips, and cut down ride search time. Riders can even schedule a pick-up on their phone, something unheard of in the traditional taxi model.

Variable or flexible pricing – Functioning as a ride-sharing company rather than a taxi service, Uber has the freedom to set a flexible pricing policy according to market demand. Riders also appreciate Uber's transparent and upfront pricing model.

Convenient and frictionless payment – Uber's cashless transaction debits a rider's credit card and credits the driver's account immediately making it unnecessary to produce cab fare or make change.

Implementing a rating system to improve service quality – Allowing customers to rate the driver, and vice versa, at the end of a ride helps maintain service quality from the perspective of the driver and customer. This encourages drivers to provide a high quality of service, thereby encouraging customers to return.

Key Takeaways:

Services Business Case Study — Uber

- Uber has been able to build a global network using the core principles of expanding access, delivering reliability, providing choice, and aligning needs.

- Uber pricing is based on three key components, including base rate, time and distance of the route, and the demand for rides in that time and place.

- Uber has leveraged the marketplace model by removing the middleman and allowing drivers and riders to transact directly.

- In the global market, Uber continues to face challenges pertaining to regulatory compliance. Local competition and poor customer loyalty are also ongoing challenges.

- Some of the key innovations put forth by Uber include the use of innovative technology, variable or flexible pricing, and increased productivity of assets.

Chapter 12: B2B Technical Case Study – Z-Tech, a part of AB InBev

---

MiMercado by AB InBev offers a more convenient, intuitive experience online for our customers. It's a core pillar of our digitization strategy, a strategy to grow our business, and an opportunity for us to strengthen our relationship with our buyers.

Luiz Gondim, CTO at Z-Tech and Global VP, Innovation at AB InBev

Introduction

Consumer Packaged Goods (CPG) companies have seen their distribution networks disrupted in the growing markets of Central and South America by big box stores and online marketplaces. This is especially true when it comes to supplying smaller grocery stores and markets. This disruption has created an emerging need among CPG companies and brands to regain control of the relationship with those smaller businesses.

The large number of small businesses who stock consumer packaged goods represent a significant part of the market share in these regions, a fact made more evident during the COVID-19 pandemic when distribution channels were slowed or stopped, causing supply shortages and outages across the region.

MiMercado is the response of Z-Tech, a part of AB InBev, to the need for a more direct line between CPG brands and the small markets that offer their products.

12.1 About MiMercado and Z-Tech

Z-Tech is the technology and innovation hub of AB InBev, the largest brewery company in the world with over $45 Billion in revenue yearly and 630 beer brands in 150 different countries. Z-Tech's mission is to empower small and medium-sized businesses to change the world through technology. They target the marketplace and fintech markets through the creation and acquisition of business ventures from those segments, and seek to introduce disruptive technology solutions that, coupled with the strengths of AB InBev, can change these market landscapes.

MiMercado is a B2B marketplace launched in the Mexican market so that corner stores, or points of consumption (POC), can buy their CPG inventory in a single platform to reduce the friction of managing multiple vendors or having to travel to procure goods, resulting in lost sales and long working hours.

The aspirations are backed by research of the Mexico City market, which has more than forty thousand POCs with a weekly AOV of Mex$3200, or about $160 US. Furthermore, other joint efforts from Z-Tech support the notion that a global marketplace engine can expand this model to other parts of Mexico and other countries in Central and South America and achieve comparable results, making this vertical of business viable even for a conglomerate the size of AB InBev.

12.2 Market Landscape

In the current market landscape, CPG and overall inventory for POCs are supplied by long-standing, often family-owned-and-operated, wholesalers with some reticence to change where and how they purchase inventory.

All eight of the largest wholesalers in this region have been operating for over thirty years and account for more than sixty percent of the market. Another crucial factor is that margins are tight for these large wholesalers, netting to less than 10% gross margin and losing much of that on logistics, sales, and service costs.

In this space, the trends indicate that a digital experience will enable self-service for the POCs and move the industry forward. Different store formats serve different markets and require different digital strategies, with a few examples shown below.

Store Format	Characteristics
Self-service	- Targets individual consumers - Store sizes vary from 400 to 2500 m2 - Primary focus: food, beverage, tobacco, non-groceries
Cash & Carry	- Offers both retail and wholesale pricing - POS serves as warehouse to reduce costs - High-volume, fast-turnover, varied merchandise
Specialty	- Specializes in select categories - Caters to niche markets - Varied brands and products - Wide range of prices
Discounter	- Focuses on limited private-label grocery products at budget prices - Store sizes vary from 400 to 2500 m2
Convenience	- Sells everyday products to individual consumers at proximity locations - Small store formats of >400 m2 - Limited mix of products
Wholesale club	- Operates on a membership fee model - Wide variety of grocery and non-grocery products - Aggressive pricing

FIGURE 12.1

For those wholesalers to be able to keep up with CPG brands and to increase margins, they have been investing heavily in an expanded portfolio of brands and private label offerings.

When Z-Tech chose to launch MiMercado in Mexico City, the Central de Abasto (CEDA) was a primary consideration. A government-owned marketplace founded in 1981, CEDA was created to be a single commercial space to supply the city. The Mexican government claims it is the largest market in the world at 327 acres, with ninety thousand people employed (mostly by private enterprises), 350–500 thousand daily visitors, and $9B USD in annual sales. It is the only place of business in Mexico that exchanges more money than the Mexican stock exchange. Large and small wholesalers use CEDA to supply goods to both retailers and end consumers, accounting for 80% of Mexico City's goods, and 45% of all wholesale food supplies in Mexico.

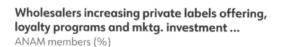

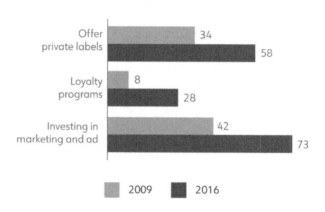

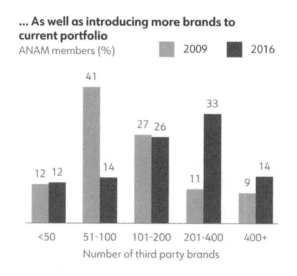

FIGURE 12.2

To compete with such a dominant player, upstarts like MiMercado must offer a unique value proposition that can rival this competition and gather interest from POCs. This example is for Mexico, but the same applies to other Central and South American markets. Additionally, some parts of the African continent are following the same trend.

12.3 Revenue Model

Currently, MiMercado operates as a 1P + 3P marketplace, and the revenue streams consist of:

- **Direct sales of owned inventory (1P):** MiMercado has direct contracts with wholesalers like Sodisa that supply distribution centers, but owns and sell those goods directly and profits from the margins.

- **Commission fees by Category (3P):** MiMercado also has onboarded sellers like Grupo Modelo and charges a commission on products sold through the marketplace. Continuous addition of sellers will scale the business on a national level.

- **Subscription (3P):** MiMercado charges a membership fee for new sellers, generating a recurring monthly revenue to sustain operations.

12.4 Challenges

Historically, POC sales have been driven by in-person processes, with a distributed, boots-on-the-ground sales team selling directly to many small business owners across Mexico. Over the past few years, AB InBev has undertaken a massive effort to rapidly digitize its business, investing significant resources in building online sales channels with a focus on emerging markets.

But digitizing existing sales channels is not enough to maintain a long-term lead in the modern, highly competitive landscape. Whether in B2B or B2C, creating a fresh, innovative online buying experience requires greater convenience, wider selection, a strong customer experience, and maintenance of a pricing model that competes with the likes of CEDA in Mexico City to be attractive to the POCs.

Another challenge Z-Tech faced was the fact that technology and digital purchasing are not as pervasive in Mexico as in the US and other developed markets. Being able to provide that strong customer experience using tools already available to all POCs, like a simple smartphone, and support through platforms like WhatsApp was crucial to increase the confidence of the POC owners in doing business with a digital Marketplace.

12.5 Solution

MiMercado was created to address the market need for a single-source digital commerce property that allows owners of small markets and stalls to easily order beverage, CPG, and other items from their mobile phones.

The marketplace is built on the Adobe Magento Commerce platform to handle all of the core eCommerce functions of catalog, search, cart, and checkout. It is integrated with the Mirakl marketplace platform to handle the third-party seller functions, such as catalog and taxonomy normalization, seller profile management, escrow payment handling, funds distribution, and offers. This cloud-based, scalable architecture forms a flexible foundation for future growth.

To address the reality that the majority of these shop owners conduct business from their mobile phones on networks that often provide a sluggish response, a headless approach was taken to the user interface. A progressive web application (PWA) front-end was built using the Vue Storefront framework in order to provide an app-like experience that is optimized for both mobile users and bandwidth-challenged connections.

PWAs are accessed via a browser, like a standard website, but have access to mobile device features that enable advanced functions like local caching of page and catalog content, push notifications, home screen shortcuts, and even offline checkout capabilities. They are also compliant with Google's Accelerated Mobile Pages (AMP) technology, which speeds up load and interaction times and improves SEO rankings.

The resulting solution provides business owners with an easily accessible one-stop-shop to re-supply their shelves, creates a community of sellers offering a broad and deep selection of items to the business owners, and positions AB InBev as an innovative leader in the food distribution space in these rapidly expanding markets.

12.6 Business Impact

While the marketplace will continue to grow and evolve, the data so far indicates that AB InBev made a wise investment in the development of MiMercado. The greater B2B marketplace space saw considerable momentum before 2020, but the COVID pandemic has positioned the market to reach $3.6 trillion worldwide by 2024. To capitalize on this trend, MiMercado's innovative business model helps the local corner store market improve profitability through a centralized, cost-effective ordering platform. While its growth has been nothing less than phenomenal, the two key challenges MiMercado faces moving forward are customer adherence and the logistical challenges of scale with small margins on sales. But the MiMercado solution was conceived and built with careful intention that provides AB InBev a repeatable and scalable model to expand its marketplace success.

Key Takeaways:

B2B Technical Case Study — Z-Tech, part of AB InBev

- An opportunity existed in the Central and South American regions where smaller food markets needed an easier and more reliable way to purchase.
- Z-Tech, beverage giant AB InBev's tech and innovation hub, decided to launch an online marketplace property in these areas called MiMercado.
- The marketplace model allows AB InBev to offer their own myriad of beverage options alongside an endless aisle of other CPG products in a single shopping experience.
- Specific user requirements—like mobile first, low bandwidth, and limited phone capability—led to an innovative headless PWA approach to the user interface.
- Shop owners have responded favorably with strong early adoption that enables MiMercado to continue expanding into new areas.

Chapter 13: Loyalty Technical Case Study- Livelo

Customer satisfaction is worthless, customer loyalty is priceless.

Jefferey Gitomer, American Author

Introduction

One of the more interesting applications of the marketplace model is that of a customer loyalty program. Too often, programs where customers redeem points for goods or services are plagued by poor selection. Customers are left feeling decidedly unappreciated and questioning the value of the loyalty program that is supposed to endear them to the brand. To solve this, Livelo Brazil decided to use the marketplace model to offer a wider and deeper selection of rewards utilized by many different brands.

13.1 About Livelo Brasil

Founded in 2014, Livelo Brasil was created to consolidate the loyalty programs of Bradesco and Banco do Brasil, two of the largest banks in Brazil. The state-of-the-art eCommerce platform gives consumers a dynamic and engaging experience when redeeming loyalty points.

Livelo enables more than 16 million customers to compare prices and redeem points for 700,000 products and services, including airline tickets, car rentals, and travel packages. They can also transfer their points to other major loyalty programs in Brazil. Towards the end of 2017, Livelo launched a B2B program called Livelo Incentivo allowing external partner companies to award loyalty program benefits to employees as a sales incentive.

13.2 The Challenge

Livelo was a small group with big ideas, but the program was not driving adoption rates quickly enough. Livelo grappled with several challenges to making the program work.

- Limited customer engagement

- Lack of Differentiation

- A siloed loyalty program experience for the consumer.

- Changing technology and consumer behavior challenges.

- Inability to demonstrate the platform's value to the customer.

To add to the complexity of the project, all the customer data from two large banks had to be migrated to the platform, the platform had to address unique rules for the accrual partners, and the entire project was on a strict, and short, timeline.

13.3 The Solution

The project began in November 2014 using the program Comarch Loyalty Management (CLM), a technology that uses AI (Artificial Intelligence) and machine learning mechanisms to monitor consumer shopping patterns and provide offers suited to their preferences.

Increased Customer Engagement – Intuitive user interfaces and engaging shopping and product catalog pages were created to increase shopper engagement.

Using the existing customer data, new user journeys were created and used to tailor experiences, offers, and messages to the loyalty program consumer. Loyalty Report of 2019 suggests that brands see three times the increase in member spend when they connect with customers in the right channels, the right places, the right moments, and with the right messaging.

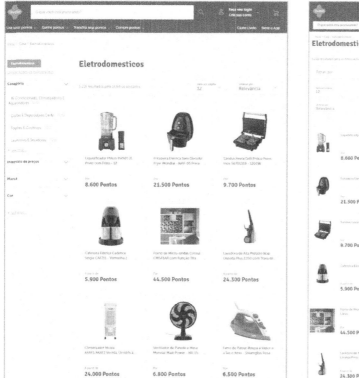

FIGURE 13.1 Desktop and Mobile user interfaces of Livelo

Differentiated Loyalty Program Offering – To offer something unique that the customers were unlikely to find elsewhere, highly personalized, frictionless customer journeys were created.

For example, using the "Cash + Points" feature, the customer could choose to split payment between Cash and Points. Points are converted to cash and custom pricing calculators were created so that discounting, adjustments, and refunds/returns all worked seamlessly.

Club Livelo offered automatic membership renewal with personalized plan options, grace periods for plan changes and cancellations, and benefit options. This page also offered the customer view of their entire membership history.

Another key feature that was introduced in the platform was the dynamic pricing to keep prices current with the supplier's marketplace. All these features alongside a highly user-friendly interface helped Livelo differentiate.

Seamless & Fully Integrated Loyalty Program Experience – To address the problem of consumers having a siloed shopping experience, the marketplace integrated the functions of accrual partners, redemption partners, transfer partners, business systems, and redemption channels. This provided a standardized product view, data normalization for SKU picker options, a full view of inventory and availability, and a record of all fulfillment interactions.

FIGURE 13.2 Seamless Integration

These integrations, along with faster checkout and eWallet capabilities, delivered a smoother customer journey.

Scalable & Ready for Future Loyalty Program – Modern consumers are used to the innovative technologies and advancements of major players like Amazon, and they expect those same advancements everywhere. So Livelo took steps to ensure their marketplace functioned well at launch and would continue to do so in the future. Some of the specific customizations included the following:

- Smooth user data migration from the primary partners with multiple customer data levels (Livelo´s Master Data)
- Creation of custom rules for authentication and fraud prevention
- Distinct and custom billing and processing rules for each partner
- Customized billing rules based on post-paid, pre-paid, and split fee
- Highly customized processing and billing for Livelo's product (cash + points, membership subscription, points renewed, and purchase)
- Automatic billing reconciliation with redemption partners
- Multi-channel option for redemption via website, mobile, ATM, and POS

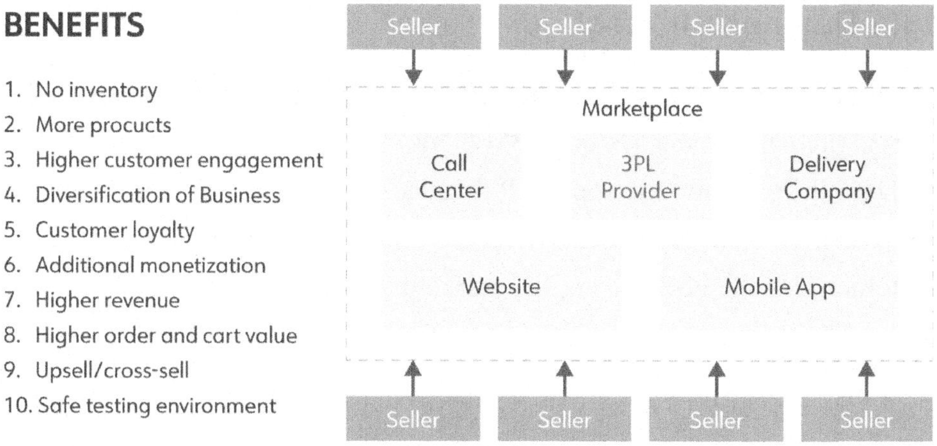
BENEFITS
1. No inventory
2. More procucts
3. Higher customer engagement
4. Diversification of Business
5. Customer loyalty
6. Additional monetization
7. Higher revenue
8. Higher order and cart value
9. Upsell/cross-sell
10. Safe testing environment
Seller
Seller
Seller
Seller
Marketplace
Call Center
3PL Provider
Delivery Company
Website
Mobile App
Seller
Seller
Seller
Seller

FIGURE 13.3 Benefits of connecting loyalty to marketplace

Connecting the Loyalty Customer to Marketplace – One of the biggest wins for this project was for the loyalty customer who now had access to the huge retail marketplace of sellers and brands. This was made possible by connecting the loyalty program platform to redemption and accrual partners. This brought the following benefit to Livelo and its customers.

- Larger Product Selection: Loyalty program participants now had access to large product selection through the marketplace's accrual and redemption partners. And Livelo never had to source, merchandising, warehouse, or deliver products.

- Deeper customer engagement: Creating a world-class loyalty program platform with highly integrated architecture and personalized customer experience resulted in deeper customer engagement. This in turn offered better targeting and customer segmentation and a higher level of customer personalization.

- Stronger customer loyalty: As a result of the enhanced customer experience, broader selection, dynamic pricing, and quality customer service, loyalty program participation increased dramatically. Overall there was a significant increase in the redemption rate once the new program was rolled out.

13.4 Business Impact

The project saw seamless integration between existing client systems with campaign management system (IBM UNIQA), eCommerce (ORACLE ATG), third-party mobile app, SAP Finance, Livelo Tax Online, and Fast Shop S.A. This integration also involved migration of over 16 million customer accounts. Benefits of the marketplace approach included the following:

- Loyal customers were given access to over 1 million products and services, including ticket searches across 750 airlines, car rentals, and travel packages.

- Integration of the wallet feature API allows Livelo points to be used in place of cash payment.

- The payment API also provides flexibility as it can be called by any site on the web (like PayPal).

Key Takeaways:

Loyalty Technical Case Study — Livelo

- The marketplace model works well for customer loyalty programs as it helps with customer engagement and differentiation.

- Implementation of the marketplace model provided a fully integrated, seamless customer experience enabled by the integration of all stakeholders.

- As a result of the marketplace implementation, loyalty program participants had access to a large product selection of products from accrual and redemption partners.

- The marketplace model significantly increased loyalty program redemptions.

Chapter 14: B2C Technical Case Study – Best Buy Canada

14.1 About Best Buy Canada
14.2 Marketplace Landscape & Challenges
14.3 The Solution
14.4 Business Impact

Our sellers win because they don't need to sustain the investment required to be successful in eCommerce. They reap the benefits of our investment. Our shareholders win because it's a profitable model.

Thierry Hay-Sabourin, Senior Vice President, eCommerce, Best Buy Canada

Introduction

One of the primary benefits of the marketplace model is that it provides the customer with a comprehensive product assortment and little motivation to leave the platform and look elsewhere. The core idea is to use third-party sellers to broaden the offerings outside the core catalog. Over time this strategy helps the retailer to achieve dominance in new categories while enabling sellers to compete and offer better prices to the end customer. In the last decade, many retailers have adopted the marketplace model with remarkable success thanks to the ready-made software packages that do the heavy lifting for the marketplace operator. Best Buy Canada is one such example, where sustained traction in some unexpected categories resulted when chances were taken with their marketplace expansion efforts.

14.1 About Best Buy Canada

Best Buy Canada is one of the largest omnichannel retailers of consumer electronics and related accessories and services in Canada. The large catalog of technology and entertainment products include home electronics, cameras and camcorders, computers, portable electronics, music, movies and games, Bluetooth headsets, phones, and other communication products. It also operates the Geek Squad, a computer support task force.

Based in Burnaby, Canada, Best Buy Canada was founded in 2002 as a subsidiary of Best Buy Enterprise Services, Inc., and operates stores in the United States as well as in Toronto and Victoria, Canada. Around the world, the Best Buy family of brands and partnerships collectively generates billions of dollars in annual revenue and includes brands such as Best Buy, Best Buy Mobile, Magnolia Audio Video, and Pacific Sales.

14.2 Market Landscape & Challenges

Best Buy Canada has always had a huge physical and digital presence. With 200 outlets, they annually average over 250 million visits by 50 million customers to Best Buy and Best Buy mobile stores across North America. They wanted to leverage the opportunity a digital marketplace presented and to give their customer a better experience and a wide array of choices. Best Buy US also had ventured into the marketplace model but had kept 1st party products and 3rd party products on separate sites, hence giving a broken experience. This was one of the lessons for Best Buy Canada and they were focused on providing a unified experience to the customer. Because of Best Buy's physical presence, in-store pickup and returns provided a natural advantage over competitors like eBay and Amazon. But offering a better assortment of product had its own challenges.

- Negotiating contracts and managing suppliers was a long and complex process.

- They had no expertise in the new product lines they considered carrying.

- Maintaining a large physical inventory required risky capital spending.

- Seller onboarding and training was a new and complex process.

- Allowing third parties to sell under their name risked erosion of the brand.

14.3 The Solution

To address these challenges Best Buy Canada decided to launch an online marketplace. This allowed Best Buy to merchandise the wider product range from trusted third-party sellers alongside its own stock. The customer found a wide array of product choices at competitive pricing in a seamlessly integrated experience.

FIGURE 14.1

One of the great successes of the rollout of the online marketplace was the time to market. With huge pressure from the competition, Best Buy Canada needed to move fast to launch and operationalize its marketplace quickly. The company considered building its own marketplace platform technology, but in the end decided to rely on Mirakl.

Mirakl brought to the table its expertise in the online marketplace business through the solutions it had delivered for over 200 clients across 40 countries. With their expertise in technology, partner ecosystems, and business operations they made the process of launching the online marketplace simple. Mirakl's marketplace automation took care of the hardest and the most complex parts so Best Buy could focus its energies on core business functions.

With Mirakl's help, Best Buy Canada was able to do the following:

- Rapidly scale the process of onboarding new sellers,

- Carry out smooth catalog integrations for the products of hundreds of sellers,

- Significantly increase the SKU count with close to zero investment inventory, product expertise, or logistics,

- Reduce time to market for new products from weeks to days,

- Operate in complimentary categories with no risks.

14.4 Business Impact

Once the marketplace implementation was completed, Best Buy Canada was able to reap the following benefits.

- In its first year of operation, its SKU counts went up by over 200% as the third-party products were added, providing a wider assortment of products. This was made possible because with the marketplace model it was easier to onboard sellers at scale.

- The marketplace model allowed Best Buy Canada to gain leadership positions across product categories like musical instruments and baby products within a brief time.

- Marketplace listing also helped drive SEO improvements and helped in cross-selling. 75% of the customers that bought products from the marketplace also purchased Best Buy's own products.

- The marketplace model meant that sourcing of sellers and products was faster when compared to retail where it took months to source. Best Buy Canada was able to bring products to market 200X times faster.

- Covering both 1st party and 3rd party products in a unified portal provided a fillip to both and made for great customer experience.

Key Takeaways:

B2C Technical Case Study — Best Buy Canada

- Launching a marketplace platform solution helped Best Buy Canada solve some of its biggest problems like quickly onboarding and training many 3P sellers.

- By adopting the platform model and encouraging 3P sales, Best Buy Canada was no longer competing with third parties but complimenting them.

- Using marketplace Best Buy Canada was able to get products to market in a matter of days which helped it build leadership across product categories.

- A marketplace platform solution can automate the hardest things about running a marketplace namely seller onboarding, catalog integration and management, and communication with vendors and customers.

SECTION III: How to Operate a Marketplace?

Chapter 15: General Architecture

If a builder builds a house for someone, and does not construct it properly, and the house falls and kills its owner, then that builder shall be put to death.

Hammurabi, King of Babylon 1780 BC

Introduction

eCommerce architectures generally serve two constituents—the eCommerce operator and the customers. Marketplace architectures add a third constituent—the sellers. It is helpful to think of the architecture in terms of customer-facing components, seller-facing components, and marketplace operator-facing components.

Usually a commercial eCommerce platform (Magento, Shopify, Salesforce Commerce Cloud, etc.) serves as the customer-facing software. Similarly, a commercial marketplace platform (Mirakl, Webkul, Unirgy, etc.) is used as the seller-facing platform. Part of a marketplace implementation project is the integration of the eCommerce software and the marketplace software.

Sometimes the eCommerce platform is called the front end and the marketplace is the back end. However, from the common 3-tier architecture viewpoint, this description is not accurate. The eCommerce platform has its own back end and the marketplace platform has its own front end for sellers.

There are a few integrated platforms that include both the customer-facing components and the seller-facing components. VTEX, Arcadier, Sharetribe, and Marketplacer are examples that simplify launching a new eCommerce and marketplace platform. However, if a business has an existing eCommerce platform, these combined platforms may face challenges integrating smoothy to avoid two user interfaces, catalogs, carts, etc.

An annual comparison of the rapidly evolving marketplace platform vendors can be found at www.MarketplaceSuiteSpot.com. The next chapter discusses the pros and cons of custom building, buying, or renting (cloud subscription) a platform.

Regardless of the software selected (or built), a foundational understanding of the software architecture and the data flow is important for a marketplace business.

Chapter 4 Marketplace Features provides a detailed discussion of basic features while Chapter 26 Advanced Technical Features covers the other end of the spectrum. However, a quick review of marketplace features and requirements can add context for discussing technical architecture:

- Marketplace Set Up and Branding
- Vendor Management
- Orders, Shipping & Returns
- Accounting & Vendor Payouts
- Product Catalog Management
- APIs for extensions
- Governance & Administration
- Performance & Scalability
- Integration Capabilities
- Mobile Experience

15.1 Marketplace Architecture Overview

Figure 15.1 on the following page provides a software vendor-agnostic view of the architecture and data flows of a marketplace platform. The customer (buyers) interface is on top, the operator interface is on the left, and the seller interface is on the bottom.

The **eCommerce Platform** is the traditional customer-facing software that consists of first-party product catalogs, search and navigation functionalities, cart features, checkout, order status, and customer service. Customer-facing pages may be added to describe sellers.

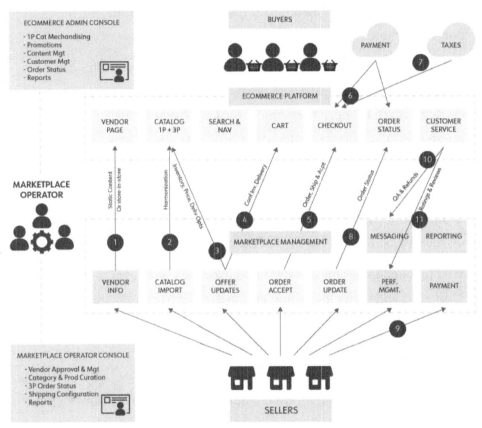

FIGURE 15.1 Marketplace Platform Architecture

Payment & Taxes are usually cloud-based services to process payment and apply the appropriate tax based on nexus inputs.

The **eCommerce Administration Console** and **Marketplace Management Module** are the tools used by the marketplace operator to manage each platform. On pre-integrated eCommerce and marketplace platforms like VTEX, there will only be one console.

The eCommerce administration console manages merchandising, promotions, product content, site search, site configuration, and some reporting. Some elements, like site search, might actually operate as a service from another cloud provider but the concept is similar.

The **Marketplace Operator Console** is the tool that allows the operator to approve and manage vendors, curate products and categories, manage 3P order status, handle shipping and fulfillment configurations, view reports, and more.

The **Marketplace platform** provides the sellers an interface to load products, harmonize catalog data, load offers, accept orders, update orders, view sales revenue, etc. These functions are usually available either through a graphical user interface, via file exchange, or via API integrations.

In the broader picture of enterprise infrastructure, there are usually additional tools like ERP, CRM, OMS, PIM, BI/DW, etc. This chapter is only focused on the architecture of the marketplace.

A best practice for architecture is to provide API interfaces to access eCommerce and marketplace services. Microservices are a popular evolving architecture approach.

15.2 Marketplace Dataflow

Figure 15.1 highlights the following numbered data flows of marketplace operation.

1. **Vendor Info** – Vendors begin by providing basic static information, like name, description, and location(s). In more advanced marketplaces, sellers may be able to configure their own branded store which can show dynamic data such as their complete catalog.

2. **Catalog Import** – The operator imports and integrates the product catalogs of the 3P sellers. An important step in this process is the

data harmonization of the catalog structure, product attributes, and other elements for smooth search and navigation.

3. **Offer Updates** – A seller offer describes that seller's price, inventory, shipping cost, shipping times, etc. A single product may have multiple offers if more than one vendor sells it. While product data like size or weight rarely changes, offer data such as price and inventory level can change quite frequently.

4. **Add-to-Cart Confirmation** – Seller inventory may change quickly, especially if a seller lists on multiple marketplaces. It is possible for offer data in the eCommerce platform to be out of sync with real-world seller status. Therefore, inventory is usually confirmed (and sometimes sequestered) when a customer adds a 3P product to their cart.

5. **Order Acceptance** – Upon checkout, the seller must either accept or reject the order and confirm quantity and shipping timeframe.

6. **Payment** – When the customer completes the transaction with payment, the payment service provider (PSP) will initially place a hold for a certain dollar amount (depending on the payment type). PSPs and alternate payment methods like PayPal or Apple Pay provide merchant services like accepting credit cards, electronic payments, digital wallets, and more. Once the shipment has been confirmed the final credit card transaction will be settled.

7. **Taxes** –Taxes are calculated based on the seller's and buyer's nexus (location) that each transaction creates. Tax calculation can get quite complex if a shopping cart includes 1P products and 3P products from multiple sellers and items with different tax treatments, such as food, clothing, and medicine. A detailed discussion of this topic is found in Chapter 17 Payment & Tax Considerations.

8. **Order Status** – Once a seller has shipped a product, they ideally update the order status with details like carrier, tracking number, and estimated delivery time.

9. **Payment Settlement** – After delivery is complete, the marketplace transfers funds to the seller, minus commissions and other fees, according to the terms and conditions.

10. **Messaging** – This communication channel enables limited interaction between customers and sellers, mostly used in the case of issues with an order. This interaction is controlled and somewhat anonymized to minimize platform leakage (customers bypassing the marketplace to buy directly from sellers). Marketplaces should also monitor this messaging to track potential issues with sellers, products, or other elements.

11. **Performance Management** – After the customer has received the product, ratings and reviews of sellers, products, and overall customer experience help to optimize the marketplace performance for more sales, better conversion, and better user experience.

15.3 More Complex Marketplace Architectures

Beyond these common marketplace architectural considerations and designs, many other unique challenges may need to be addressed with different architectural approaches. The solutions are beyond the scope of this book, but the following is a list of more complex issues to consider.

- Internationalization of seller content (e.g. language, images, prices, shipping, tax) for a global customer base

- Integrating seller promotions with marketplace operator promotions

- Mixed shopping carts when some products are fulfilled locally from store and others are shipped by third-party sellers

- Marketplaces which offer services like installation in addition to products. Services must be scheduled, performed by a 3P provider, and validated by the customer.

- Orders with multiple ship-to addresses coming from multiple sellers. B2B marketplace orders may include large quantity purchases which must be split and sent to different locations. This may also complicate tax calculation with multiple source and destination tax nexus points.

- Global enterprises that have different eCommerce engines for different geographies

- Selling used or refurbished goods of varying condition and managing customer expectations and satisfaction

- Digital rights management and licensing for selling digital goods

- Selling controlled goods, such as alcohol, which have shipping restrictions

- Punch-out requirements to a seller site for features like configuring a computer to add to cart

- Federated marketplaces which enable sellers to white-label and manage their marketplace store as their own branded store (without marketplace branding)

Key Takeaways: General Architecture

- It is helpful to think of marketplace components from the viewpoint of the three constituents they serve—customers, sellers, and operators.

- Usually a customer-facing eCommerce platform is integrated with a seller-facing marketplace platform. There are also platforms like VTEX which combine both, but those may have challenges integrating with existing eCommerce platforms.

- Product data like size, weight, and color are generally static. Offer data like seller inventory level and seller price can vary frequently and must be tightly coupled between the marketplace platform and the eCommerce platform.

- Marketplaces provide sellers with an interface to load products, harmonize catalog data, load offers, accept orders, update orders, view sales data, etc.

- A controlled messaging system that enables limited communication between customers and sellers must balance the goals of improving customer satisfaction and reducing platform leakage.

- There are many advanced business models and use cases that can drive substantial changes to the basic architecture presented in this chapter.

Chapter 16: Build, Buy, or Rent a Platform?

16.1 Understanding "Cloud" and "as a Service"
16.2 Building a platform
16.3 Buying a platform
16.4 Renting a platform

Start with the end in mind and work backward.

Michael Stelzner, CEO, Social Media Examiner

Introduction

Consider three approaches to new housing.

Build: The homeowner can get exactly what they want, but it will take a long time and require a lot of money up front. Payments go to ownership, not rent, but the homeowner is responsible for all maintenance.

Buy: The homeowner probably will not get exactly what they want, but they can customize it for additional expense after buying it for some money up front. Payments go to ownership, not rent. The seller is responsible for a limited amount of maintenance, but that does not cover customizations.

Rent: The tenant probably will not get exactly what they want and will be limited in how much they can customize, but there is very little money up front and it will be available quickly. Recurring payments go to rent, but somebody else will be responsible for most maintenance.

The decision will be influenced by budget, timeframe, and unique requirements.

The same pros and cons apply to building (custom code), buying (perpetual license / on-premise), or renting (Cloud / SaaS / PaaS) software platforms.

This analogy applies equally to both the eCommerce platform and the marketplace platform discussed in Chapter 15 General Architecture. Many organizations are opting for a combination of approaches. For example, a common architecture involves buying Magento eCommerce software and renting a Mirakl marketplace SaaS subscription. Alternately Magento Cloud can be rented as a PaaS cloud and a perpetual license of Webkul marketplace software can be bought.

For the most recent comparison of marketplace platforms, see a detailed annual assessment on www.MarketplaceSuiteSpot.com.

A high-level comparison of factors in the build v. buy v. rent decision is shown below.

Evaluating Software Approaches			
Consideration	**Build**	**Buy**	**Rent**
Upfront cost	High	High	Low
Recurring costs	High	Medium or High	Medium or High
Flexibility	High	Medium	Low
Time-to-Market	Slow	Medium	Fast
Cost Predictability	Highly variable	Medium variability	Fairly consistent
Accountability (including PCI)	In-house/SI Partner	In-house/SI + S/W vendor	SaaS vendor
Risk	High	Medium	Medium
In-house tech skills	Strong	Medium	Limited
Business Model	Unique	Standard or unique	Standard
Example	Java code on AWS, or assembling multiple tools like commercetools	Magento Commerce, SAP Hybris.	Magento Cloud, Shopify, Salesforce Commerce Cloud, BigCommerce

TABLE 16.1

16.1 Understanding "Cloud" and "as a Service"

The term *cloud* is one of the most over-used technology terms of the past decade. It is important to understand the varying levels to which a solution is "in the cloud." The terms on-premise (not cloud), Infrastructure as a Service (IaaS), Platform as a Service (PaaS), and Software as a Service (SaaS) are more descriptive. Figure 16.1 below provides an overview of the four approaches by indicating which elements of the platform are managed by another party as a service.

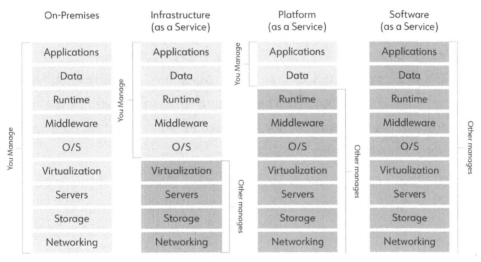

FIGURE 16.1: Different levels of "as a Service"

On-Premise – In this model everything must be purchased and managed. Most companies started with on-premise data centers where they purchased racks, servers, UPS, switches, and all software. When the on-premise term is applied to just software, it often means "perpetual license." Today when perpetual license software is purchased, it is usually hosted on top of an IaaS or PaaS environment from a cloud provider. Early monolithic eCommerce platforms like ATG, Hybris, and WebSphere Commerce were on-premise perpetual license software.

IaaS – These platforms offer services like virtualization, networking, and pay-as-you-go storage. Typically, an IaaS provider hosts the infrastructure components traditionally present in an on-premise data center. IaaS providers usually deliver services like detailed billing, monitoring, log access, security, load balancing, and clustering. Example benefits of IaaS include not having to worry about a server disk failing or having to configure firewalls or switches. Some IaaS platforms are multi-tenant, which means a co-tenant could monopolize bandwidth or CPU and affect your workloads.

PaaS – In this model, additional services are managed but not the actual business application or data. For example, PaaS provides an operating system, Windows or Linux, and is responsible for applying patches and maintaining a healthy O/S. Sometimes perpetual license software is hosted on PaaS and provided as a cloud offering. However, the business can customize the perpetual license software. Magento Commerce Cloud is an example of PaaS eCommerce. The Magento software can still be heavily customized, but the merchant does not need to worry about the hardware, operating system, or other infrastructure.

SaaS – SaaS platforms are the primary topic in Section 16.4 Renting a Platform. SaaS includes PaaS but adds a fully functional business application available for rent. The turn-key business application, database, and everything underneath is managed and updated as a service for the subscriber. The subscriber usually does not have any access to the application source code or direct access to the database, but usually some level of customization is available.

The same SaaS application source code usually applies to all customers, so when new functionality is rolled out, all customer platforms are updated universally, or within a short timeframe. The SaaS model is managed entirely in the cloud and eliminates the need for hardware acquisition, provisioning and maintenance, software licensing, installation, and support, so minimal IT staff are needed by the subscriber. Backups of data and code are usually performed by the SaaS provider.

Some advantages of SaaS solutions are budgeting as a predictable operating expense, ease of use, and automatic updates. Drawbacks include limited control over features and limited extensibility. A thorough understanding of the vendor **service level agreement** (SLA) can help to mitigate downtime or slow performance risks which are often outside the control of the merchant. SaaS providers are also usually liable for security and PCI DSS compliance.

Shopify and Shopify Plus are fully hosted, cloud-based SaaS eCommerce platforms. Lightweight and affordable, they allow businesses to quickly create online shops with no coding, hosting, or software installation. All the software licenses, upgrades, and hosting costs are covered in a fixed monthly subscription fee. Like many SaaS eCommerce platforms, Shopify also charges a percentage of GMV, which is often called "rev share." As enterprises scale their GMV, this fee can become quite large.

16.2 Building a Platform

Early eCommerce and marketplace solutions were typically custom-built before commercial platforms were a proven approach. Most of today's largest merchants and marketplaces (over $1 billion GMV) also use custom-built solutions. However, unless there are very unique requirements, the custom-build approach is probably not the best approach for today's small and mid-sized businesses.

Building a marketplace eCommerce platform from scratch has its appeal. Every aspect is customized, from the coding language to the programming framework, the hosting/cloud environment to the front-end design, and everything in between. However, this also means the development team is responsible to make, execute, and take credit or blame for those decisions.

Often a systems integrator is engaged to help build a custom platform due to the need to quickly ramp up a large development team with very specialized domain experience. To ensure the platform keeps pace with the conveniences and features of the competition and to provide a smooth customer journey, development cannot stop at basic set-it-and-forget-it features but must continue to innovate over time. This means maintaining a development team, planning feature enhancements, scheduling regular update cycles, and continuous testing and performance tuning.

Many new features are being offered by cloud providers like Amazon Web Services (AWS) or Microsoft Azure Cloud. Modern software design typically incorporates many cloud services.

A forward-thinking approach to building a platform involves combining composable commerce tools following the MACH Alliance approach. MACH is a Microservices based, API-first, Cloud-native SaaS, and Headless architecture. An example MACH framework could start by combining tools like headless API-driven commercetools with a Vue Storefront "head" front end and Contentful for content management. More information is available at www.MACHalliance.Org.

Custom building will always be an option for the very large eCommerce and marketplace players, but several critical factors should drive the decision.

Total control – Building a custom eCommerce platform provides complete freedom and ownership of the eCommerce presence and the development team remains the ultimate decision-maker on the smallest and largest details of how the site runs.

Flexibility – Custom platform development allows flexibility to meet unique requirements and create differentiating features without relying on a platform provider for feature updates and product enhancements.

Complex legacy systems – When multiple homegrown legacy systems exist, an in-house build makes more sense for easier integration.

Valuable Resource – When the in-house development team creates a software platform, they become a valuable resource for future system design, planning, and implementation.

16.3 Buying a Platform

Buying an eCommerce or marketplace platform offers much of the control of building a custom platform with the advantage of gaining the support of the platform provider, a regular feature release schedule, far less coding, and even optional interface themes for many modern platforms. It is important to distinguish the heavy monolithic legacy platforms (ATG, Hybris, WebSphere Commerce) of the past from the next generation platforms based around APIs with rich user interfaces, management tools, and very extensible architectures.

Buying a platform is often a good compromise between the build and the rent approaches. Substantial functionality is available out of the box, but organizations can still heavily customize the platform. Most of the eCommerce and marketplace platforms have been in development for five to fifteen years, often with development teams of over a hundred people. These solutions also have already been refined (bugs, features, performance) based on the experience of having many clients operating in production for years.

An example of buying an eCommerce platform and a marketplace platform is purchasing Magento Commerce for the front-end eCommerce and buying a Webkul marketplace extension. Magento Commerce works well for fast-growing and large businesses and has an ecosystem of hundreds of third-party extensions. The entire source code is provided so it can be easily customized and extended. Magento Commerce is an on-premise offering while Magento Commerce Cloud is PaaS hosted by Magento on top of an AWS stack.

Most purchased software will have an annual support and maintenance cost which may be around 30% of the purchase cost.

Several important factors make buying a platform the right choice for some companies.

Price – While an in-house build may look more cost effective on paper, schedule delays and cost overruns, along with future feature additions, tend to skyrocket the cost. With more predictable costs and timelines, an industry-ready solution is generally less expensive over time.

Accountability – A stable, experienced vendor can be held accountable for maintenance and updates to a purchased platform, freeing the marketplace operator to run the business without the expense and effort of maintaining an in-house development team.

Speed – A purchased eCommerce solution can be customized and launched far more quickly than a ground-up build. Additionally, with a paid maintenance agreement, the provider will respond to platform bugs and provide updates and enhancements.

16.4 Renting a Platform

Renting a platform refers to a SaaS or PaaS platform subscription where the solution is hosted in the cloud and managed by the software vendor. The software is licensed for a fixed number of years (with options to extend) with a predictable cost.

Subscribing to a SaaS platform will typically have less risk than a custom build. However, it provides less opportunity to differentiate from competitors. For example, about a million merchants are using Shopify and most B2C sites offer a similar customer user experience.

Another advantage of SaaS solutions is that the cloud provider continues developing its solution and rolling out new features and functions. Merchants are sometimes surprised when new features appear in their platform, but most SaaS vendors send release notes in advance of upgrades.

In addition to a fixed recurring fee, many SaaS platforms also charge a revenue-share fee which may be 1%-4% of total GMV. When launching a new marketplace, this may not be substantial, but as GMV grows over

$100 million, the rev-share fees can be millions of dollars. There is usually also a one-time initiation fee, but it is typically far less than the cost of buying software.

Some benefits of renting a platform include the following:

Time to Market – Cloud platforms tend to be the fastest to market and can sometimes be launched in a matter of several weeks or months.

Functionality – SaaS platforms have the benefit of many business and technical refinements after lessons learned from their use by many other merchants. A successful marketplace requires a lot of moving parts to work in harmony, including integrations, needs of the sellers, and ever-changing customer expectations. Business processes can be implemented across diverse areas like seller onboarding and management, catalog harmonization, offer management, and order management.

Technical Know-how – Building a marketplace is complex and needs specialized business knowledge and technical skills. In competitive labor markets, it is often hard (and expensive) to find talent with the proper experience. These factors can affect time to market, costs, and feature development.

Overall Risks & Costs – In addition to development and hosting risks, SaaS providers usually also take on security and PCI risks, and perhaps some liability. SaaS subscription costs are usually very predictable. The risk of technical obsolescence is usually lower as the cloud providers continually update their platforms. Lock-in risk can be high if a merchant realizes a year into a 5-year subscription that a platform is not the right fit.

An example of renting a marketplace solution could be a Shopify Plus cloud eCommerce front end with a Mirakl marketplace cloud back end.

Key Takeaways: Build, Buy, or Rent a Platform?

- The build v. buy v. rent decision factors for software platforms are similar to housing: up-front budget, recurring expenses, timeframe, and unique requirements.

- A custom-build approach may be best when total control and flexibility over the solution are required and the operator has the resources and time to build.

- Buying a platform can offer an extensible and feature-rich solution that shares responsibility with the software vendor.

- Renting a cloud solution provides predictable up-front and recurring costs with fast time-to-market for proven cookie-cutter capabilities but limited ability to customize for unique requirements or differentiated user experiences.

Chapter 17: Payments & Taxes

---

*A Nigerian prince left you $10 million of inheritance. Send
me your account number and social security number and I
will transfer the funds to you.*

Distant Relative

Introduction

While traditional eCommerce consists of one seller and multiple buyers, a
marketplace involves multiple sellers and multiple buyers. This core
difference inherently requires different methods of collecting and
disbursing both payments and taxes. As each marketplace transaction
includes three parties—seller, buyer, and operator—marketplaces require
more complex payment and taxation functions and processes.

17.1 Traditional eCommerce v. Marketplaces

In a traditional eCommerce environment, the transactional relationship
between a seller and customers is simple. A customer receives goods or
services directly from the eCommerce store and the store receives
payment directly from the customer. While the payment needs of a
traditional eCommerce merchant are not without complexities, the direct
payment service denotes a straightforward relationship.

Figure 17.1

Within a marketplace environment, the platform is effectively acting as a commercial broker or trading floor for sellers and buyers to interact more easily. Because both the seller and the buyer are essentially customers of the marketplace, significant payment services are required to support the three-way relationship.

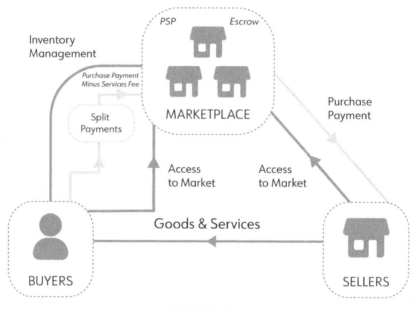

FIGURE 17.2

Further complicating the relationship between marketplace, seller, and buyer is the business model that the marketplace chooses to operate. Three distinct models have a significant impact on the operation, relationships, and compliance implications for the marketplace.

Payment Facilitator (PFac) – As an **aggregator** of small merchants, the marketplace operator becomes the payment acceptance provider between the buyer and seller. This model, used by Amazon, requires the operator to have a payment institution license and adhere to regulatory compliance.

Merchant of Record (MOR) – The marketplace operator is the master merchant carrying all liability for transactions processed on the platform, while individual sellers are considered sub-merchants.

Broker or Commercial Agent – Acting only as an intermediary between buyers and sellers, the operator is not involved in the exchange of funds but employs a third-party PSP who assumes liability for transactions.

Escrow Accounts

Marketplace operators need to establish a trusted environment that ensures obligations are fulfilled by all parties. Escrow payments/accounts offer a payment solution for all sizes of marketplace. Escrow involves holding funds for the parties until the transactions are complete. For example, when a buyer places an order and makes payment, the funds are not transferred to the seller account immediately but can be held in an escrow account. Once the buyer receives the order and is satisfied, funds are released from the escrow account to the seller. Escrow acts as a third-party platform offering trustworthy services to sellers and buyers. Most of the leading marketplace platform solutions integrate escrow services.

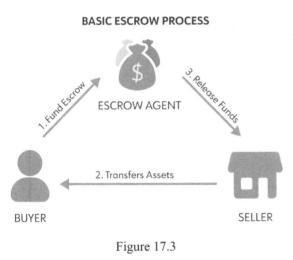

Figure 17.3

Escrow accounts are especially helpful for B2B marketplaces where buyers purchase in bulk and payments are large. Escrow acts as a safe vault from which money is released only when the products are received in the agreed quality and quantity and without damage. Should damage occur, the money is automatically withheld in escrow. Overall, escrow accounts have many benefits for both buyers and sellers.

- Parties who are unknown to each other can transact business through a safe and transparent window.

- The buyer is protected from fraud, such as paying for damaged, faulty, or substandard products and services.

- The seller can provide products and services with the confidence that full payment is on the way.

Cross Border Payments & Taxes

Cross border transactions are a complex, but valuable, driver of marketplace scale. They offer a truly global marketplace without physical boundaries where buyers and sellers can participate regardless of where they live and where they want to sell. However, cross border payments and taxes are extraordinarily complex as they face key challenges in regulatory compliance, operating costs, currencies, and taxes. And the complexity increases with each cross-border market added.

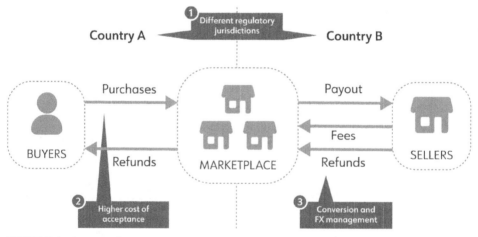

FIGURE 17.4 Image Source: Cross-Border Payments and Commerce Report 2019 – 2020

Regulatory Compliance – Every country has its own set of compliance and licensing regulations. So, every cross-border marketplace transaction needs to comply with two sets of regulations instead of just one. For a marketplace to scale up in a particular country, it will be worthwhile to develop a good rapport with the local regulatory bodies or even establish a legal entity in the country.

Operating Costs – While the cost of payments has been drastically reduced in the US, there is less regulation cross border payments. As a result, each cross-border transaction could add up to 4–5% on the operating costs, along with significant risk and bottom-line expense.

Currencies – Marketplaces should focus on currencies that are the most pervasive and viable for international trade rather than focusing on 180 currencies around the globe. Building both internal financial infrastructure and customer-facing services will optimize currency conversion and mitigate foreign exchange rate risks.

Taxes – Taxes and international duties are an equally complicated component of cross-border transactions with many variables and changes in the sales tax landscape. It is important to identify and evaluate the risks and address them properly. It may be wise to commission a transaction tax risk assessment or a nexus study. Plans should cover current needs and future changes, like where the business will be in the next three to five years. Many third-party applications, like FedEx Cross Border and UPS iParcel, offer full automation of tax and invoicing, are compliant with legislation across multiple countries, and allow marketplace operators focus on their core business.

17.2 Payment Considerations

Typically, in eCommerce, payment is charged to the customer when the seller ships the product or accepts the order. For marketplace scenarios where a single order ships from multiple sellers, the PSP may move separate line item amounts to the operator's escrow accounts for each seller, but the customer will see a single charge to his credit card. Similarly, when a customer requests a return or refund, the funds may be pulled from the operator's escrow account even if the return is facilitated by the seller.

Apart from the split payment processing, there are additional considerations when selecting a payment service provider.

- Liability for KYC

- PCI DSS liability for stored credit card information

- Subscription, recurring, and scheduled payments

- Custom payment flows allowing customers to see single complete payments or individual payments to various sellers

- Support for multiple currencies

- Availability of documentation and support during implementation and updates

- Responsiveness and technical support

- Integrations with 3P platforms, including plugins to various eCommerce and marketplace platforms

- Fraud protection tools, such as built-in or add-on modules

17.3 Movement of Money

In a 1P eCommerce store, the transaction flow ends once the money is transferred from the customer. Because of the multi-part relationships in a marketplace, varying amounts of money must be moved at different times and in different ways to complete a transaction. The following diagram shows an example flow of funds for a customer ordering three items—one 1P product from the marketplace operator inventory and two 3P products from different 3P sellers—for a total of $100.

FINANCIAL FLOWS: MARKETPLACE

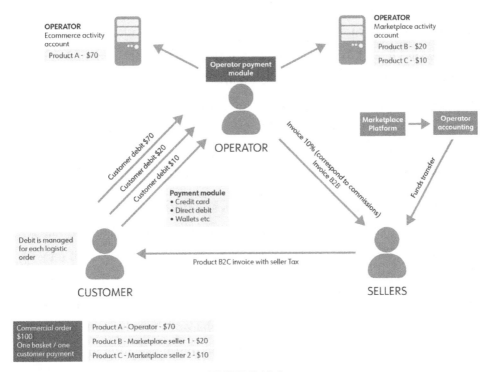

FIGURE 17.5

When to move the money – The simplest method is to pass the money from the buyer directly to the seller at the time of payment, but this is not the best option for most situations. Both buyer and seller are relying on the marketplace operator to act in their best interest, so the operator must ensure customers get what they order and sellers get payment.

Once the marketplace operator decides the role it will play in the exchange of funds—payment facilitator, merchant of record, or broker—the next decision is when the customer's credit card or other payment form will be debited and when the merchant will receive that money. The customer may be charged at the time of order, when the product is shipped, or after receipt confirmation. The seller may receive payment at the time the customer is charged or after the customer agrees the transaction is complete. It should be noted that any scenario which includes holding the money in an escrow account or moving it through the operator's own account may be heavily regulated.

How to move the money – Moving money between multiple parties is a complex and heavily regulated function. Beginning with the Know Your Customer (KYC) process, every national government has its own systems to prevent money laundering, tax avoidance, terrorist funding, etc. Operating in multiple countries and with multiple currencies adds another layer of complexity. Best practice is to begin operation in one country and expand gradually.

Commission is another arena that garners significant regulatory inspection. Rather than receiving the customer's full payment into the operator's account and then transferring the seller's portion out, it may be better to split the payment at the time the customer pays so that the seller's portion goes to an escrow account. Another method is to direct the full amount to the seller and the operator then charges the seller a transaction fee after the fact. Because of these regulatory burdens, some marketplaces like OfferUp and Wallapop launched without an in-app payment system, instead relying on 3P payment platforms like PayPal.

17.4 Fraud Detection & Prevention

Fraud in eCommerce has increased significantly in the last few years. Criminals now have access to more advanced technologies that help them navigate loopholes in the system. Additionally, the variable international rules regarding internet crime mean marketplaces face an immense challenge to track and combat new tactics in online fraud. For every measure, there is a countermeasure. The primary objectives of fraud include stealing product from the operator, stealing customer data, and selling customer data to third-party cyberthieves. Following are some of the most common methods of marketplace fraud.

Chargebacks – A customer can dispute an item or service charged to their account by claiming they did not receive the product or service. Payment is returned to the customer's credit card and the seller or operator is charged that amount. A history of chargebacks can cause irreparable damage to the business reputation of a merchant or marketplace operator, including being dropped by a PSP or subject to rate increases. While genuine chargebacks are unavoidable, adherence to best practices around customer service, KYC principles, and merchant accessibility can reduce the occurrence. Payment validation, transaction authorization, and biometric identification such as facial and fingerprint recognition are gaining popularity as powerful fraud prevention tools, particularly for mobile payments. Google Play already uses this technology to authenticate purchases made in their store.

Identity Theft – As implied by the name, this type of fraud involves impersonation. Criminals access the user information and make purchases on their behalf. It affects both the buyer and seller. The customer usually ends up seeking a refund as soon as they discover the fraudulent transaction.

Return Fraud – In this type of fraud, criminals claim that they never received the product and seek a refund. Sometimes they replace the good product with a faulty one and seek a return. The seller ends up making the refund as well as losing the inventory.

Merchant Fraud – In this scenario, the criminal creates a fake merchant account as a front for a legitimate business. The front is used to collect debit card and credit card information to withdraw money.

Clean Fraud – This technique is harder to detect as the criminals use stolen card information to make online transactions. If they can provide valid card information, they can go undetected for a considerable length of time.

Phishing – Criminals collect personal information from users by posing as a business, bank personnel, or other person of authority. They seek user

ID, passwords, and card information via emails and SMS's containing phishing links.

Some of the red flags to look out for are larger than average order values, cash on delivery orders, incomplete addresses, large quantities of the same product, many different cards linked to the same IP address, overseas orders, and unexpected order velocity. Fortunately, the latest breed of PSP and fraud detection and prevention vendors solve a lot of these problems with artificial intelligence and large data sets. Such solutions help merchants minimize fraudulent orders.

17.5 Challenges & Best Practices

International & Cross-border Payments – Payments coming from other countries can be expensive, slow, and inefficient. National banking infrastructures that are not equipped for cross-border payments in combination with non-uniform technologies and payment software platforms sometimes make the process of transacting business as complex. But as global eCommerce grows, new developments in cross-border payment requirements and transnational systems will decrease reliance on correspondent networks. Trends to look for in the future include the following:

- Payments and fee structures will be government regulated.

- Payment systems will better handle costs, liquidity, and credit risk.

- MNC's will achieve economies of scale and consolidate and reduced credit risk.

- Outsourced specialists will drive down costs and increase process efficiency.

Card Data Security – When accepting credit and debit cards both online and offline, the PCI DSS standard requires merchants to build and maintain secure systems and networks, safeguard cardholder data, maintain a strict program to manage system vulnerabilities, maintain strict access control measures, periodically monitor, and test networks, and maintain a clear information security policy.

Recent breaches in financial services, healthcare, and retail have highlighted the importance of securing customer information and card data. Addressing online payment security issues is critical for any online merchant, but more so for a marketplace that runs on trust. To do so, marketplace operators must be prepared to adhere to PCI DSS Level 1 certification standards or use a PSP-hosted payment page.

Payment Methods & Multi-currency – Operating a global digital marketplace means accepting a variety of currencies and payment methods. Electronic payments systems such as credit cards, eWallets, and mobile payments allow customers to transact in their native currency. Global marketplace operators can choose to set up new bank accounts, establish new business entities, and abide by regulatory frameworks for each national market. Or the operator can select a PSP with the requisite payment infrastructure already in place. This enables the merchant to collect payment in the buyer's currency and disburse payment in the merchant's currency.

Privacy & GDPR – As data privacy laws like General Data Protection Regulation (GDPR) become more prevalent, it is important to ensure processes and integrations are compliant. While GDPR is mostly a European law (also adopted by other countries), there are other applicable laws, like the California Consumer Privacy Act (CCPA).

Technical Integration – Online payment systems are required to run proprietary programs across hardware and software platforms. Often this process can be cumbersome due to lack of interface between processing systems. This leads to difficulties for a PSP to connect with other systems, which results in lost transactions, payment delays, and expensive fees. Integrated systems and gateways provide real-time processing, help address liquidity issues, and minimize delays. They also help in preserving the integrity of online transactions.

A **payment processor** supplies immediate and individually processed transactions. This helps in avoiding delays that are often an inherent component of automated clearinghouse processes.

For online marketplaces and consumers alike, the bottom line is clear. Seamless, secure, and easy transactions are mostly provided by a PCC DSS Level 1 payment processor.

17.6 Essential Criteria for Selecting a PSP

When considering a payment service provider, some features are preferred, and some are mandatory.

Marketplace-specific Solution – The best PSP holds a deep understanding of the dynamics and best practices of a marketplace environment. Beyond basic eCommerce merchant offerings, the PSP should have marketplace-specific solutions. Some of these include managing the process of splitting payments to multiple sellers, a high level of flexibility while managing commissions, and secure and seamless routing of funds to multiple sellers.

Regulatory Compliance – A quality PSP is licensed in your country, has not been reported to or sanctioned by any regulatory bodies, and follows US Anti-Money Laundering (AML) laws and Europe's General Data Protection Regulation (GDPR8).

KYC Support – The ideal PSP helps its partners through the KYC verification process. This is particularly significant for marketplaces that frequently onboard new sellers as the process can be both time and money consuming.

17.7 Taxes

As the marketplace industry grows, local and federal governments will change the legal and tax requirements to adapt. All parties involved in a marketplace transaction—seller, shipping agency, operator, customer, etc.—bear some level of responsibility to pay applicable taxes.

Typically, the customer pays sales tax as part of the order payment, either because the tax is added onto the displayed product price or the seller rolls the tax into the displayed product price. Whether the seller or operator, in turn, pays that tax amount to the government is determined by the nexus. In a marketplace model, the originating shipping location is called the nexus, and tax is calculated based on this nexus and the destination.

If the seller location is declared the nexus, then the marketplace disburses the tax amount to the seller and the seller is responsible to pay the applicable taxes to the government. If the marketplace operator location is declared the nexus, then the operator is obligated to pay the applicable taxes.

Best practice dictates using a 3P tax integrator who carefully watches tax changes for federal, state, and local entities and then applies the correct percentage of tax to each transaction. In the US, there are many robust tax calculation engines available, like Avalara and Vertex. In countries without robust tax plugins available, the platform can monitor and apply taxes manually or the sellers can be required to roll the taxes into the displayed product price.

17.8 South Dakota v. Wayfair – Economic Nexus

For more than half a century, the Supreme Court held that a seller was required to have people, property, or some physical connection to a state for that state to validly compel the seller to collect and remit sales tax. The state of South Dakota appealed this long-standing ruling and successfully convinced the court to expand a state's authority to impose tax obligations on out-of-state, remote, and online sellers through its economic nexus rule.

On June 2, 2018, the US Supreme Court ruled in the case of South Dakota v. Wayfair that the physical presence of a seller is not a constitutional requirement for a state to impose sales tax. This meant that any state could impose sales tax on an out-of-state seller whose goods were shipped to a customer inside the state. This landmark decision clearly broadened the scope and ability of states to levy taxes on interstate sales by out-of-state sellers. In the wake of this decision in favor of South Dakota, many other states imposed similar tax collection laws.

What are the sales and transactions threshold requirements that trigger economic nexus in South Dakota?

For an economic nexus to trigger in South Dakota, an eCommerce seller must fulfill either of the following criteria:

- The gross revenue of seller from the sale of tangible product, personal property, or service delivered, either physically or electronically, into South Dakota exceeds $100,000 or

- The seller has 200 or more separate transactions through personal property, any product transferred electronically, or services for delivery into South Dakota.

The state of South Dakota considers selling $100,000 worth of goods or services inside South Dakota to be equivalent to selling $30 million nationwide.

South Dakota's law of economic nexus applies to remote online and offline sellers that may not be registered with the state currently but meet the threshold requirements that trigger economic nexus.

Apart from physical presence what other nexus-related laws should an online seller be aware of?

South Dakota's law applies to taxable sales made to consumers within the state, including the following situations.

- The law applies to wholesalers and manufacturers who sell direct to consumers.

- The law applies to both physical products and intangible services.

- The law does not have any bearing on items that are tax exempt.

Are other states imposing similar laws? If yes, when will they go into effect?

Other states with similar economic nexus rules include Alabama, Connecticut, Georgia, Hawaii, Iowa, Illinois, Indiana, Kentucky, Louisiana, Massachusetts, Maine, Mississippi, North Dakota, Ohio, Pennsylvania, Rhode Island, Tennessee, Vermont, Washington, Wyoming. Each state has its own requirements that trigger economic nexus.

Does physical presence still trigger nexus?

Yes. The Supreme Court ruling states that nexus is enforced when companies and sellers have a significant physical presence in another state.

How do online sellers ascertain whether they have nexus in South Dakota and other states?

It is best to work directly with a state and local tax advisor or a service like Vertex or Avalara to determine how nexus laws apply.

Key Takeaways: Payments & Taxes

- The three major relationship models in the marketplace payment system are payment facilitator, merchant of record, and broker/commercial agent.

- Managing multiple countries and currencies in a single marketplace can be a daunting task. Best practice dictates launching in one country and expanding gradually.

- When choosing a payment service provider, the three factors you should consider are marketplace specificity of the solution, regulatory compliance, and payment support.

- South Dakota's law of economic nexus applies to remote online and offline sellers that may not be registered with the state currently but meet the threshold requirements that trigger economic nexus, which is either sales over $100,000 or 200 or more transaction in the state.

- Sample payment, tax, and fraud detection vendors are listed in Appendix A.

Chapter 18: Seller Acquisition & Management

Building and sustaining community is a never-ending part of doing business.

Gary Vaynerchuk, American Entrepreneur

Introduction

At the heart of any successful online marketplace is a large supply of high-quality sellers. Building a two-sided marketplace should always begin with the supply side for two primary reasons. 1) Sellers have the incentive of finding new sources of revenue while customers have no motivation to visit a marketplace with few or low-quality sellers. 2) Sellers can bring their existing customer base to the marketplace. But beyond simply bringing in any sellers, consideration should also be given to finding the right sellers. Poor customer experience can cause great damage to the marketplace reputation, so sellers should be vetted carefully.

18.1 Seller Acquisition Process

Similar to a marketing and sales funnel, a seller acquisition consists of steps like acquiring, onboarding, and retaining the best quality sellers for your marketplace. Moving potential sellers through the funnel identifies the sellers which best fit the marketplace. For example, just 5% of the sellers on Amazon account for over 40% of the revenue.

Establishing an effective seller success funnel requires thoughtful and methodical time and effort but will save time and money in the long run. A structured and refined funnel can easily and rapidly attract high-quality sellers.

There are five steps to the seller acquisition process.

Define Seller Acquisition Goals – Begin by determining the number and type of sellers needed based on the categories planned and an assortment of products per category. While it is important to provide customers a variety of product choices, too having multiple sellers with overlapping product offerings will dilute the customer experience. One strategy is to onboard fewer vendors with large varied product catalogs.

Define Target Seller –Next create ideal seller profiles of the sellers who best match the target categories and audiences of the marketplace. These theoretical profiles define the traits which are common to the kind of seller the marketplace needs to recruit.

Following is an example of profiling for qualifying the sellers.

- Seller is experienced

- Has a presence in my geographic region

Define Goals

Identify Core Categories
No of Sellers Needed

Define Target Seller

Create Ideal Seller Profile
Top and Bottom Seller Profiling

Seller Identification

Utilize Sources of Information
Market Intelligence for Seller
Qualification

Reach Out & Offer

Seller outreach - Attractive Offer
Clear T&C, Logistics Support

Track Progress

Measure against quantitative
and qualitative goals

FIGURE 18.1 Seller Acquisition Process

- Offers a wide variety of sizes and colors and frequently runs special offers

- Has high seller rating, consistently positive reviews of 95% and/or 4 stars or more.

- Has shown consistent sales growth of 50% or more over the last 12 months

Seller profiles can also be created from the bottom up, meaning look for existing sellers who are already selling well on other marketplaces. To build a diverse marketplace, it is important to create multiple profiles for the various types of sellers carrying products that are a fit for the marketplace and its audience.

Seller Identification – With a clear understanding of the product categories and the ideal sellers use AI-powered algorithms and other resources to search other marketplaces, countries, and brands. By inputting the defined search criteria, these tools will identify sellers who fit the marketplace.

Reaching Out & Recruiting – Develop a proposition to attract sellers to join the marketplace. To set the stage for a mutually beneficial long-term relationship, key elements of the proposition should include a clear fee structure, effective logistics support, business tools to maximize sales, and an outline of the seller-friendly terms and conditions. If the seller is already succeeding on another marketplace, provide a clear value proposition for switching to a new marketplace.

Track Progress Through Metrics – The final step in the acquisition process is to track qualitative and quantitative metrics. Evaluating the seller acquisition program will refine the process to continue bringing in better quality sellers. Some important evaluation questions include the following:

- Have you reached the target number of sellers for each category?

- Did you recruit the top sellers that you aimed for?

- Was it difficult to find the sellers that perfectly matched your profiles?

18.2 Seller Onboarding Process

Onboarding, that is the process of integrating new sellers into the platform, ensures new sellers have the necessary knowledge, information, and tools to succeed in the marketplace. The process begins when a seller who wants to sell on the marketplace visits the registration page, fills out the form, and uploads required documentation.

Onboarding Initiation

Start of the on-boarding process
Seller register business entity

Next the onboarding team verifies the business documents furnished by the seller and reviews the seller's business model and product catalog to ensure a fit for the marketplace. If for any reason the onboarding team determines the seller is not a good fit for the marketplace, the seller is notified that the application has been rejected.

Seller Registration

Registration form filled
Required information uploaded

Seller Verification

Due Diligence
Document Verification

If the seller registration is approved, notification is sent, the seller dashboard is activated, and the seller can begin uploading the product catalog.

Onboarding Approval

Seller Registration - Approved
Seller Panel Activation

FIGURE 18.2 Seller Onboarding Process

18.3 Common Mistakes of Seller Onboarding

Signing new sellers can look like growth, but if the marketplace does not develop a strong relationship with the sellers at the outset of the relationship, the sellers will churn and the market will not expand. To ensure new vendor relationships get off on the right foot and develop into long-term partnerships, use a consistent and repeatable vendor onboarding process. Here are some common mistakes to avoid while you get sellers on board.

Poor communication – Nothing sours a relationship more quickly than unmet expectations. So communicate clearly at every stage what sellers and the operator can expect of one another. Additionally, an operator who practices good communication at the beginning of the relationship sets the example for the duration. It is essential that the operator frequently asks sellers what they need to be more successful.

Process Standardization Overload – While an efficient and standardized process is critical to a smooth-running marketplace, rigid adherence to the standards can create unnecessary stress for all parties. Leave room for flexibility as needed.

Incomplete Due Diligence – A new seller's reputation becomes the marketplace's reputation, so due diligence must be given meticulous time and effort. A seller's business practices, history, and products should be examined for quality, as well as confirming the company is not involved in child labor or illegal practices.

Failure to Plan – A marketplace that does not have plans in place to help sellers grow will not be able to retain sellers for long-term relationships. Before signing on new sellers, develop a clear path and incentives for their growth. A marketplace that seeks the health and growth of its sellers builds trust and goodwill.

Not Training Enough – If new sellers cannot understand how to use the platform and its tools for growing success, they will be unlikely to remain.

Good training will not only teach sellers how to get started but will also help them expand their presence and increase revenue over time. Additionally, provide an avenue for sellers to give feedback on their pain points and what kind of continuing training will help them.

18.4 Creating Seller Policies

When creating seller policies, the marketplace operator should consider four key pillars.

- General Terms and Conditions
- Seller Product Creation
- Options for Shipping
- Customer Care Service

Different marketplaces require different information at the time of registration. Figure 18.3 above shows that Walmart seeks extensive information from sellers as part of registration. The marketplace operator must decide how open or restricted marketplace account creation will be. Generally speaking, horizontal pure-play 3P eCommerce sites are more open as they are looking to scale. Amazon takes this approach, even encouraging sellers to register and start selling as quickly as possible. When it comes to terms and conditions for sellers, the following items need to be explained clearly and without any ambiguity.

Return Policy & Refunds – Return and refund policy comes into play when a purchased item does not match the description, has a defect, or otherwise does not satisfy the customer. Usually the liability remains between the seller and the buyer and does not include the marketplace operator.

	Amazon	Walmart	Rakuten	Newegg	Best Buy CA
Business Name	✓	✓	✓	✓	✓
Business Contact	✓	✓	✓		✓
Technical Contact		✓			
Bank Account Details	✓				
SSN / ITIN / EIN	✓	✓			
Business Structure	✓				
Employees					
Stores					✓
Website	✓	✓	✓		✓
Referred By					
Other Marketplaces	✓	✓	✓	✓	✓
Product Categories	✓	✓	✓		✓
Top Brands		✓			✓
Top Products		✓			
Estimated SKUs	✓	✓	✓	✓	✓
Estimated Sales Volume		✓	✓	✓	
Seller Reviews		✓			
Seller Type	✓	✓		✓	
Shipping Methods		✓			
Return Policy		✓			
Aggregator(s) Used		✓		✓	

TABLE 18.1 Seller registration information required by top marketplaces

Pricing Parity – Here the marketplace operator ensures that a seller is not selling the same product in some other marketplace at a lower rate. Some large marketplaces use an advanced algorithm to track prices and potentially remove a product listing if it is discovered to be listed elsewhere at a lower price.

Tax Collection – Tax collection and remittance terms should be clearly defined, applicable laws identified, and methods of charging tax assigned.

Product Images – In this section, the operator should specify image formats, size, resolution quality, and file naming convention. Figure 18.4 below is the product image requirement for Amazon, which covers both technical specifications and site standards.

TECHNICAL REQUIREMENTS

- Product image submitted to Amazon must meet the following technical specifications.
- TIFF (.tif/.tiff), JPEG (.jpeg/.jpg), GIF (.gif) and PNG (.png) format
- Image pixel dimensions of at least 1000 or large in either height or width preferred
- sRGB or CMYK color mode
- File names must consist of the product identifier (Amazon ASIN, 13-digit ISBN, EAN, JAN, or UPC) followed by a period and the appropriate file extension (Example: B000123456.jpg or 0237425673485.tif)

Note: Spaces, dahes or additional characters in the filename will prevent your image from going online.

AMAZON SITE STANDARDS FOR PRODUCT IMAGES

For images named by product identifier without a variant code or named with the MAIN variant, and display as the main image on the product detail page, Amazon maintains the following site product image standards:

- The image must be the cover art or a professional photograph of the product being sold. Drawing or illustrations of the product are not allowed.
- The image must not contain gratuitous or confusing additional objects.
- The image must be in focus, professionally lit and photographed or scanned, with realistic color, and smooth edges.
- Books, Music, and Video/DVD image should be the front cover art, and fill 100% of the image frame. Jewel cases, promotional stickers, and cellophane are not allowed.
- All other products should fill 85% or more of the image frame.
- The full product must be in frame.
- Backgrounds must be pure white (RGB 255, 255, 255).
- The image must not contain additional text, graphics, or inset images.
- Pornographic and offensive materials ate not allowed.

FIGURE 18.3 Technical Requirements

External URLs – Most marketplace terms and conditions stipulate that no external URL can be provided in the product description page of the seller storefront in either link or image forms. If external links are provided, then a disclaimer below the link should clearly state that the marketplace operator is not responsible for the availability of such external sites or resources and does not endorse and is not responsible or liable for any content, advertising, products, or other material on or available from such sites or resources.

Excluded Products – State clearly what items are prohibited or excluded from sale on the marketplace. For instance, Amazon doesn't allow products that are in direct competition to Kindle. Exclusion items may also differ based on specified criteria such as season.

Credit Card Fraud – This section defines unauthorized usage, liability in case of a dispute, and liability due to errors. It also details a step-by-step procedure in the event of an unauthorized transaction and how to raise a security issue.

Credit Card Chargebacks - Chargebacks are a forced transaction reversal initiated by the cardholder's bank. They are meant as a consumer protection mechanism but are sometimes misused. Guidelines here should define a standard procedure around chargebacks and how to dispute if necessary.

Delivery Errors – This section outlines liability in case of a delivery error due to willful act, default, omission, misstatement, or misrepresentation by the consignor, consignee, or any other party claiming interest in the shipment. In most cases, liability for errors in fulfillment is placed with the fulfiller, whether that is the marketplace operator or the seller.

Seller Payment – This section clearly identifies how and when a seller will get paid for the products they sell on the marketplace. For example, Amazon first settles the account balance (initiates payment to the seller's bank account) fourteen days after a seller registers their account. Subsequently, the settlement process repeats every 7 days.

Seller Product Creation – In terms of product creation, the marketplace operator needs to declare the level of autonomy the seller will have. For example, Amazon lets the sellers create products on their own for most categories, while sites like Best Buy Canada and Rakuten require approval.

Shipping Methods – This section should clearly discuss the type of shipping, whether the seller is solely responsible or if the operator can provide assistance, and expected shipping time frames.

Shipping Charges – This policy should provide a framework under which the sellers can set the shipping charges. If the marketplace operator provides shipping on behalf of the sellers, charges should be clearly discussed in weight or units and define how the distance from the shipping location will factor into the charges.

Shipping SLA – The service level agreement is a commitment between the marketplace operator and the seller which defines quality, availability, and responsibilities expected of each party. The agreement includes definitions of a fulfilled or breached SLA, as well as the terms for dispute, arbitration, and penalties.

Customer Care Service – Because the customer experience directly correlates to the success of the marketplace, the operator needs to draft a clear policy around customer service. The policy should address questions like who will provide front end customer service and will the seller have direct access to the customers. The best practice is to have level 1 issues addressed by the seller and level 2 issues addressed by the operator.

Level 1 Issues

- Product information
- Shipping & delivery information
- Order cancelation
- Request an invoice

Level 2 Issues

- Right to retract
- Shipping issue
- Issue with item received
- Item not received

18.5 Creating a Marketplace Seller's Guide

While seller policies inform all parties of the same rules and expectations, sellers still need to be trained on marketplace functions. To create an environment where sellers feel empowered for success, a seller's guide outlines ways to accelerate sales on the marketplace.

Product Catalogs – Encourage sellers to make their entire catalog available on the marketplace and include detailed information on how sellers can map their products to the marketplace catalog.

Pricing – Allow sellers flexibility to price their items as they see fit. At the same time, guide them in market competition by advising them to perform regular audits of their prices.

Visibility – Explain clearly to sellers how products are ranked within the marketplace, and educate them on how to improve product visibility through promotions, discounts, etc. The seller should be empowered to optimize their product listings to appear in the right categories.

18.6 Supporting Sellers for Growth

Sellers are the primary asset of any online marketplace, so the wise operator manages them effectively through their lifecycle with the marketplace. The level of assistance a seller needs varies depending on the growth stage within the marketplace.

Early-stage Seller – These sellers typically need extra handholding in many areas, but one critical step is product showcasing and its effect on conversion. This is the primary reason for picture specifications in the seller policies. Because the operator is onboarding many new sellers in the early days of a new marketplace, managing and controlling seller listings effectively will ensure counterfeit and repetitive products are removed from the site and maintain trust with the sellers. Additionally, sellers from different countries should be carefully monitored to ensure they are in compliance with local laws. The operator should communicate regularly with all new sellers to cultivate a sense of ownership in them that drives them to supply better quality products and excellent customer service.

Mid-stage Seller – These sellers have become comfortable with the platform, but the operator would be wise to regularly monitor the quality of goods, order processing times, and order delivery processes. At this stage, customer feedback and ratings are a valuable tool for establishing seller rankings and encouraging sellers to follow performance standard guidelines. The operator should also monitor customer disputes to find and fix breakdowns in the system.

Monitoring transactions and seller activities will help the operator find and stop fraud. In particular, activities that should raise a red flag include high-dollar activity, an unusually high number of new listings from a single seller, recently changed email or a bank account, or a rapidly falling reputation score on the marketplace. To head off fraud before it starts,

- Attach bank accounts and financial relationships data to seller profiles in the marketplace platform

- Always carry out multi-factor authentication

- Use the social media profile as an extra identity validation of the seller.

The operator's overall goal for mid-stage sellers should be to align the entire marketplace organization toward customer satisfaction.

Mature-stage Seller – When sellers have reached a level of maturity, the operator's objective should be to watch seller KPIs to help them maintain product quality and customer service while looking for further optimization opportunities.

If you're not a Power Seller yer, you can always work your way up by meeting these requirements:

- Have an eBay account in good standing that's been active for at least 90 days

- Follow all eBay policies

- Maintain a positive feedback score of 98% or higher

- Have a minimum of 100 transactions and $3,000 in sales with US buyers over the past 12 months

---

FIGURE 18.4 eBay's performance guidelines for becoming a Power Seller

These performance standards can also become quality **benchmarks** to build credibility with customers. Flipkart places an "Assured" badge on its top sellers so customers see the rating easily.

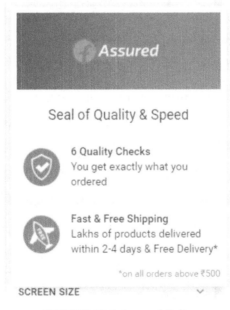

FIGURE 18.5 Assured Seller

Key Takeaways: Seller Acquisition & Management

- Because quality sellers are the most critical element in the success of a marketplace, the operator needs a seller acquisition funnel for continuous acquisition, activation, revenues, and retention.

- The two key steps of the seller acquisition process are defining seller acquisition goals and creating Ideal Seller Profiles.

- Seller onboarding and registration, though critical, should be a simple process for the seller to follow.

- The three critical components of onboarding are continuous communication, complete due diligence, and proper training and enablement of the seller.

- Seller Policy should focus on four key areas: Seller Terms and Conditions, Seller Product Creation, Options for Shipping, and Customer Care.

- The key elements of a Marketplace Seller Guide are product catalog, pricing, and visibility for the seller.

Chapter 19: Data – Catalog, Offers, & Orders

19.1 Product Catalog
19.2 Seller offers
19.3 Order Data and Workflows
19.4 Additional Data Tools

Information is the oil of the 21st century.

Peter Sondergaard, Gartner Research

Introduction

If data is the new oil, then starting a marketplace is like uncovering a massive old reserve. However, proper planning and robust refinery systems are needed to monetize oil with end customers. And in terms of a marketplace, three core areas of data must be refined—the product catalog, seller offers, and orders.

At the database level, enterprise marketplaces have hundreds of tables and thousands of data elements. There are also other major categories of data like customer information and promotions, but these do not vary substantially from eCommerce to marketplaces. To avoid an overwhelming amount of detail this chapter focuses on just three foundational data topics.

Product data includes its categorization in catalog hierarchy ("Clothing>Men>Western Wear>Shorts) and the product attributes (size, weight, color), which is generally static. Offer data (seller inventory level, seller price, shipping cost) can vary frequently. Orders record a customer purchasing an offer(s) from a seller(s) for a product(s).

Application business logic and user experiences are driven by data; data is the foundation on which platforms are built. Poorly organized data will inevitably limit application functionality and cause poor user experiences.

High-level marketplace data flow is covered in Chapter 15 General Architecture. Chapter 21 Key Performance Indicators addresses metrics and insights that can be gleaned from data.

19.1 Product Catalog

While first-party eCommerce operators often have challenges defining the best structure and attributes for their own catalog, marketplaces amplify that complexity as they merge catalog structures and attributes from hundreds or thousands of 3P seller catalogs. Defining the proper catalog taxonomy at the start of a marketplace project is critical as it is very difficult to reverse or undo poorly structured data after it has been entered into a system.

Catalog management can be performed in an eCommerce platform's merchandising tool, a product information management (PIM) tool, or a marketplace platform's catalog management tool, such as Mirakl Catalog Manager. First-party basic catalog management can be done upstream in an ERP, but that data is generally sparse and often is neither user friendly nor SEO optimized. Third-party product data generally is not ingested directly into ERP systems.

For ingesting third-party product data, the marketplace platform ought to provide this merging capability. eCommerce platform merchandising tools are generally not well suited for harmonizing third-party catalog data. The harmonization process can include category selection and product attribute mapping. Enterprise marketplace platforms like Mirakl offer intelligent mapping tools that are very helpful when importing thousands or tens of thousands of products.

Catalog structure is the combination of categories, attributes, and value lists as defined by how they interact with each other. Catalog data is also often syndicated to many systems, such a Google Product Search.

Taxonomy

A taxonomy is a knowledge organization system used for navigation, indexing, and retrieval. Defining a quality product taxonomy, or hierarchical classification, is a critical step toward helping customers and sellers find categories and products. Haphazard taxonomy results in lost sales and a poor reputation, while carefully structured taxonomy based on deep knowledge of users and products creates a logical search structure to improve sales. A Forrester study found that poorly architected eCommerce sites sell 50% less than well-organized sites.

Taxonomies should consolidate the data across unstructured and structured information and provide the organizing principles behind the metadata used for faceted navigation and search. They can also provide a foundation for up-sell and cross-sell opportunities based on semantic relationships. A sample apparel taxonomy is shown on the next page.

The taxonomy can also be used for the overall website design in the form of skeleton wireframes, navigation maps, and user interface design. Top-level categories often get dedicated category pages. Product detail pages can be presented differently for different categories to highlight the data most relevant to that category.

After the taxonomy is populated with content and integrated with the existing content management process, site search can be tuned based on the structure and data. Ideally a customer should be able to find what they are looking for in no more than three clicks.

Finally, the most crucial step is to maintain the taxonomy structure. As the marketplace grows and expands to new categories the basic taxonomy model must be updated to accommodate new information, context, content, and data to provide the proper user experience for the new categories.

Sample Taxonomy

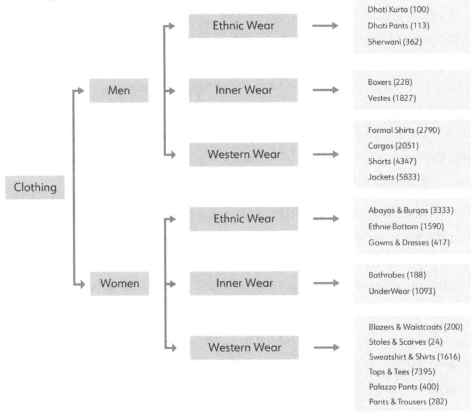

FIGURE 19.1 Sample taxonomy. Source: https://lionbridge.ai/articles/5-must-read-papers-on-product-categorization-for-data-scientists/

Product Attributes and Value Lists

Product attributes store the metadata about a product. Different product categories have different attributes. For example, important attributes for the TV category are brand, screen size, screen technology, resolution, input ports, etc. Alternately, attributes for a book include author, publisher, page count, cover type, and ISBN code.

Value lists define the options available for an attribute for a category. For example, the value list options for TV screen type could be plasma, LCD, LED, or OLED. The value list options for book cover types could be paperback, hardcover, or wire bound.

Consistent usage of value lists is important for catalog navigation and search. For example, challenges could arise if one seller uses the term "paperback" and another uses "softcover." It is important to select the proper entries in the value list that will be most useful to customers and most aligned with seller data.

Data Harmonization

The marketplace and the sellers may have field names to describe the same attribute. For example, one seller might call the field Screen_Tech and another seller may call it Screen_Type. The marketplace might use a field called Display_Tech. Alternately, the text used in seller value lists may not match the marketplace value lists. The process of harmonization maps, and perhaps transforms, these seller fields and data into a consistent structure in the marketplace.

Advanced marketplace platforms have intelligent tools to help automate the data harmonization process.

SKU Variants

One product may have multiple variants that can each have their own SKU number. For example, one particular brand of AA batteries might be available in 2-packs, 4-packs, or 12-packs and each pack size variant could be considered a different SKU, resulting in three SKUs for that brand AA battery product. Similarly, a specific shirt might be available in four sizes and five colors which results in a two-dimensional matrix of 20 SKU variants of that shirt product. Batteries could also be organized in a two-dimensional matrix with size (AAA, AA, C, D) and pack count (2-pack, 4-pack, 12-pack) as the two dimensions.

SKU variants are a typical feature of eCommerce platforms. However, depending on the business, different approaches to marketplace integration should be evaluated. SKU variants are very common in the apparel industry. However, some organizations may consider the 2-pack and the 4-pack to be different products, not SKU variants. Consider the user base, the marketplace's value proposition, and the type of sellers engaged when determining how to structure SKU variants (if at all).

Images and Video

Images and videos are generally related to the product and not to a seller offer. However, often the first seller to upload a product may include their images which should be seller-neutral.

Product Details

Since consumers can physically touch or see marketplace goods, the product information provided by the seller is often their only basis for decision making. To ensure a positive customer journey and ease of finding products, marketplace operators should provide sellers a well-defined set of product information standards. Some basic product properties most marketplaces require include the following:

- Product attributes relevant to the category

- Product images and videos

- Warranty information

- Return information

- Product Q&A

Tax inclusion – Most sellers assign a tax code to their product so the operator can apply appropriate tax at checkout, but another option is to include tax in the displayed item price. This decision is based on the market demographics and statutory regulations, and the seller would need to send that tax-inclusive price in the product information uploaded to the marketplace management software.

Shipping inclusion – Some marketplaces display only the item price to garner consumer attention. Once the customer visits the product details page, the shipping details are revealed. If the seller handles their own inventory and shipping, they may choose to include the shipping price in the product price.

Marketplace operators should encourage competitive pricing to maintain and increase traffic to the site. A poor pricing strategy could lead to three significant problems.

- Disintermediation or Leakage – Some customers and sellers use the marketplace for discovery, but then complete the transaction outside of the platform. Pricing restrictions, heavy processing fees, convenience fees, and shipping charges may force consumers to look for cheaper alternatives.

- Multi-tenanting – If products are identical across multiple platforms, shoppers will search all platforms for the same product and then purchase from the platform offering the lowest price.

- Monogamous buying – If transactions routinely happen between the same buyer and seller, they may decide to take their relationship off the marketplace.

19.2 Seller Offers

Within marketplaces, shoppers often have multiple options or offers for purchasing the same product at different prices, shipping costs, shipping times, etc. from different sellers. Product characteristics (attributes) cannot change from seller to seller. Example product attributes include:

1. Product name
2. Brand
3. Images
4. Description
5. Product ID, EAN, ISBN, UPC, etc.
6. Color, size, dimensions, etc.
7. Other category-specific attributes

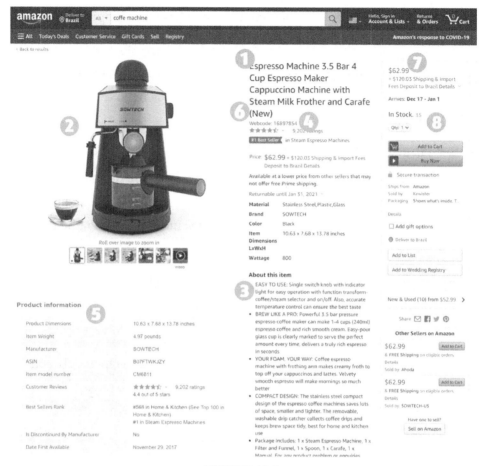

FIGURE 19.2

Product offers vary from one seller to the next and may include:

1. A reference to the specific product

2. Item condition (new, used, renewed)

3. Item Selling Price

4. Item Stock Quantity (may be qty per fulfillment location)

5. Shipping Cost (may be a table lookup)

6. Shipping Time (may be a table lookup)

7. Promotion terms (price, timeframe, conditions)

8. Volume discounts

In some marketplaces, sellers can set up their offers with seller-specific information, but many marketplaces are strict about standardizing product information to ease comparing offers from various sellers. Under the buy box, most marketplaces list offers from other sellers, if available. Aggressive sellers will continually update their offer price (sometimes with automated repricing engines) in attempts to win the buy box. Marketplaces need the processing ability to receive and prioritize these dynamic feeds in near real time.

Advanced sellers usually have API integrations (or other integrations) between the marketplace and their inventory and order management systems. Marketplace offer status tends to be more accurate for integrated sellers. Less sophisticated sellers who might use a marketplace GUI interface to manually update their inventory and order status tend to be less accurate.

Offer data must also be linked to items added to the shopping cart to ensure that the proper seller is used at checkout for fulfillment. Offer data may be displayed on the product listing page, product detail page, cart, checkout, and order status pages. See Chapter 22 User Experience for details about UX best practices for marketplaces.

19.3 Order Data and Workflows

Marketplace orders require more data and processes than simple first-party eCommerce orders. Offer data must be included in the shopping cart and the checkout process to ensure the appropriate association of each line item to a seller and price.

Upon checkout, a shopping cart may contain 1P goods stocked by the operator and several 3P goods fulfilled by multiple third-party sellers. Each item in the cart might have different shipment tracking information and different credit card settlement times. In these scenarios, one checkout might result in multiple order records and processes.

This data must also be stored in the order history for easy lookup by the customer.

If order-level promotions (e.g. 5% discount on orders over $100) are included, it is important to consider what happens if a seller cannot fulfill one item in the cart or the amount of credit if an item is returned.

An Order Lifecycle contains the following elements:

- Order breakdowns

- Data verification

- Alerts/Email communication to customers, sellers, and operators

- Order expiration time limits

- Incident management

- Order messaging & communication

- Order evaluation & assessment

- Customer debit requests

- Customer cancellation requests

- Customer refund requests

Typical Order Features

Payment Workflows come in several different forms. Pay on acceptance means the order amount is debited as soon as the order is accepted. Pay on Delivery means the order amount is debited only after the customer receives the delivery. Pay on Due Date, usually applicable for B2B, means the order amount is debited on a specified date after receipt of the order.

Taxes must be paid by either the operator or the seller, but they can choose whether to call out those taxes on the order or simply roll them into the displayed product price. The choices are no taxes, product and shipping taxes, product taxes only, or shipping taxes only.

Shipping is usually calculated on a shipping grid that divides the country into regions with costs per region, often with ground and air options.

Shipping can be processed free of charge to the customer, but the operator and sellers should define a threshold for orders to qualify for free shipping.

Lead time to ship is the space where sellers define their time to pick, pack, and ship exclusive of the carrier's time requirements.

Returns and Cancellations should have individual features to enable customers to cancel or return an order for a full or partial refund.

By integrating marketplace checkout with the seller's inventory system and listing calendar, the operator can prevent overselling and potentially long delays in shipping. A double-check system can also help to confirm that the product customers are paying for is the product they want. It is the operator's responsibility to split orders into seller specific suborders and export that information to the seller OMS via integrated APIs.

19.4 Additional Data Tools

This section describes some additional tools which can be helpful in data and related content management.

Product Information Management (PIM)

If a marketplace platform does not include powerful data ingestion and harmonization tools it might make sense to integrate a PIM solution like Akeneo, Salsify, or Stibo STEP. Some eCommerce operators have a legacy PIM solution in use before launching a marketplace.

Medium to large sellers may also have a PIM or other in-house system to manage their product life cycle, while small businesses likely have only a basic system (or simple spreadsheets) in place. Whatever the case, sellers should use an automated system to send updated product information regularly. Since the source of information varies by seller, data formats and product attributes are likely to vary. To address this, the marketplace must have a well-defined and structured integration architecture.

Beginning with product attributes and associated media, the operator must declare what file types are supported, restrictions on file size, and legal or regulatory information that is required. Sellers will be required to send their data only in the operator defined formats, such as JSON, XML, or CSV. The marketplace can receive the information either by direct integration or via a marketplace management software.

Master Data Management (MDM)

Master Data Management is usually a function of IT to create a centralized "golden record" of reference data across domains. While PIM (product information management system) is a business-led subset focused on product and merchandising information, MDM encompasses data for products, vendors, customers, financial, etc. and creates a master for each. For example, an MDM product master can serve the following functions, much like the PIM.

- On-boarding products, hierarchies, relationships, and classifications.

- Collaborating with partners to author correct content the first time.

- Managing and governing policies, dictionaries, rules, and references.

- Correlating product data with media assets and other domains.

- Seamless publishing of product data to eCommerce, marketplaces, print catalogs, and data pools.

Digital Asset Management (DAM)

Digital Asset Management solutions maintain images and digital content for centralized and easy access. Having all assets in a single location enables the marketers and marketplace operators to build and launch product information across all channels in the most efficient manner. The best current platforms offer cloud, AI, and machine learning as part of the DAM solution. Similar to the way PIM handles product information,

DAM handles digital assets like images, logos, videos, documentation, presentations, metadata, and even branded and promotional items. PIM and DAM systems work together to store, manage, and distribute digital assets along with product information.

Product Search / Site Search

A robust search feature, either keyword or typeahead, will not only improve user experience but also provide a more direct path to purchase. Marketplace operators can use search configuration to assist in sellers generating more sales while opening another revenue stream for the platform itself. Operators usually charge for

- paid ads at the top of search suggestions,

- premium listing in search results for specific keywords,

- product promotion on specific product listing pages, and

- top product placement in category navigation.

Some customers are unsure of what they want and browse product listings to see what is available, while other customers know exactly what they want and want to find and purchase it quickly. Quality site architecture and navigation tools will accommodate both kinds of shoppers and provide the operator informative data for making decisions on site traffic, commonly searched categories, and top-selling products.

Key Takeaways: Data – Catalog, Offers & Orders

- Data is the foundation upon which business logic and user experiences are built. Poor data will cause poor applications and poor user experiences.

- Product catalog data includes its categorization in the hierarchy (taxonomy) and the product attributes, which is generally static. Offer data (seller inventory level, seller price, shipping cost) can vary frequently. Orders record a customer purchasing an offer(s) from a seller(s) for a product(s).

- The core catalog structure elements are the category hierarchy, product attributes, and value lists.

- Data harmonization is the process of consolidating varying hierarchies, attributes, and value lists from sellers into the marketplace operator standard.

- Designing the optimal product taxonomy requires deep knowledge of the customer base, the products, and the marketplace strategy.

- Search is a primary tool for customers to explore product catalogs, however, search depends on good data. Robust search tools also provide the operator with valuable data (e.g. null search results) to help improve user experience.

- By integrating the marketplace checkout process with the seller's automated inventory system, the operator can minimize overselling and potentially long delays in shipping.

Chapter 20: Organizational Structure

20.1 Organization of Team Relationships
20.2 Organization for Growth Stages
20.3 Shared Support Functions
20.4 Key Marketplace Job Role Descriptions

---

*It's tough when markets change and your people within the
company don't.*

Harvard Business Review

Introduction

Many business experts can agree that eCommerce and marketplaces are going to be the main growth engines for consumer goods and services in the next decade. And while considerable data and research shed light on technologies and business strategies to make the best of the opportunity, very little emphasis has been placed on organizational structure as a means to help a marketplace succeed in today's 24/7 connected world.

For organizations already operating in digital commerce, some roles need to be augmented to cover marketplace functions. For companies new to the eCommerce space, new roles need to be created all together. From catalog management to merchandising, managing sellers to complex customer service solutions, and overall marketplace management, staffing needs depend on the company's existing capabilities and growth plans. And while organizational structure can set a new marketplace on the path toward growth, there is no guaranteed success. Ultimately, marketplace companies will need the right talent and culture to win.

20.1 Organization of Team Relationships

In a large eCommerce organization selling 1P products alongside 3P products, the functions of the marketplace will resemble Figure 20.1

below. In this straightforward structure, the marketplace manager oversees all marketplace operations, including seller support and seller acquisition. Merchandising, marketing, technology, and other functions are considered parallel, and all are supported by underlying business functions like marketing, merchant operations, IT, and business operations.

FIGURE 20.1 Sample Functions in a Marketplace Organization

Any strategic partnerships with big brands and retailers fall under strategic partnership management. Depending on the overall revenue potential of the partner and the value of the relationship, a dedicated manager could be assigned to nurture it.

It is important to note that the marketing department of an eCommerce marketplace serves a two-fold strategy. They must create demand for the products on the platform, while at the same time attracting best of breed sellers across product categories.

20.2 Organization for Growth Stages

Launch Phase

As the name suggests, this is the first year of operation. An early-stage marketplace resembles a science experiment. Rather than building big teams, the focus should be on acquiring the concoction of skills and talents to address fundamental challenges like onboarding new sellers, facilitating smooth transactions between customers and sellers, and creating value for shoppers.

MARKETPLACE ORGANIZATIONAL SIZE BY MARKETPLACE SCALE

FIGURE 20.2

The team set up is foundational. For a marketplace of 10-100 sellers, a full-time marketplace manager and one to two seller acquisition managers should be aggressively pursuing new sellers and a wide assortment of products. Seller acquisition and optimization will remain a key area even during the growth and maturity stages of the marketplace.

With so few sellers on board at this stage, the marketplace should retain thin staffing levels around support functions, such as technical support, accounting and finance, marketing and merchandising, and customer service. For an optimum operation, 1 full-time employee should be able to handle these four functions. With a structure of this type, $ 1- 5 million in sales makes a great start for scalable and sustainable marketplace operations. In this most difficult phase, team members wear many hats, learn hard lessons, sometimes feel as though things are not going anywhere. For instance, Airbnb struggled for four years before taking off. However, through adversity and perseverance, innovation is born.

Growth Phase

A marketplace in the growth phase—generally between the second and third years of operation—has built an initial user base and stabilized basic operations, but now aims for that virtuous cycle. By increasing efforts to bring high-quality sellers, more customers are attracted to the platform, which in turn brings in more sellers. The growth phase could be reached anywhere between two and four years after launch and generates revenue of $5 to $20 million from a seller count of 100–500.

With the significant increase of sellers, transactions, and revenue, the marketplace operations team should focus on three primary areas—seller acquisition, seller account management, and customer service. At least two to three seller acquisition managers should devote full-time focus to onboarding high-quality. This process should follow the funnel model of training many quality sellers; those who meet the high-performance standards to help the marketplace will be rewarded and retained.

Account managers will be added as the number of sellers increases, and top-tier sellers (based on sales volume, number of transactions, customer ratings, etc.) will have dedicated account managers to service their needs. And with more customers and transactions comes the need for more customer care representatives who handle customer queries and disputes.

At-Scale Phase

Having sustained rapid growth during the first few years, the marketplace should be ready to develop long-term stability structures. After about 4 years of operation, a healthy marketplace can expect to support 500–2000 sellers and maintain a sales volume of $20 to $50 million or more.

As the marketplace grows substantially in terms of revenue, sellers, consumers, and transactions, an experienced hand will be required at the top. A marketplace director will lead big picture planning for the marketplace, includes annual operations planning, model level planning, seller SKU planning, and budgets. Additional oversight is needed for quarterly and monthly revenue reviews, inventory requirements, selection across stores and sellers, as well as product and category profitability measures. This role acts as a governance mechanism to steer the large operation into profitability. As this is a cross-functional role, the ideal candidate will be able to work with diverse teams to drive results.

The at-scale stage also means the addition of personnel in seller management functions. Three to Four seller acquisition analysts should report to a single seller manager, while four to five account analysts report to a single account manager. In the long term, a team of 10-20 people will manage a marketplace with more than 1000 sellers.

20.3 Shared Support Functions

Four main functions support the marketplace teams. Particularly in the early stages of marketplace growth, a single person or a few people can share these responsibilities rather than paying for a full-time employee in each position.

Customer Service

- Handles customer complaints and incidents between sellers and customers

- Records and processes orders and inquiries received by mail, telephone, and through customer contact.

- Provides pricing, availability, and schedule information within established guidelines.

- Suggests alternative products or services to meet customer needs.

Technical Support

- Answers seller questions about API integration, test, and production

- Handles all technical queries around the platform and troubleshoots problems

- Helps seller with portal login issues

- Assists seller with uploading inventory feeds

- Helps seller with general account questions

Marketing & Merchandising

- Broadly manages the quality of the product catalog and the resulting customer experience.

- Manages projects like product data quality and attribute and image collection.

- Integrates the marketplace offers within the traffic acquisition strategy of the site (SEO, SEM, Social)

- Handles marketing activities across channels and creation of marketing assets, either internally or in collaboration with external agencies.

- Initiates, defines, plans, and manages the seller self-registration pipeline.

Accounting/Finance

- Controls transaction flows and payment runs

- Provides full accounting services for all expenses, B2C and B2B invoicing, bank transactions, payroll, reconciliation with cash on delivery, payment gateway, and also help in monthly financial projections.

20.4 Key Job Descriptions

Marketplace Manager

Responsibilities

- Lead the marketplace growth and the team

- Become the ambassador of the marketplace in the company

- Ensure full visibility of marketplace offers inside and outside the website

- Recruit and develop strategic partners, key brands, retailers

- Drive business analysis and recommendations to improve the business

Qualifications

- Excellent analytical skills

- 5+ years sales and management experience

- Preferably experienced in marketplace business

Seller Acquisition Manager

Responsibilities

- Target future top sellers through relevant acquisition channels

- Recruit sellers quickly and efficiently using a mastered sales pitch

- Train sellers in use of back-office, functional tools and quality criteria

- Develop accounts until fully self-sufficient

- Objective: 25 sellers activated per quarter

Qualifications

- Excellent communication and negotiation skills

- Prior business development experience preferred

- Passionate for the e-business sector

- A Master's degree is required

Account Manager

Responsibilities

- Develop 100 strategic accounts and build loyalty

- Ensure the update of seller catalog online, promote sellers offers in marketing mediums, analyze seller performances and provide training and recommendations

- Drive business analysis and develop strategic recommendations to improve the product area's turnover

- Lead the growth of a specific product area

Qualifications

- Excellent communication skills: ability to work closely with sellers and internal teams

- Analytical skills

- Retail eCommerce experience and knowledge

- Bachelor's degree is required

Seller Support Manager

Responsibilities

- Onboard seller catalogs on the platform

- Train sellers on using the back-office tools and functions

- Help sellers migrate their products

- Monitor seller quality of service and take necessary actions

- Be the first point of contact for sellers on functional issues

Qualifications

- Strong problem-solving skills with service orientation

- Experience within a customer service environment

- A Master's degree is required

Key Takeaways: Organizational Structure

- In the launch stage, lean teams should focus on fundamental functions to ensure smooth transactions.

- At the growth phase, focus on establishing a virtuous cycle by bringing in high-quality sellers who attract new customers who, in turn, attract more sellers.

- At a more mature stage, bringing in senior staff begins with a marketplace director who will guide the marketplace into profitability and long-term growth.

- Somewhere along the journey, consider scaling beyond the initial niche by expanding categories, your audience demographic, or the market itself.

Chapter 21: Key Performance Indicators

The price of light is less than the cost of darkness.

Arthur C. Nielsen, Modern Marketing Research Pioneer

Introduction

WHICH LEVERS TO PULL TO CHANGE PERFORMANCE?

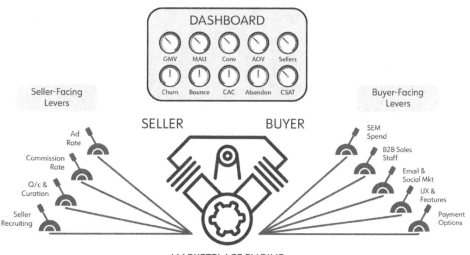

MARKETPLACE ENGINE

FIGURE 21.1

As with any business model, studying Key Performance Indicators, or KPIs, helps a commerce site operator evaluate marketplace performance by weighing the effectiveness of various functions against the operational and strategic goals. The insights gathered from KPIs help inform action steps to compete, improve, grow, remain strong, etc. The key is to examine performance through a variety of lenses. Beyond simple growth of the consumer base or number of transactions, all angles of the platform, sellers, catalog, logistics, and back-office functions must be examined for efficiency and effectiveness. But first, understanding core concepts of the marketplace model will allow the operator to define success in a marketplace environment and then develop a list of KPIs to track the health of the business.

21.1 Core Concepts around Marketplace Business Model

The Virtuous Cycle – As Jeff Bezos dubbed it, the Virtuous Cycle demonstrates how fantastic customer experience is at the forefront of success in a marketplace business. Great customer experience attracts more customers, attracts more third-party sellers, enhances product selection, lowers the cost of products and innovation, attracts more customers. Therefore, examining and acting on KPIs should aim to magnify the flywheel repeatedly and create a network effect.

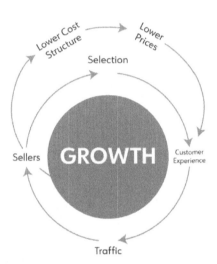

Figure 21.2

Critical Mass – This scientific concept states that for transactions to occur on a marketplace, there must be a minimum number of sellers, products, and buyers. Theoretically, only one of each could result in a transaction, but the odds of the right single buyer wanting to purchase the right single product from the right single seller are extraordinary. Therefore, there must be a good volume of supply and demand to make a marketplace function, much less grow.

Building Trust – While consumers have mostly grown accustomed to the idea of entering their credit card information on a website, a marketplace of any type still must exert a good amount of effort to foster trust between all the stakeholders. An excellent example is Airbnb, which had to convince both renters and property owners that renting a private home instead of a hotel room was a good and safe idea. Early adopters may be drawn to the novelty factor of a new marketplace but gaining the trust of a larger market requires significant reputation management.

How did Airbnb achieve its network effects?

Corresponding Questions: How to build liquidity/Solve the chicken-egg problem?

FIGURE 21.3

21.2 Liquidity Metrics

Liquidity, in terms of a marketplace, applies to both providers and customers. In its most basic form, liquidity is the reasonable expectation of being able to sell what you listed or find what you are looking for. In KPI terms, provider liquidity is the percentage of listings that lead to transactions within a certain time period, whereas customer liquidity means the probability of a visit leading to a transaction on the marketplace website. Insights gained by the study of liquidity metrics include the ease of the customer journey and path to purchase, as well as whether marketing dollars are being spent on the right audiences.

Basic liquidity metrics:

- Search to fill – Percentage of searches or requests that lead to a transaction

- Supplier utilization – Percentage of suppliers experiencing heavy customer traffic

- Time to Fill – Speed at which orders are filled or services are performed

Advanced liquidity metrics:

- Buyer-to-Seller Ratio - Number of buyers one seller can serve. There is no single right ratio for all marketplaces; rather, this ratio can vary greatly by industry and marketplace type.

- Repeat Purchase Ratio – Percentage of transactions by customers who have previously purchased on the platform. A higher repeat purchase ratio translates to a higher customer lifetime value and lower customer acquisition costs.

- Average Order Value (AOV) – This self-descriptive metric can inform promotional activities like recommending complementary purchases.

21.3 Trust Metrics

Like liquidity metrics, trust metrics can also be observed from the customer perspective and the seller perspective. The importance of these KPIs cannot be overstated as they provide the most direct picture of whether customers will continue to shop on the marketplace.

Customer Retention Rate shows the percentage of customers who continue doing business with the marketplace over a given time period. By contrast, Churn Rate shows the percentage of customers a marketplace has lost over time. This metric is also a good indicator of the effectiveness of customer loyalty and customer service programs.

Net Promoter Score is a simple format, devised by Fred Reichheld of Bain & Company and Satmetrix Systems in 2003, which asks the customer "How likely are you to recommend our marketplace to a friend or colleague?" By choosing a number or smiley face, the customer tells a story about their overall satisfaction.

FIGURE 21.4

Customer Resolution Time is how long it takes to resolve a consumer's problem. Ideally most marketplace businesses aim for first contact resolution (FCR), that is, resolving the issue in a single interaction thereby eliminating the need for them to reach out a second time. While it is important to resolve matters quickly, of equal importance is resolving issues correctly and to the customer's satisfaction.

21.4 Business Scale Metrics

Business metrics or scale metrics answer questions related to big picture costs, revenue, and profitability.

Gross Merchandise Value (GMV) is the total value of products or services transacted on the marketplace platform, exclusive of returns and cancellations, during a specific time period. This depicts the total scale and overall health of your business.

Net Revenue is calculated by multiplying GMV by the per transaction commission rate.

Customer Acquisition Cost (CAC) is the total hard and soft costs that go into acquiring new customers (usually mostly sales and marketing costs) divided by the number of new customers. Best practice is to start with a target CAC target that nets a positive return on the investment. Ideally, this cost would be zero based on the organic network and referral effect of the marketplace, however, that is not the case in the real world. Even if you do not spend much on marketing, you are likely to spend money on sales, support, community management factors that influence things like referrals. Some of the levers to bring down the customer acquisition costs include increasing conversion rates, increasing customer retention rates, and use of marketing automation and other platforms to keep customers and potential customers engaged. A comprehensive referral program is another way to lower the CAC, as referrals from existing customers tend to carry the lowest cost of all.

Customer Lifetime Value (CLV) is the total amount of revenue expected from each customer throughout the duration of their relationship with the marketplace. To be profitable, CLV must be higher than CAC. Overall CLV is an estimate calculated through many variables, but the result still provides a valuable snapshot of the viability of a marketplace. The formulas below detail the calculation of CLV.

Average Purchase Frequency Rate (AFPR) = Number of Purchases/ Number of Customers

Customer Value = AOV x AFPR

Customer Lifetime Value = Customer Value x Average Customer Lifespan

21.5 Profitability Metrics

Profitability metrics incorporate data about both sellers and buyers to give an overall picture of whether the marketplace is making a profit.

Concentration Analysis is used to highlight relationships between users and sellers. For example, the bulk of sales may be concentrated with certain top sellers or customers within a certain geographical region may be purchasing a concentrated group of products. Concentration analysis reveals areas of significant growth, business aspects that may need greater effort, and where time and money are being wisely or poorly invested.

Seller Acquisition Cost is calculated similarly to CAC, but its application is quite different. A basic example makes this easier to understand. If the marketplace operator spends $5,000 on seller acquisition efforts and gains 5 new sellers, the operator has spent $1000 per seller. If each seller completes 1,000 transactions, the operator shows a seller acquisition cost of $1 per transaction.

That SAC is then applied to the margin. If each transaction pays the operator a $10 gross commission less the $1 SAC, then the operator's net margin is $9 per transaction.

Seller Lifetime Value estimates how much revenue a particular seller will generate over its lifetime. You can calculate this metric using the average order value, transaction frequency, and the average lifetime per seller.

Monthly Recurring Revenue is a predictable revenue that a marketplace can count on receiving each month. Often applicable to a subscription business, the simple calculation multiplies average revenue per customer by the total number of customers using the subscription service.

21.6 User Behavior Metrics

Applicable to marketplaces, eCommerce, and websites alike, behavior metrics help the website owner understand what visitors do while on the site and whether their experience was positive or negative.

Monthly Active Users (MAU) tracks the number of unique users to visit a site and should depict growth.

Bounce Rate shows the percentage of users who visit the site and leave right away. The operator's goal should be to keep this rate very low. This metric can be tracked per web page to discern where the customer journey breaks down or leads to purchase. As a benchmark, Amazon and eBay have bounce rates of around 20% to 25%.

Problem	Possible Cause/ Action
Low number of visitors	Increase acquisition budget
High bounce rate	Redefine target audience
	Improve landing page design
	Refine core value proposition
Listings are visited but no transactions	Customer liquidity issue, get more relevant providers or more relevant customers
Right products but lack of buyers	Problem with product discovery. Adjust UI, category page layout etc.
Many listings visited but few purchases	Increase quality of products
	Increase special offers
Cart abandonment	Examine purchase process

TABLE 21.1 Common insights from user behavior metrics

Time spent on site, as it sounds, refers to how much time users are spending on the site, but it is also important to consider how exactly are they engaging with it. Track categories, products, and purchase patterns to determine if users are spending a long time searching for products they cannot find, enjoying browsing the site, or bouncing immediately in frustration.

Conversion Rate is a critical KPI that deserves significant scrutiny as it tracks how many visitors complete a transaction. In combination with bounce rates, click-through rates, and time spent on site, the conversion rate shows the operator where the bottlenecks are, whether that is content that does not engage, a cumbersome checkout process, or a shipping policy that is not clear. This KPI should be continuously studied for constant optimization.

Key Takeaways: Key Performance Indicators

- When looking at marketplace KPI's, it is important to understand the fundamental concepts of the virtuous cycle

- , liquidity, and building trust.

- Liquidity KPIs relate to whether the platform makes transactions easy. Provider liquidity is the percentage of listings that lead to transactions within a certain time period, whereas customer liquidity means the probability of a visit leading to a transaction on the marketplace website.

- Some of the key metrics that fall under trust metrics are Net Promoter Score and Customer Retention Rate.

- GMV is the total sales value of the products or services sold through a marketplace over a specific time period. This metric should be examined in concert with other metrics like Net Revenue, and Customer Acquisition Cost.

- Profitability KPIs for sellers include Concentration Analysis, Seller Acquisition Cost, and Seller Lifetime Value.

Chapter 22: User Experience

Remember - every 'Mistake' a user makes is not because they're stupid, but because your website sucks.

Peep Laja, Founder, Conversion XL

Introduction

Marketplace design encompasses far more than simply building an eCommerce store. Today's savvy online shoppers expect a beautiful appearance, easy operation, and efficient function. But insufficient technical expertise, lack of an effective strategy, and absence of proper product-market fit can spell disaster for an early-stage marketplace. Quality user experience (UX) design is a critical piece that enables a marketplace to deeply connect with consumers and give them a clear path to purchase. Here are some numbers that show why it is a critical piece to the success of the business.

- Visitors form an opinion about a site's visual appeal in about 50 milliseconds.

- Good user experience can increase conversion rates by up to 400%.

- Over 75% of users abandon their shopping carts.

- Up to 88% of online consumers do not return to a site after a bad experience.

22.1 UX Approach to a Marketplace v. 1P eCommerce

UX design for marketplaces and eCommerce websites shares several of the same principles, such as creating a seamless path to purchase, facilitating impulse purchases, and reducing cart abandonment. However, the differences between 1P eCommerce and a multi-party platform mean marketplace UX must have a broader focus to ensure a quality experience for users on both sides of the transaction.

Two types of users – A marketplace must design a good experience for both sellers and buyers. Merchants want easy technical integration, attractive showcasing of their products, and informative tracking of their sales, while customers want to quickly find and purchase the products they need. These two audiences use the marketplace very differently, but the UX design must bring their experiences together in a way that drives conversion.

Trust – Thanks to poor customer service, fraudulent claims, and fake reviews, many consumers have begun to lose trust in online retailers. Unfortunately, this lays the burden on the UX team to establish trust from the beginning of the customer's journey and strengthen it at each stage on the path to purchase.

Testing and updating – With so many moving parts to a multi-vendor marketplace, a handful of completed purchases does not represent success. Rather, it begs the question of how many other purchases were not completed. Gathering feedback from customers about their purchase experience will inform the UX team to make needed changes, A/B test the updates, and ultimately drive growth.

22.2 Design Focus Areas

While user experience design is an iterative process that calls for continuous improvement, some key focus areas should be examined. The user experience design should help enhance the below-mentioned areas.

These focus areas are fundamental and remain more or less the same, whether you are designing a product, a portal, an eCommerce store, or a marketplace.

Visual Identity – Quality UX should create a digital experience that closely compares to an in-person shopping experience. High-quality pictures and video, informative descriptions to answer questions, and the overall look and feel of the pages will build trust and ease the path to purchase.

Easy Navigation – The goal is to provide simple maneuverability, fast and accurate searches, and a purchase path with the fewest clicks possible. These steps will increase sales among new customers while generating a positive experience that encourages them to return.

Relationship Building – Because positive customer reviews build trust and encourage new visitors to purchase, make it easy for purchasers to leave a review. Then use those reviews to build new relationships and bring in new consumers.

Security – With hackers growing in number and sophistication every day, data security must be a top priority in order to protect both sellers and buyers. Demonstrating tight security will give both types of users confidence to continue transacting on the marketplace.

22.3 Creating a Smooth Customer Journey

With so much digital content and so many online purchase options, how can consumers move from marketplace strangers to repeat shoppers? The UI/UX team needs to focus on the goals of both the operator and the customer during the four main stages of the customer journey: awareness, product discovery, purchase, and loyalty and advocacy. By considering the perspective and intent of both parties, each of these segments can be enhanced for better engagement and conversion.

The table on the following page provides some examples of a customer's intent, the possible actions they may take, and potential UX improvements to help meet both the customer's and the operator's ultimate goals.

	Awareness	Discovery	Purchase	Advocacy
Customer Activity	Learn how your platform works Research your products Compares prices	Review Prices Browse Products Compare Products Read Reviews	Add product Create an order Make Payments	Add Review Share Experience
Customer Goal	Find the optimal solution	Find out and select best, easy and fast way to transact	Create a quick order and get all the detailed info	Provide feedback and receive feedback
Brand Goal	Build trust and project platform in best light	Make the customers tay on platform. Show value	Provide safe and secure transaction environment	Act of feedback Improve service
Channels	About Us FAQ Terms & Cond	Product Page Booking Page Filter & Search	Shopping Cart Payment Page	Customer Survey Reviews Page Customer Support
UX Improvement Ideas	Desc Homepage Intuitive Nav Prominent CTA's	Adv Search Filters Product Comparisons Detailed Product Info	Easy Payment UI Reliable Payment Provider One Click Payment	

TABLE 22.1 Example Customer Journey

22.4 Best Practices for Marketplace UX Design

Designing a marketplace requires plenty of knowledge on what a user expects from the platform. It is a place that connects the consumers with businesses so there are two key aspects to UX design—helping sellers showcase their products and services and walking customers easily through the process of finding what they are looking for.

Multiple offer display – When multiple sellers are offering the same product, display all the sellers on the product page along with seller profile information like seller name, rating, total sales, and pricing or promotions. This allows the customer to comparison shop, which in turn creates competition among sellers, boosts customer service, and lowers prices.

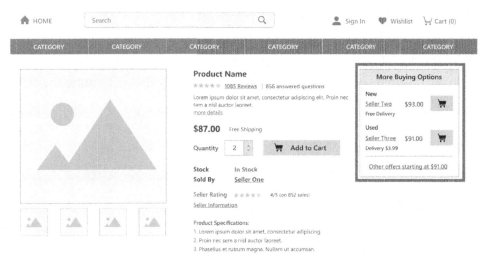

FIGURE 22.1 Multiple Offer Display

Variant Presentation – A product may have several variants (size, color, etc.) that affect the price. Displaying the lowest and highest prices offered gives the customer a general understanding of the price of the product at the beginning of their journey.

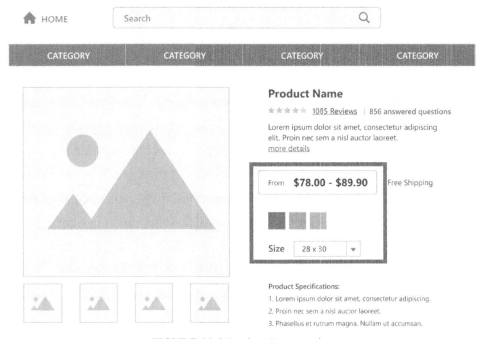

FIGURE 22.2 Variant Presentation

Based on this understanding, the customer can choose to move ahead with selecting variants. As the customer selects and narrows the variations, the price range can adjust until there is only one price applied to the customer's final selection. Variant selection would also determine the seller's list and other offers.

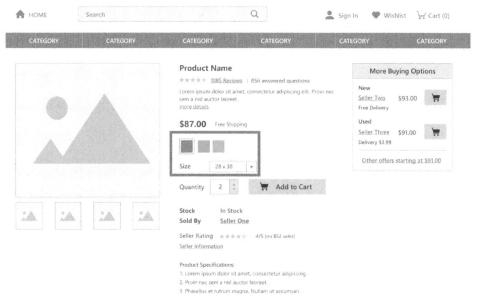

FIGURE 22.3 Product Page After Variant Selection

Buy box win criteria – The buy box contains the Add to Cart button and is linked to only one seller, typically the seller who lists the product at the lowest price. Other factors affecting the buy box include fulfillment method, stock availability, customer service, and the seller's performance. While other sellers can be found in the multiple offer display, customers are more likely to use the buy box for a smooth shopping experience, so winning the buy box is a great advantage for sellers. Figure 22.4 below also highlights the product details (price, delivery date, ratings, and description) and the multiple offer display (other sellers offering the same product).

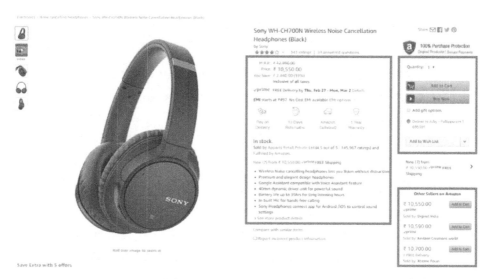

FIGURE 22.4 Amazon Buy Box

Search – A robust search feature is critical for a marketplace. Customers who cannot find the products they want may become frustrated and abandon the platform. But an effective and intuitive search algorithm easily leads customers to the right products.

- Refined in-site search and ranking algorithms – The search engine should be intuitive enough to return good results with use of natural language.

- Standardized presentation – The search box should ideally be located near the top of the page in a clear format. A simple empty box with a Search button or magnifying glass icon is common and easily understood.

- Faceted search – Instead of complicated advanced search methods, allow users to narrow their results by filtering the attributes of the product. A common way of displaying facets is down the left side of the page next to the search results.

- Search suggestions – An intuitive dropdown that lists suggests as the customer types will both save them time and help them avoid typos that may affect search results.

- Sorting options – Hick's law states that the more choices a person has, the longer it will take them to make a decision. To create a smooth path to purchase, allow customers to sort search results in ways that will help them compare products, such as price, alphabetical order, or rating.

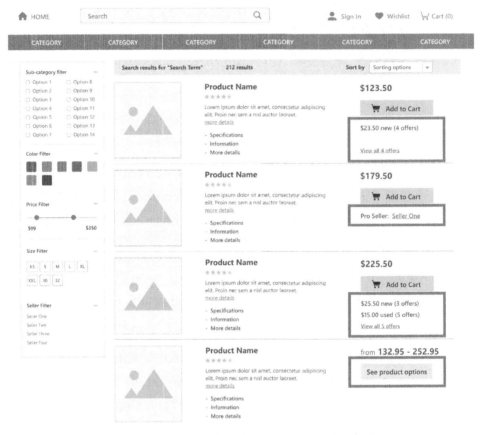

FIGURE 22.5 More options for customers to choose from

When search results are displayed, provide enough information for customers to understand the differences and want to continue to purchase.

- Product Name

- Partial description followed by a More link to the full product page

- Price (or price range for product variations)

- Number of results

- Sorting options

- Pagination (or lazy loading)

- Add to Cart button

- Option to switch between List view and Grid view

Additional information that could be displayed in the search results may include the following:

- Links to offers

- Showing Buy Box seller name

- Detailing offer conditions

22.5 SEO for Marketplaces

While users may feel their experience with a marketplace begins when they land on the home page, the reality is that the customer journey begins with their initial online search for a product. Because most consumers rely on internet search engines such as Google, the first goal for the UX team should be to ensure that the marketplace shows up when consumers search. A quality-built, user-friendly marketplace with bad SEO cannot be found.

Marketplace SEO should focus on the three key focus areas—on-page, off-page, and content marketing—while balancing the buyer intent and seller.

On-Page SEO

Technical or on-page SEO addresses how search engines read content, down to each URL, so that the most relevant results are returned when users search. An SEO audit of the marketplace will identify areas to begin work.

Following is a list of common tactics for optimizing a web page for search engines.

- In all page titles, meta descriptions, and page content, include keywords by which customers might search for products. This will help the search engines ready and understand the marketplace content.

- Format all the headings and content following Google guidelines on H1, H2, and H3 tags.

- Use original images and optimize the size along with appropriate alt tags.

- Optimize the URLs for search engine friendliness.

- Ensure strong internal links throughout the platform to help the search engine crawl and understand clusters of information.

- Improving page load time can reduce bounce rates and garner higher search rankings. Research shows that a one-second delay in page load time yields 11% fewer pageviews, a 16% decrease in customer satisfaction, and a 7% loss in conversions.

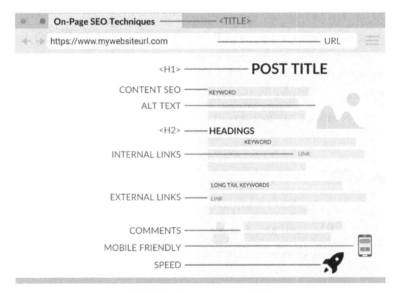

FIGURE 22.6 On Page SEO

Here are some ways to ways to improve page load time.

- Minimize HTTP requests
- Minify and combine files
- Use asynchronous loading for **CSS** and **JavaScript** files
- Defer JavaScript loading
- Reduce server response time
- Choose the right hosting option
- Enable compression
- Enable browser caching
- Reduce image sizes
- Use a CDN (Content Delivery Network)
- Optimize CSS delivery
- Prioritize above-the-fold content (lazy loading)

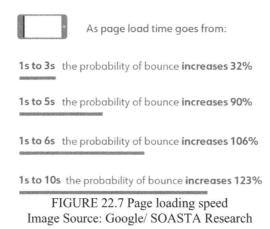

As page load time goes from:

1s to 3s the probability of bounce **increases 32%**

1s to 5s the probability of bounce **increases 90%**

1s to 6s the probability of bounce **increases 106%**

1s to 10s the probability of bounce **increases 123%**

FIGURE 22.7 Page loading speed
Image Source: Google/ SOASTA Research

Off-Page SEO

While on-page SEO refers to the content actually on the marketplace pages, off-page SEO is about linking to other high-quality websites, as their credibility adds to the credibility of the marketplace. More backlinks (both quality and quantity) give the search engine more opportunity to establish a ranking based on trust. One easy way to build off-page SEO is to leverage network partners by linking to their websites.

FIGURE 22.8 Off-Page SEO

Content Marketing

When strategically placed, quality content—photos, videos, white papers, case studies, etc.—can provide value to relevant audiences and establish the publisher as a thought leader in the industry. In the case of a marketplace, content like product explainer videos and blog posts about ways to shop online and save will attract and engage customers. When the content is distributed in places where the audience is already present, such as social media, the content becomes easily sharable for long-lasting and far-reaching effect.

Top 5 SEO Tactics for Marketplace

1. **Identify a Niche** – Using top-level keywords for the marketplace industry may seem obvious, but a smarter strategy uses more specific **long-tail keywords** that have lesser competition and higher conversion chances.

2. **Consolidate** – Focus on driving all traffic to a single domain and building that single online brand. Over time this strategy will build authority and credibility.

3. **Be Consistent** – Publish smaller pieces of content more frequently to show the search engine healthy activity.

4. **Leverage user-generated content (UGC)** – Rather than spending precious time and money creating extensive original content, provide opportunities for sellers and buyers to create content in the form of reviews, testimonials, DIY videos, etc.

5. **Invest in keyword research** – Investigate the keywords users search on Google in relation to your products and services as well as the competition. Then use those keywords in content and on the marketplace.

22.6 Customer Support & Returns

In a world where a single share, rant, or complaint posted to social media can go viral, the importance of quality customer service cannot be overstated. One review has the potential to launch a business into the stratosphere or damage a reputation beyond repair. If a good offense is the best defense, excellent customer support is the best reputation management system.

Best Practices for Customer Support

Develop a multi-channel strategy – Every customer communicates differently so the customer service department should communicate in many ways as well. Create opportunities for customers to contact and work with customer service representatives via web, email, social, and mobile. Easier communication generates faster response times and improves the customer experience.

Proactive Customer Service – According to one report, 50% of customers want to solve product or service issues themselves and 70% expect a company's website to include a self-service application. An FAQ section gives customers access to instant solutions without needing to contact customer support.

Personalized email campaigns – A study has shown that 94% of businesses agree that personalization is critical to their success. Because most people receive dozens of emails each day from someone they do not know, impersonal emails are easy to ignore, while a personalized message which includes the customer's name is shown to boosts email open rates.

Optimize and automate online order fulfillment – Manual order fulfillment systems are slow, inefficient, and prone to human error. Using an automated system to manage the process saves time, improves productivity, and increases customer satisfaction.

Connect and engage with mobile customers – Millennial and Gen Z customers prefer to shop on a mobile device. As these generations mature into money controlling buyers, optimizing search and checkout functions for mobile use will become increasingly important.

Measure customer satisfaction – Short surveys or asking customers for a brief review is an easy way to collect testimonials and measure the effectiveness of the customer service department at the same time.

Returns

The existence or lack of a fair and comprehensive return policy can be the determining factor for customers choosing where to shop online. 95% of customers will purchase again from an eCommerce retailer if they have had a positive return or exchange experience. The fact is that customers are inclined to be more forgiving of a damaged package or mis-shipped product if the marketplace is quick to take corrective action.

Best Practices for Returns and Refunds

Make the returns policy easy to find – Include multiple prominent links that make the marketplace return policy easy to find, understand, and engage.

Include clear deadlines – A clear returns policy states a specific time period during which customers can return an item so that customers know what to expect of the process.

Provide pre-printed return labels – Including a pre-printed return label in the shipping box saves the customer the effort of searching for the address or printing out the label themselves. A simpler, faster return process eliminates hassle for the customer and improves their customer service experience.

Pay for return shipping – Web Retailer reports that 88% of consumers surveyed would rate free return shipping as "important" or "very important" to their purchase decisions. So, while paying for return shipping lands in the cost column, lost sales and customers is a greater cost.

Illustrate the process – A page of dense, fine print is unlikely to be read, much less understood. Graphics, icons, and images will make the policy and instructions faster and easier to grasp.

Re-engage customers – A return does not have to be the end of the relationship. Continue to reach out to the customer, invite them back to the marketplace, and perhaps give them the incentive to purchase again.

Continuously review and update the return policy – Online retail changes continuously, and the return policy should as well. Track and analyze returns data to evaluate the relevance of returns policies and ensure they continue to serve sellers, customers, and the operator.

22.7 Seller UX

Seller UX consists of two stages, first is the discovery/ onboarding stage and the second is the interaction with the platform on an ongoing basis. Let's look at each of these in a little more detail.

Discovery/ Onboarding

While marketplace UX predominantly covers the end user's experience with the platform what is equally important is to have a smooth and frictionless experience for Sellers wanting to join the marketplace. Seller UX covers the areas the marketplace offers the sellers to onboard and register their businesses. A positive UX has a direct impact on conversion, but it also sets the stage for a long-lasting relationship between the sellers and the marketplace. For example, when you Google search "Sell on Amazon" it would take you to a page like this below. If one wants to become a seller Amazon answers most of the questions progressively and breaks the entire journey into logical steps.

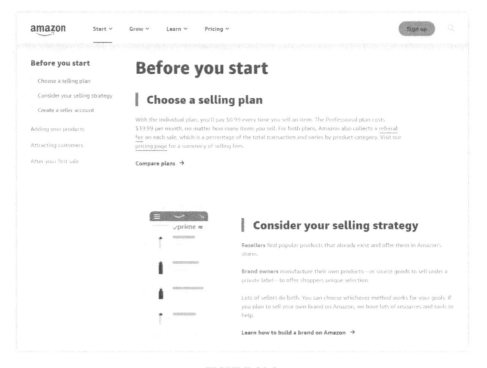

FIGURE 22.9

Here are some best UX practices a marketplace operator can follow to create the best possible experience for sellers interested in getting on-board.

- Create automated onboarding tours that help sellers achieve immediate results.

- Create segments based on the sellers' end goal and create an approach tailored to that.

- Support sellers directly through the application with step-by-step guides and ensure they don't abandon the registration process.

- Automatically launch interactive guides when the seller is about to embark on a complicated process.

- Don't do information overload, it is best to keep the information necessary and concise at the beginning and reveal more and more as the seller progresses.

- Make the entire process more conversational and less instructional.

- Show users how long they have left, use progress indicators and navigation icons.

- Get to the point quickly and help the seller attain the value they are seeking.

Post Onboarding

Once a seller is onboarded the objective of the platform user experience should then be to help them effectively manage their operations and grow their sales. The design of the seller interface should be seamless and intuitive and have various sections that offer multiple viewpoints for the sellers to view their business.

Store - From a store perspective, the seller should be able to view store status. This can be open, closed, or suspended Usually a store goes into suspended mode because of failure to comply with quality control criteria predefined by the operator. The store also needs the option to view account balance. This can either be Pending (amount for all of the store's orders debited by the operator but not yet received by the customers), Payable (shop's orders received by customers but not yet paid to the store), or Paid (this is the amount for all of the orders paid to a store by the operator).

Customers - When it comes to customers, the sellers should have a view to look at total orders, total expenses, total incidents (total number of tickets opened by the customer), and incident rate (number of order line items that had an incident out of the number of line items that were approved). There should also be a way to view all the customer information in a single place.

Orders – Ability to manage orders should feature payment workflows, application of taxes, shipping, currencies, refund, cancellations, and specific order use cases. When it comes to payments there are three options. *Pay on acceptance* where payment is debited once the order is accepted, *Pay on Delivery* where payment is debited at delivery time, and *Pay on Due Date* (used more in the B2B world) where payment is debited after the receipt of the order by the customer.

Product & Offers – The marketplace platform should offer the seller a place to manage their products and offers. The product should have at least one mandatory characteristic which is the product name. While an offer is always linked to a product, a product can have several offers associated with it. The sellers should be able to create products that feature title, description, category, brand, image, and associated logistics as well as propose offers for a product referenced in the operator catalog. The platform should facilitate creation of product variants, these are variations of a product such as the color or the size of a dress. The offers interface should provide a view to offer conditions, selling price, discounts on offers, offer visibility.

Catalog – Being able to manage the product catalog effectively is the key to success in the marketplace. The UX design should facilitate creation of product categories and attributes (an attribute defines a product. There can be several attributes per product.) A seller should be able to view both marketplace categories and catalog categories.

Messaging – The UX design should facilitate communication between Marketplace operators, sellers, and customers. Communication should pertain to only orders and offers. Sellers and operators should not be given access to start new conversations on offers. They should be only able to reply to customer queries.

Key Takeaways: User Experience

- One of the core functions of UX for a marketplace is to foster a positive, valuable, and profitable relationship between the consumers and the merchants.

- The four key design focus areas for UX in a marketplace are visual identity, ease of navigation, building relationships, and providing security assurance.

- The four stages of a customer journey on a marketplace are awareness, discovery, purchase, and loyalty. UX should focus on the customer goals at each stage to help them easily navigate to the next step.

- Three key elements of SEO for a marketplace are on-page, off-page, and content marketing while balancing the buyer intent and seller intent.

- Marketplace design should provide customers easy access to customer service and returns.

Chapter 23: Marketing an Online Marketplace

Even when you are marketing to your entire audience or customer base, you are still simply speaking to a single human at any given time.

Ann Handley

Introduction

Launching and promoting an online marketplace involves many of the same considerations as a traditional eCommerce property with an additional audience to consider—the sellers. As with any successful marketing effort, it comes down to the target audiences requiring engagement. With traditional eCommerce, the primary audience is the end-customer making the purchase. Marketplaces also need to speak to the third-party sellers to keep them informed, inspired, and engaged.

The heart of effective marketing is clear and timely communication. Getting the right message to the right person at the right time is an extremely effective way to positively influence behavior and keep people interested. This applies to consumers as much as it does to sellers. Creating a comprehensive communications plan that includes audience identification, some level of persona development, and key journey mapping helps to deliver a consistent message across all major audiences. These steps are all too often skipped in the name of expediency, even though they provide a mechanism to ensure that the message being conveyed is the message the audience needs to hear.

Since a message is only effective if delivered and understood, it is important to communicate with the audiences where they already seek information. This will vary depending on audience, location, industry, etc. The communication channels for site launch or ongoing promotion are likely to include outbound email, social media, public relations, print advertising, in-store advertising, SMS, physical events, outdoor, and paid search. An omnichannel communication strategy informed by the audience, persona, and journey building exercises will save the marketing team time by leveraging the same messaging and branding across audiences while presenting a consistent brand experience.

There is no singular right or wrong way to market and promote a marketplace property, but there are best practices to engage consumers to drive sales and engage sellers to drive adoption.

23.1 Know the Audience

Audience identification exercises are frequently overlooked but are key to marketing success. Identifying target audiences, developing key personas within those audiences, then developing maps for the most important journeys are exceptionally reliable ways to create a meaningful marketing communications plan, whether a retail merchant, conducting business-to-business transactions, or both.

Audience identification is the broadest category of the communications plan. Many online marketplaces have the two primary audiences of consumers and sellers, although it is possible to have more depending on the focus and maturity of the marketplace. To set the stage for the rest of the planning, identify broad characteristics in terms of what each audience wants, what goals the marketplace has for each audience, what the key milestones or gates are to drive each audience toward.

Persona development is the next step. Break down the groups within each audience in ways that content and messaging can be meaningfully personalized. For **buyer personas**, look at categories like personal background, goals, challenges, and even shopping preferences to get to know each consumer audience segment better. For a seller persona, consider the personal background factors and considerations, but also look at roles within the organization, professional challenges, and goals for selling on a marketplace.

There should be at least two persona groups within each audience to start, although having more is common as maturity progresses. The point of the exercise is to assign a designation to each persona with the goal of dialing in content and messaging to increasingly narrow groups as more personas are added. Journey mapping is the next step in the process. For each persona within each audience, map out a few key journeys they might make on the platform.

BUYER PERSONA PROFILE

PERSONA NAME	PERSONAL BACKGROUND	COMPANY BACKGROUND
	- Age - Education - Marital Status	- Industry - Revenue - Size
	ROLE INFORMATION	GOALS & CHALLENGES
	- How job is measured - Job skills - Reports to - Responsibilites	- Success means... - Values most... - Biggest challenges... - Biggest objections...
	SHOPPING AND CONTENT PREFERENCES	
	- Prefers to communicate by... - Conducts buying research by... - Frequently checks these sites and news sources... - Social media network preferences...	

FIGURE 23.1 Buyer Persona Profile

Examples of such journeys are the "account creation process" for a consumer and the "onboarding process" for marketplace sellers. Each journey maps the stages the audience traverses, the actions they take, the goals they have along the way, what they may be feeling and experiencing at that time, what messages or content can be provided at that time, and what results they expect at each step. Charting what someone needs while being driven toward a desired outcome helps focus messaging on what is most important and becomes the primary driver of the content and messaging.

23.2 Content and Messaging

After identifying the audience, their major journeys, and what will help them along the way, it is time to create the campaign messaging and content. This is where the branded content touts the features, functions, and benefits of the new marketplace—the things that make it a great property—and meets the audience's perspective and specific journey needs. The planning is often best broken up into multiple levels, with each level becoming increasingly individualized.

Journey maps, such as the (highly simplified) Customer Journey Map in Figure 23.2, are useful when planning which content needs to be delivered at what time. This example looks at a customer's motivations, goals, interactions, and opportunities for engagement along the Y-axis while making a purchasing decision (stages along the X-axis).

CUSTOMER JOURNEY MAP

	AWARENESS	CONSIDERATION	DECISION	LOYALTY
MOTIVATION	RESEARCH	COMPARE	TRY	SUSTAIN
GOAL	CLICK POSTS	GIVE PII	FREE TRIAL	CONTINUE TO PAY
INTERACTION	SOCIAL MEDIA	SITES AND ADS	LIMITED OFFERS	24 HOUR SUPPORT
OPPORTUNITIES	ADVERTISEMENTS	SHOW ADVANTAGES	PROMOTIONS	LOYALTY PROGRAM

FIGURE 23.2 Customer Journey Map

Top-level messaging

This is the highest-level detail that needs to be communicated about the marketplace—the overall purpose, mission, and universal value propositions. This messaging is largely the same across all audiences, but with a slightly different lens for buyers or sellers. Both audiences need to know the general benefits and focus of the marketplace, as consumer interest will drive demand for the seller's products.

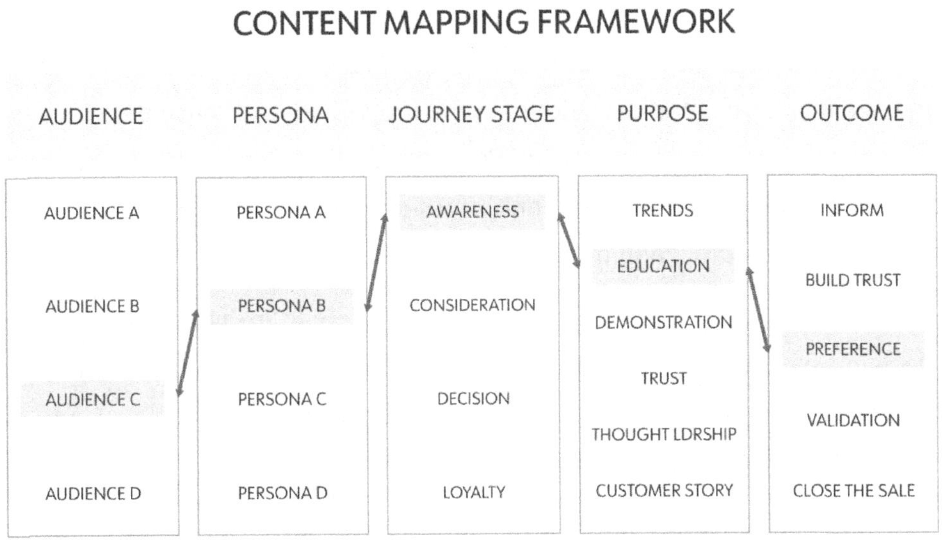

CONTENT MAPPING FRAMEWORK

AUDIENCE	PERSONA	JOURNEY STAGE	PURPOSE	OUTCOME
AUDIENCE A	PERSONA A	AWARENESS	TRENDS	INFORM
AUDIENCE B	PERSONA B	CONSIDERATION	EDUCATION	BUILD TRUST
			DEMONSTRATION	
				PREFERENCE
AUDIENCE C	PERSONA C	DECISION	TRUST	VALIDATION
			THOUGHT LDRSHIP	
AUDIENCE D	PERSONA D	LOYALTY	CUSTOMER STORY	CLOSE THE SALE

FIGURE 23.3 Content Mapping Framework

Audience-level messaging

The audience level is where personalization becomes a factor. Each audience has its own motivations, needs, goals, and channel preferences. A site launch announcement targeting customers, sellers, and internal constituents may contain similar content, but the timing of the message, the secondary points, and the call-to-action will be completely different.

For instance, when launching a new marketplace, the customers need to know what this new marketplace will offer them and when, while the sellers need to know why this marketplace is a profitable channel to offer their items and how to get started.

Persona-level messaging

The persona-level is where personalization of the message starts to enter the communication stream. After all, messages are communicated to individuals, not groups. Personas are designed to help focus marketers on delivering specific enough messaging that it speaks to the reader on a deeper level. This can be as simple as including camping imagery featuring young women when communicating with a young female outdoor enthusiast or including industry-specific and role-specific terminology in a B2B communication. Sophisticated personalization uses artificial intelligence and machine learning to analyze and predict based on the persona group, and even down to the individual level once enough data is available. This is where tracked digital body language correlates to more accurate product recommendations, cross-sell, up-sell, bundled items, lifestyle information, and more.

Consumer personas should focus on factors likely to influence a buying decision such as age, economic status, geography, and interests, while seller personas should focus on industry, title, decision-maker level, and categories offered.

Journey-level messaging

These communications tend to happen when customers take key actions, hit certain milestones, or otherwise trigger the need for a message. Examples include signing up for a new account, placing an order, placing a first re-order, inquiring about a product or service, going dormant for a period, etc. The key to effective messaging in these cases is to map which persona is in which portion of the journey. These transactional messages tend to be brief and focused with a clear call-to-action, but the more personalized the message, the more valuable it will be to both the recipient and the organization.

A consumer-based account sign-up journey will have specific messaging that encourages the buyer to set up an account, instructs them how to sign up, welcomes them when they do sign-up, and follows up appropriately depending on whether they have placed an order or not. A seller-based onboarding journey takes place once they have agreed to become a seller on the marketplace. That messaging should welcome them to the marketplace and set next steps, then also include clear communication for each step, in terms of setting up a storefront, importing the catalog data, setting their first promotion, etc.

23.3 Messaging Cadence

Trigger-based

This type of messaging is based on key events within a mapped customer journey that trigger a communication to be sent. As an example, if a customer places a new order, that will trigger a receipt of the purchase followed a few days later by a request to review the item. If a new seller is onboarded and added to the marketplace site, this would trigger a message welcoming them to the program and providing key details about the program and helpful reference links.

Nurture

Nurture messaging, also referred to as drip messaging, works by creating messaging tracks designed to educate the audience by conveying a series of messages over time. Audience members can be manually entered into an informational nurture track by the site operator or could be entered into such a track via a trigger, such a requesting more information about a site launch or a product, usually via form submittal. A customer nurture track may involve a series of four messages triggered by a product information request, with the four messages covering primary product information, secondary benefits, a review or case study, and finally an opportunity to purchase.

Ad Hoc

This type of messaging is usually promotional or informational in nature, rather than transactional. These messages are not triggered by a specific event, nor are they part of a nurture stream; they are sent to the audience as needed to promote products or services, announce new features, or convey any information that the site operator wants to communicate to the customers, sellers, or internal audiences.

23.4 Messaging Channels

Following are some of the best marketing and communication channels to leverage to ensure a new marketplace is successfully launched and continually promoted via an omnichannel strategy.

Public Relations (PR) and Media Activities

Traditional PR and media activities such as press releases, media placements in publications, interviews, and appearances may be old-school, but they are also highly effective at spreading a message. Aside from the physical distribution channels, the digital aspect of the placements has clear SEO benefits, in addition to the buzz-building effects. A traditional PR effort will vary depending on the size of the organization and the intended audience. As such, publications targeted will range from national level to industry trade level. Media interviews and televised appearances may also be appropriate targets for higher profile, bigger budget launches.

Use PR and media early and often to set the tone for other channels. The messaging should be clear and concise while presenting the value of the offering to the intended audience.

This is a tactic that extends from the pre-launch hype stage, through to the innovation and iteration stages of site development. This messaging brings customers and sellers awareness of the marketplace and shows internal constituents that the Marketplace is being promoted publicly.

Organic Social Activities

Social media is firmly in the "must-have" category when it comes to any modern business, but it plays an increasingly significant role in the launch of new web properties. While the audience will dictate exactly which social networks to focus efforts on, the goal is to build excitement for the new property, promote and reinforce the PR and media activities, and to engage the audience with interactive content such as polls or contests.

Concentrate efforts on consumer-focused sites like Facebook, Instagram, and Twitter, adding the likes of Pinterest and Snapchat, depending on the target audience. Business-focused sites will usually concentrate on LinkedIn, Twitter, and Facebook.

The other aspect of organic social that organizations need to prepare for is the inevitability of social media as a customer service channel. This is especially true for consumer-focused eCommerce operators. Social media has become one of the most important customer service functions. Whatever social properties are utilized, it is wise to have both processes and personnel in place and empowered with the technology and knowledge to quickly respond to customer inquiries and issues.

This tactic applies to the pre-launch hype phase and should be an ongoing engagement effort through launch and post-launch. Like with PR and media, organic social should target both customers and sellers, knowing that internal audiences will also see the outward branding.

Search Marketing and Paid Social

Paid search marketing, especially via Google AdWords, is quite possibly the most important method of driving traffic to a new eCommerce property, with paid social ads and sponsored content growing in importance. Planning an effective AdWords and paid social marketing effort means understanding the target audience and setting an aggressive budget from launch-time forward.

Starting a new AdWords effort for a new property lacks the benefit of historical data, so use information about the target audience from the persona exercise. That information, combined with keyword research using Google's Keyword Planner, can provide a great starting point. Google offers a new feature called Dynamic AdWords that will automatically match the content on a site with a customer's actual search terms. This is an effective way early on to see exactly how real customer search terms match with the content. Be sure to stay on top of adjusting things like negative keywords (keywords that match content but are not worth spending money on) and creating tightly focused campaigns based on the keywords that are driving traffic and converting into sales.

Paid social is still much newer than Google's AdWords and the various networks have been undergoing rapid iterations and improvements to their targeting capabilities. The most important consideration when advertising or sponsoring content on social networks, is the purpose of each network. Ask why the various personas are using that social network, and then tailor the message and imagery accordingly. A potential customer is likely to be in work mode when browsing LinkedIn, meaning more business-focused information and content will be relevant, whereas that same person may be more likely to interact with a poll or a contest on Facebook.

Retargeting is the other key aspect of advertising on social media properties. It is possible to start with broader, category-based retargeting ads for those who have visited a category or product page and work up to retargeting individual products if a detailed effort is not feasible off the jump. In addition to the product or category-based retargeting efforts, an abandoned cart campaign is also likely to perform well early on.

These tactics apply much closer to the actual launch of the site and should be a primary source of lead investment from launch through ongoing operations and iterations.

Print Advertising

The popularity, metrics, and effective targeting of digital engagement methods have led many marketing strategists to shy away from print advertising, but it can still serve as a valuable channel for brand building and lead generation. Print advertising can be utilized in many ways—national, regional, and industry-specific publications, along with circulars and direct mail.

The key for success in print advertising, as with the other channels, is to select the publications relevant to the audience and craft visually impactful ads with a succinct message and a clear **call to action**. If the organization utilizes circulars, they represent an ideal opportunity to promote the new eCommerce property, especially in conjunction with a one-time offer code that incents customers to create an online account or place their first order. Print-specific offer codes and unique URLs help to track ROI from print advertising.

Print advertising can be used to build-hype, promote the launch, and continually reinforce the brand value of the site by touting new products, categories, and innovations.

In-Store Promotions

Brick and Mortar retailers stepping into the eCommerce arena with a new property have the distinct advantage of leveraging their foot traffic to drive awareness of the new site. These tactics can range from banners, graphics, printing on receipts, ads on shopping carts, endcap displays, and apparel or pins for the staff.

The key to successful in-store advertising is to develop messaging that clearly expresses how the digital experience adds benefit to the in-store experience. This could mean online-only items, in-store stock information, ordering for delivery, exclusive online promos/coupons/sales, rewards programs, etc. Clearly communicate the benefits and give the audience a call-to-action. Just as with print advertising, unique codes or URLs can help track the ROI of this effort.

In-store promotions can be used lightly to generate hype and should be primarily used for site launch promotion, then ongoing to announce online promotions, new features, sales, etc.

Email Marketing

The death of email marketing as a means of revenue generation has been exaggerated. Email remains a vital channel for those willing to put in the work to make it effective. That work includes knowing the audience and personas, plotting their journey, then creating relevant messages sent at the right time.

Email marketing can certainly be used to send sales-focused email messages, but an over-reliance on that tactic encourages a customer to click Unsubscribe. The most effective email marketers provide valuable information to their prospects and customers at the time when they need it most. This includes not only marketing emails, but transactional emails surrounding key events like a new account sign-up, a first order, a **cart abandonment** message, a shipping confirmation, etc. Similarly, email marketing can be an effective way to regularly communicate with sellers, especially using trigger or event-based messaging that keeps them up to date with site features and promotions.

If a marketing team understands their audience, what they care about, and the major journeys they will embark upon (discovering the site, placing the first order, creating an account, leaving their first review, re-purchasing, winning back an inactive customer, etc.), it is possible to design more meaningful communications that provide value while also making up-sell or cross-sell suggestions. Having a subscription center where visitors can select what types of communications to receive and how frequently to receive them helps cut down on the number of outright unsubscribes and informs the marketing team what certain individuals are interested in hearing about.

These email marketing tactics can be used sparingly in the hype stage of the launch but are most effective at site launch and in continually engaging those who use the site in both seller and consumer audiences.

On-Page Search Engine Optimization

Last, but certainly not least, is Search Engine Optimization (SEO). A marketplace has certain inherent advantages over traditional eCommerce sites in that the depth and breadth of categories and SKUs tend to be higher, therefore providing more opportunities for high-ranking terms. The primary marketplace-specific issues relate to potential duplicate content, which will harm rankings, so it is vitally important to ensure a clean catalog free from duplicates and with a clear consistent taxonomy.

With Google and Bing, et al, continually changing their indexing algorithms, SEO is part art and part science. However, it is known that the search engine operators are obsessed with relevance and very much against anyone trying to game the system. Initially, focus on the fundamentals of search optimization. Start simple, then iterate into more complexity.

Ensure page titles reflect the primary product/category/topic clearly; URL structure contains the product, category, or topic; meta descriptions contain the terms in the page title; those terms are repeated within a header tag; images have alt tags; and that those alt tags contain the same keywords or phrases used within the other meta fields. This consistent use of the same keywords and key phrases helps the search engines gauge the level of relevancy of the page content, leading to higher organic placements.

The other, equally important, part of SEO preparation is to think of everything in a mobile-first fashion. Google is leading the charge in ranking sites through the lens of a mobile user, meaning if the site is not truly mobile responsive and has the other SEO fundamentals handled, that site will not garner a favorable ranking in organic results.

Using Google's Webmasters Tools and Bing's Webmaster Tools help with the organic search planning and optimization activities.

These search optimization tactics occur during the site build stage of production but go into practice once the site is live to the public. After launch, they should become a foundational operational activity of generating traffic to the site.

Off-Page Search Engine Optimization

Inbound links from trusted sources are a major contributing factor to metrics like Domain Rank and Page Score, calculated measurements meant to impart trust in a particular domain or page against competitors. This does not mean that all inbound links are created equal, as links from sites with extremely low scores across these rankings can harm the site's rankings. For instance, traffic from "link farms," sites created specifically to harvest and create off-site links, were once an effective way to boost search engine trust but are now highly discouraged.

The best way to optimize off-page SEO considerations is to have a clearly defined off-site linking strategy with weekly monitoring in place to track link quantity while ensuring quality, disallowing anything that may be harmful. For established brands, having prominent links from any site with potentially relevant traffic is a straightforward way to get started. Another crucial step is to encourage all the sellers to link to the marketplace from their own web sites and social accounts. Additional link outreach can include any brand/CPG partners, social campaigns that encourage sharable, clickable content, and a public relations strategy that earns links in media publications and blogs.

23.5 Marketing Technology

A properly implemented and integrated marketing technology stack should provide marketplace operators with a true 360-degree view of both their end-customer and their third-party sellers. This means that any marketing technology implemented needs to have the ability to segment and quantify the different types of interactions had by customers and sellers. This technology stack should be fully integrated with automated data synchronizing processes to prevent data silos and potential errors being introduced by manual data operations. Following are the core components of an integrated marketing technology stack.

CRM Platform

A customer relationship management platform such as Salesforce, Microsoft Dynamics, or SugarCRM should be the hub for customer data and the integrated systems that use that data. Setting distinct record types to segment end-customers from marketplace sellers is an important delimiter in how both audience's records are utilized. Ensuring that seller-specific fields such as type of seller, category of goods offered, total sales, and any key rating metrics are present in the CRM system ensures readily available access to that data when segmenting the audience for relevant messaging.

Marketing Automation Platform

An enterprise-grade marketing automation platform handles much more than just email communications. Modern platforms such as Marketo, Salesforce Sales Cloud, Oracle Sales Cloud, and many more have the capability to send and track emails, SMS messages, social media messages, and even integrate with search engine advertising and retargeting capabilities. Like with the CRM platform, the marketing automation platform needs to be sophisticated enough to distinctly communicate with both end-customers and third-party sellers. Some platforms will provide the option to completely segment all assets, campaigns, and messages within their interface, which is especially useful if audience engagement is handled by disparate teams. Another key capability specific to marketplaces is the ability to run multiple engagement scoring schemes, often referred to as lead scoring.

Social Engagement Platform

Whether brand building, syndicating content, announcing new features, or promoting products, social media has become a vitally important communications channel. Customers look to social networks like Facebook, Twitter, and Instagram for product and site information, while sellers will look to platforms like LinkedIn or WhatsApp to stay connected. Having a dedicated social engagement platform to manage cross-network posting and having a centralized inbox is one of the secret weapons of effective marketplace marketers. Ensure that the platform chosen functions well with the networks that customers and sellers use and integrates well with the rest of the marketing technology stack.

Ad Tech Platform

Many marketplace operators can get by using the native social media and search engine paid advertising tools or leveraging such capabilities built-in to marketing automation or social engagement platforms. For those who wish to get more sophisticated, a dedicated ad technology platform may be the better option. These platforms allow more granular targeting, retargeting, and A/B testing capabilities than comes with native tools, plus they provide more management and analytics tools to help manage and measure paid efforts at-scale. Targeting customers with product and service promotions while targeting sellers with recruitment messages carries a level of sophistication that one of the dedicated ad tech platforms may help to manage. As with the other components of the marketing stack, ensure that the selected platform integrates tightly in order to provide the most value.

Remember that marketing an online marketplace does not have to be an all-at-once proposition. The most important thing is to create a realistic plan that addresses key consumer and seller audiences. The more cohesive, relevant, and timely these messages are, the more engaged the audiences will become. Keeping the customer messaging and promotions in-sync with a well-informed and actively engaged seller base ensures that traffic is being consistently generated via multiple channels. Start small, communicate often, and continue to measure and iterate these tactics. That way, the customers will buy more and the sellers will list more, creating a rising tide of profitability and satisfaction across the board.

Key Takeaways: Marketing an Online Marketplace

- There are two primary audiences for an online marketplace site—customers and sellers.

- Knowing the target audiences for consumers and sellers, including building out personas and journeys, is vital to effective marketing and communication.

- Creating meaningful content and messaging for each audience keeps people engaged.

- Deliver content and messaging on multiple relevant channels

- Create and manage an integrated marketing communication stack consisting of a CRM platform and digital engagement platforms to provide a 360-degree view of audience engagement.

Chapter 24: Conversion Rate Optimization

It's much easier to double your business by doubling your conversion rate than by doubling your traffic.

Jeff Eisenberg, American Businessman & Former Ice Hockey Executive

Introduction

While the earlier decades focused on bringing traffic to the online store, more recent years have aimed to convert that traffic into paying customers. The science of conversion rate optimization (CRO) has grown wide and deep as operators attempt to cover all touchpoints of customer interaction.

Google defines conversion rate as the ratio of transactions to sessions, expressed as a percentage. For example, a ratio of one transaction to every ten sessions would be expressed as an eCommerce Conversion Rate of 10%. Simply put, a conversion is someone who visits a site and completes a transaction, so the conversion rate is the percentage of visitors who purchase.

A well designed and executed CRO strategy can help discover new growth methods, saving time and effort through minor adjustments that cumulatively yield huge results. By highlighting the usability of the marketplace and identifying customer behaviors, a continuous CRO effort gives the operator insights to drive growth and profitability.

24.1 What to Look For

For decades, behavioral scientists have studied consumers to understand what motivates them to purchase or walk away. Much of that study centered on reading body language and face-to-face interaction with a salesperson—none of which applies to an online transaction. The new generation of behavioral scientists has begun to examine the marketplace platforms themselves to help operators understand what makes a customer put an item in the cart, complete the purchase, or navigate away. Begin examination of the marketplace in these primary areas.

Page Design

Because most of the customer journey so frequently navigates through the product page before purchase, these pages have the highest impact on conversion rates. The example below demonstrates why Amazon's conversion rate can go as high as 74%. Plenty of white space, easy to view photos, clear descriptions, and brightly colored Add to Cart and Buy Now buttons all work together to give the customer the information they need to decide on purchase and easily close the sale.

FIGURE 24.1 Amazon Product Page

Website Copy

While a well-designed and attractive website creates a first impression for immediate engagement, the words on the page have the power to hook visitors and convert them. Engaging copy should give audiences the information they need and direct them to their next steps to purchase.

- Headline – An impactful headline catches the reader's attention and delivers the right information to keep them reading. Also, the font, color, and size should allow for easy reading. This headline on Fiverr tells the consumer exactly what they can expect to find on the website.

FIGURE 24.2 Fiverr Landing page

- Body Content – Well-written body content should remain consistent with brand messaging while delivering clear, precise information to help the consumer understand value and move forward on the path to purchase. As always, small paragraphs, subheadings, and bulleted lists increase readability and help the audience absorb pertinent information at-a-glance.

Call to Action

Whether the desired action is to request a quote, book an appointment, or make a purchase, the call-to-action button should clearly state the goal, should be a bright color and should be prominently located for the consumer to find easily. When ADT changed the text of the CTA button from "Book a Survey" to "Get a Free Quote," conversion rates jumped to 60%.

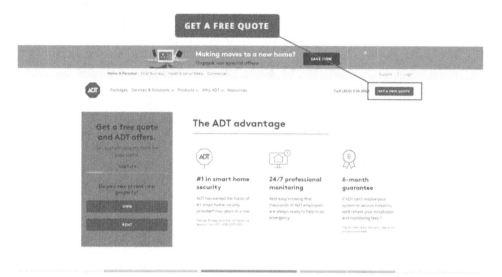

FIGURE 24.3 ADT Call to Action button
Source: https://vwo.com/success-stories/adt/

Forms

Because investment is shown to increase engagement, asking visitors to take a few minutes to fill out a simple form will increase their buy-in on the marketplace while providing the operator valuable data. Forms could be a basic customer satisfaction questionnaire, signing up for an email newsletter, or creating a user ID. Here are four tips for increasing conversion while balancing many low-quality leads against a few high-quality leads.

- Number of fields –Fewer fields are better in most cases simply to avoid annoying potential customers.

- Appearance – Good design should include consistent styling, pleasant colors and images, and easy readability.

- Password – Guide the users to make strong yet easy-to-remember passwords.

- SSO – Single sign-on allows users to log in without learning a new password, but also allows the operator to use APIs to pull user information from existing accounts such as Facebook or Google.

Site Navigation & Structure

The primary goal is to help the user navigate the path to purchase in as few clicks as possible. Proper site design focuses on UX and making it easy for users to find the information they want and take the actions they need.

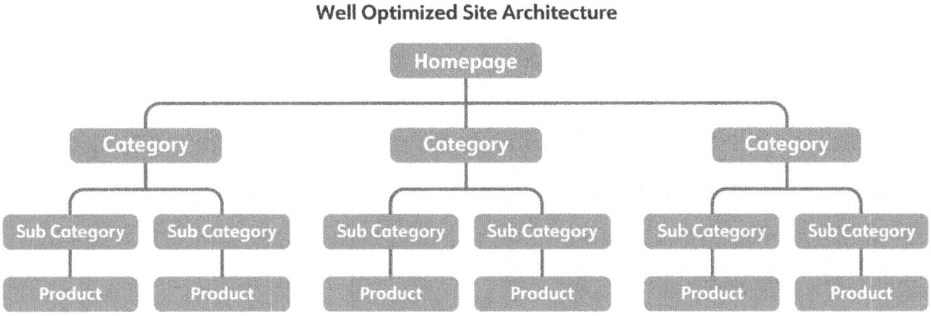

Well Optimized Site Architecture

FIGURE 24.4 Site Navigation and Structure

Chapter 22: User Experience is devoted to a broader exploration of this topic.

24.2 Looking Beyond Conversion Rate

While conversion rate can be a very telling metric, it should be considered within the context of other key metrics to make it more meaningful. Following are some of the common misconceptions about conversion rate. Higher conversion rate equals higher performance. Conversion rate alone does not give a complete picture of performance. An example:

- Marketplace A: 6000 visits ÷ 250 sales = 4% conversion rate

- Marketplace B: 1000 visits ÷ 100 sales = 10% conversion rate

Clearly Marketplace B has a far higher conversion rate, but if all transactions have the same dollar value, Marketplace A more than doubled the revenue of Marketplace B.

More engagement means higher conversion. Increased engagement cannot overcome the challenge of a small catalog or outreach to the wrong audience. If a customer visits a marketplace three times before purchasing the single item of interest to them, a triggered reminder message may encourage them to revisit the site and view more products, but if they cannot find products they need or want, five or ten visits will not be enough to encourage more purchases.

The conversion rate applies to all audiences. In the same way that different customers view and purchase various products based on need and interest, different customers will visit a different number of times before purchasing. For this reason, conversion rate should be studied per audience, rather than a single conversion rate for the entire marketplace. After examining and understanding the conversion rate for various audiences, different adjustments to the CRO campaign should be made to speak to each audience.

24.3 Top 20 Best Practices to Optimize Marketplace Conversion Rates

1. **Increase page load speed.** Over 40% of users drop off a website that takes more than 3 seconds to load. This first step towards CRO is crucial and non-negotiable. Tools like Google's PageSpeed Insights can audit marketplace pages and provide tips for improvement. Start with lightweight themes, avoiding unnecessary plugins, and compressing JavaScript and CSS files. Additionally, cache plugins and a content delivery network provide for smooth operations.

2. **Make checkout easier.** Remove distractions like forcing visitors to create a login, opting into marketing messages, or reviewing the privacy policy. Such information can be dealt with after purchase, so give the customer the easiest, and shortest path to purchase.

How many users who add a product to their cart complete checkout?

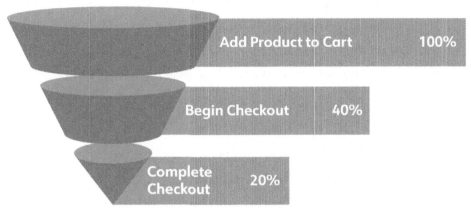

FIGURE 24.5 Users completing checkout

3. **Make the CTA beneficial.** Instead of enabling users to take a basic action step— Download, Click Here, or Continue—give CTA buttons that are meaningful and beneficial. Get My eBook and Send Me a Free Quote tell the customer what they will receive as a result of clicking the button. AB testing copy, placement, and design will also lead to higher conversion rates.

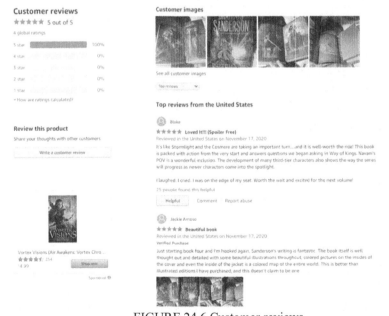

FIGURE 24.6 Customer reviews

4. **Build trust with customer reviews.** Displaying customer reviews on product pages so customers can read them before purchase builds credibility and increases trust. Amazon has taken this a step further by allowing customers to ask question of each other. This both increases engagement and saves the operator and vendor the time of answering customer queries.

5. **Have a sale.** Big sales and special pricing have drawn customers into brick-and-mortar stores for hundreds of years. Online marketplaces are no different. Amazon has Prime Day, Flipkart has Big Billion Days, and Alibaba has Singles Day. But sales of any type and at any time of year will increase conversion. In addition to low prices, free or one-day delivery and exchange offers can boost conversion.

6. **Play the Scarcity Game.** Create a sense of urgency by displaying how many items are left in stock or adding a timer to show when special pricing or free shipping end.

FIGURE 24.7 Product page improvements

7. **Make product pages helpful.** Keywords and tags optimize product pages for search engines, while quality images and

descriptive information entice the consumer to purchase. Also, complimentary product recommendations and create upsell and cross-sell opportunities.

8. **Navigation should be simple and obvious.** A smooth customer journey includes the fewest clicks possible. Smart search, clear navigation labels, and bright CTA buttons make for excellent customer experience and increased conversion rates.

9. **Support multiple languages.** Consumers around the world are willing to shop on marketplaces based in another part of the world, but only if they can read the content. Use AI that auto-detects the user origin and gives the option upfront to change the website language.

10. **Accept a variety of payment methods.** While it is important to have site security for those who choose to type in a credit card number, eWallets and mobile payment options have gained in popularity. Accepting different payment forms ensures customers can complete their transactions in a way they feel comfortable. And like choosing a language, give users the freedom to pay in their home currency. Chinese marketplace giant Ali Express allows for both in the top bar menu.

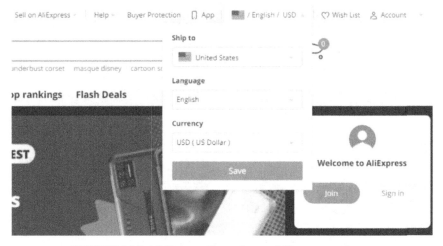

FIGURE 24.8 Ali Express Location and Currency selector

11. **Optimize the mobile experience.** Mobile traffic first exceeded desktop traffic on retail websites in 2017. According to Wolfgang Digital's KPI Report 2019, 53% of traffic comes from mobile devices, but mobile accounts for just 32% of revenue.

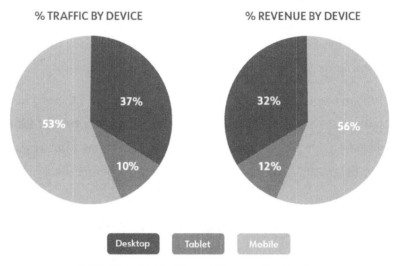

FIGURE 24.9 Traffic and Revenue by Device

Mobile users and desktop users are the same consumers, mobile optimization must apply to both the marketplace website itself as well as all marketing strategies.

FIGURE 24.10 Share of Mobile Commerce Sales

12. **Use chatbots & 24/7 support to improve customer experience.**

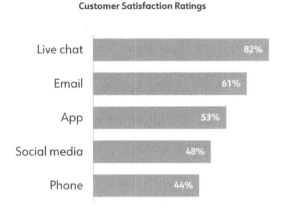

Customer Satisfaction Ratings

Live chat	82%
Email	61%
App	53%
Social media	48%
Phone	44%

FIGURE 24.11 Users prefer chat over other communication forms

Since 73% of consumers prefer chat over other forms of communication, real-time responsiveness can make the difference between a sale and a lost opportunity. Facebook, WhatsApp, Twitter, Google, and many others have integrated bots into their instant messaging platforms to help with shopping, bookings, and customer service.

13. **Offer expedited delivery.** Amazon's mastery of logistical efficiency has spoiled modern consumers, but other marketplaces must comply if they wish to compete. Evaluate shipping procedures and costs and be prepared to offer shoppers an excellent deal.

14. **Make returns easy.** A clearly written, customer-centric return policy will give customers confidence to complete their purchase without risk.

15. **Accept and incorporate customer feedback.** Beyond asking customers for simply product reviews, ask for their opinion about the marketplace as well—what is working, what needs work. A discount code or special coupon pricing can encourage customers to spend a few minutes of their time answering the survey questions.

16. **Use A/B testing. landing pages**, CTA buttons, product placements, and site copy are a few of the areas which benefit most

from A/B testing, and tools like AB Tasty, Optimizely, Visual Website Optimizer (VWO), and Crazy Egg make the process simple.

17. **Retarget customers who abandon their cart.** A recent survey showed that up to 88% of shoppers regularly abandon their carts. To stop revenue leakage, retargeting shows ads to people who have visited that marketplace in the past. Search abandonment retargeting is a related tactic that can also stem revenue leakage and improve conversion.

18. **Optimize for different personas.** The marketing team developed shopper personas not only for the initial site build and launch campaigns but also for updating and optimizing. Revisit those personas, adjust them as needed, and then optimize the marketing campaign and website to capture each persona.

19. **Track customer behavior using analytics.** Customer behavior can provide significant insight about the marketplace website. For example, examine how customers interact with the site, what posts or products get the maximum traction, which are the hottest selling products, or where customers come from. One of the most powerful and easy to use tool is Google Analytics.

20. **Have a well thought out content strategy.** Content marketing is critical for developing brand awareness of the marketplace. Author articles, create videos, publish photos, and produce social media content that differentiates the marketplace from competitors.

Some Conversion Benchmarks

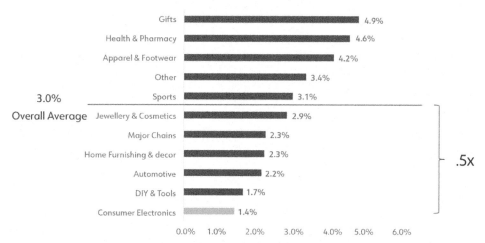

FIGURE 24.12 Conversion by Orders/Visits
Source: Adobe Digital Index 2020

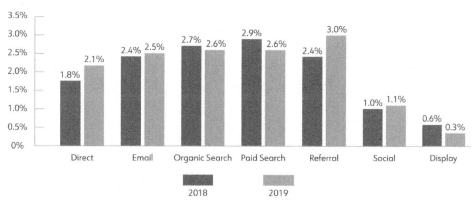

FIGURE 24.13 Conversion rate by Traffic source
Source: Research from Episerver Retail Clients 2020

Conversion Rate by Device

		Q2 2018	Q3 2018	Q4 2018	Q1 2019	Q2 2019
Global	Desktop	4.12%	4.26%	4.79%	4.04%	3.90%
Global	Mobile Phone	2.00%	2.03%	2.23%	1.88%	1.82%
Global	Other	0.17%	0.15%	0.13%	0.06%	0.06%
Global	Tablet	3.72%	3.84%	4.05%	3.54%	3.49%
US	Desktop	4.50%	4.55%	5.23%	4.44%	4.14%
US	Mobile Phone	1.81%	1.85%	2.18%	1.79%	1.53%
US	Other	0.09%	0.09%	0.14%	0.06%	0.05%
US	Tablet	3.68%	3.82%	4.21%	3.58%	3.36%
GB	Desktop	5.12%	5.56%	5.28%	4.40%	4.97%
GB	Mobile Phone	3.30%	3.33%	3.27%	2.97%	3.35%
GB	Other	1.26%	0.98%	1.70%	1.30%	1.34%
GB	Tablet	4.65%	4.74%	4.50%	4.23%	4.48%

FIGURE 24.14 Conversion rate by Device
Source: Monetate Ecommerce Quarterly Benchmarks

Conversion Rate by Operating System

	Q2 2018	Q3 2018	Q4 2018	Q1 2019	Q2 2019
Android	1.96%	2.03%	2.27%	1.93%	1.81%
Chrome OS	3.14%	3.57%	3.72%	2.95%	3.01%
Linux	0.47%	0.47%	0.68%	0.69%	0.41%
Macintosh	3.87%	4.11%	4.74%	3.58%	3.67%
Windows	4.49%	4.65%	5.12%	4.52%	4.41%
Windows Phone	1.49%	1.43%	1.40%	1.25%	1.14%
iOS	2.37%	2.37%	2.53%	2.15%	2.11%

FIGURE 24.15 Conversion rate by Operating System
Source: Monetate Ecommerce Quarterly Benchmarks

Key Takeaways: Conversion Rate Optimization

- Conversion rate is a powerful metric but should not be taken in isolation. To get a complete picture, consider other customer engagement metrics like visits and time spent on site.

- The five basic elements to optimize the user journey are landing page design, website copy, forms, call to action, and site navigation.

- Some of the key areas that have indirect impact on conversion rates are logistics (same-day delivery, BOPIS, etc.) and use of AI and machine learning in areas of customer support and inventory management.

- Conversion rate optimization is an ongoing process of continual testing and adjustments and is to be thought of as an ongoing program rather than a periodic effort.

Chapter 25: Customer Service

Your most unhappy customers are your greatest source of learning.

Bill Gates – Co-Founder Microsoft

Introduction

Customer service has long been recognized as a critical component of revenue growth. Given the power of digitally enabled, modern customers to voice their opinion, online businesses need to reinvent the customer experience to drive loyalty, build trust, and protect the reputation of their marketplace. This refers to all customer contact before, during, and after purchase which helps them navigate the marketplace and achieve their goals. Here are some numbers from the recent Salesforce survey that emphasize the importance of customer service and how it can strengthen your marketplace brand.

- 70% of the customer buying experience is about how they feel they are being treated.

- Counteracting one negative customer experience requires up to 12 positive experiences.

- Close to 89% of customers never come back after a poor customer service experience.

- Over 50% of customer do not mind paying extra for better customer experience

25.1 Primary Functions of Customer Service

As the marketplace model becomes increasingly popular, standing out from the crowd becomes more difficult. Excellent customer service can be a significant distinguishing factor. Figure 25.1 below show delivery tracking and payment methods are features that users consider the most important.

E-Commerce Account Features Most Important to Users

Feature	Percentage
Check delivery date, track order, check status of delivery	63%
Manage credit card / payment method	40%
Review order history (past orders)	31%
Return an item	30%
Contact customer service (call, live chat, e-mail)	26%
Edit / update order	18%
Cancel order	16%
Reset password	16%
Print, download invoice / receipt	15%
Manage wishlist, saved items	13%
Manage addresses	7%
Give feedback to the e-commerce site	5%
Manage newsletter subscriptions (unsubscribe, update)	5%
Other	2%

FIGURE 25.1 Source: https://baymard.com/blog/order-returns-ecommerce-ux

While customer service representatives should be prepared to handle nearly any customer need, there are four areas that are frequent customer requests.

Where is my Order (WISMO)?

Order tracking allows the operator and seller to monitor the progress of orders and shipments and communicate the status to customers. Marketplace order tracking includes features like packaging status, shipment tracking, estimated delivery dates, and even notification of delays.

FIGURE 25.2 Order tracking option on Amazon

The extent of order tracking services provided by the marketplace varies depending on the technology capabilities of the stakeholders in the ecosystem. Larger marketplaces, like Amazon, provide end to end tracking to keep customers informed of the order progress from the time they order straight through to delivery confirmation.

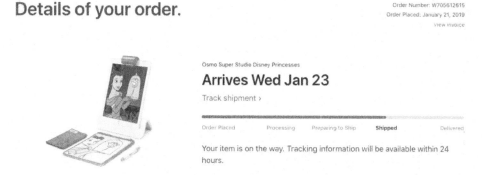

FIGURE 25.3 Shipment status on Amazon

Tracking has become standard in the shipping industry, so once the shipper has received the package and generated a tracking number, this number should be shared with the customer. The shipment status can then be tracked by the customer on the marketplace site or directly on the shipper's website.

Delivery By Amazon

Tracking ID Q21130114274

Saturday, 23 February

3:45 PM	Delivered
	Richmond, VA
7:59 AM	Out for delivery
	Richmond, VA

Friday, 22 February

11:53 PM	Package arrived at the final delivery station
	Virginia, VA
10:19 PM	Package departed an Amazon facility
	Virginia, VA
	Package has shipped
	Virginia, VA

UPS

Locations | United States - English ∨ | Sign up / Log in | Search or Track

Quick Start   Tracking   Shipping   Services   Customer Support

Tracking Details

LZ038Y412915676690   Updated: 12/04/2020 11:54 A.M. EST

Delivered

Delivered To
Richmond, VA, US

Left At: Residential
Received By: ID Verified
Proof of Delivery

Delivered On   **Delivery Time**
Wednesday   **at 7:24 P.M.**
11/04/2020

Send Updates

We care about the security of your package. Log in to get more details about your delivery.

Shipment Progress			Shipment Details
	Date	Location	**Service**
			UPS Next Day Air Saver®
Delivered	11/04/2020 7:24 P.M.	Richmond, VA, US	Show More +
Out for Delivery	11/04/2020 8:51 A.M.	Chantilly, VA, United States	Track
Shipped	11/03/2020 6:49 P.M.	Latham, NY, United States	Help
Label Created	11/03/2020 3:18 P.M.	United States	Track

Customer Service	This Site	Company Info	Connect with Us
Help and Support Center	Tracking	About UPS	Facebook
Get Started with UPS	Shipping	Media Relations	Twitter

FIGURE 25.4 Shipment Tracking

Marketplaces should strive to provide the highest level of customer service with a comprehensive view of order status available on the marketplace website so that customers do not need to navigate to different sites.

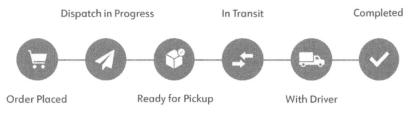

FIGURE 25.5 Shipment Tracking

Order Cancellation

This option allows both sellers and customers to cancel orders. Sellers may need to cancel an order only if they are not able to fulfill the order due to lack of inventory. By contrast, customers may have several reasons for canceling an order—the item was not available, they changed their mind about ordering, or the order was fraudulently placed through their account. Whatever the reason for cancellation, the operator should provide a clear policy for how and when orders may be canceled, such as before payment has been collected, before the order has shipped, or within a specified timeframe after the order is placed. Cancellation of orders by either seller or buyer should take place on the Manage Orders page within the accounts.

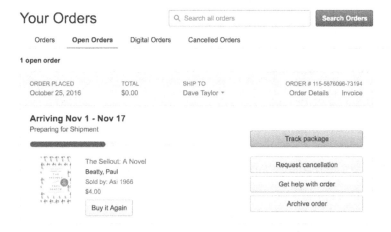

FIGURE 25.6 Order Cancellation option

Some marketplaces facilitate either complete or partial cancellation of customer orders. Partial cancellation is usually performed by allowing customers to update the quantity of the order. Once an order is canceled, the order status is updated and an email is sent to notify the customer. In some cases, cancellation by phone may also be an option.

FIGURE 25.7 Returning or replacing items

To improve customer experience, some marketplaces allow customers to cancel an order after they have been shipped by calling the package back from the shipper without executing delivery.

Returns

Returns are an inevitable part of selling online. According to the National Retail Federation in 2018, customers returned 30% of all online purchases. The most frequent reasons for return include the following:

- changed mind

- wrong item shipped

- purchase arrived too late

- damaged or defective

- found a better price

- did not match description or meet expectation

- wrong size

- wardrobing (wearing an item and then returning)

Considering the fact that 73% of consumers told UPS that the returns process directly impacts the likelihood that they will shop with that retailer again (2019 UPS Pulse of the Online Shopper), managing the returns process well is a critical part of any marketplace business strategy.

A returns process designed for excellent customer experience should strive for the following:

- Make the process easy to understand and initiate.

- Request a reason for the return.

- Provide return shipping labels or a digital solution

- Keep the customer informed of the return status via a tracking mechanism.

Fraud

All the features that make marketplace shopping an excellent experience for consumers—ease of placing an order, anonymous payment, and fast shipping—have also enabled robust criminal activity, to the tune of $1.5 trillion a year, according to research out of Surrey University. The financial losses affect operators, sellers, and customers alike, while reputation damage and loss of customer trust can translate to long term detriment to the marketplace platform.

Some of the more common forms of fraud impacting marketplace operations include the following:

- Fake sellers – Fraudulent sellers copy the profile of legitimate sellers and fool victims into paying for products or services they will never receive.

- Money laundering – By creating fake buyer and seller accounts, individuals can order product through the buyer account and pay the seller using stolen credit cards. The products or services do not exist, but the very real money is lost.

- Payment fraud – When real products or services are purchased with stolen credit card numbers, the seller, the credit card owner, or the bank backing the card loses the money.

As customer service on a marketplace has limited exposure in identifying and preventing sophisticated fraud, their role would be primarily to process the complaint and pass it to the authorities.

25.2 Communication Channels

Any successful customer service strategy must enable customers to communicate in the manner they are most comfortable. The Critical Channels of Choice study, conducted by the CMO Council in partnership with Pitney Bowes, determined that today's consumers across all generations want and expect companies to offer a blend of physical and digital communication channels. Survey respondents expect businesses to communicate via email (86%), telephone (65%), website (53%), text (52%), and in-person (48%). But when asked which communication forms they could not live without, the top two answers were surprising— telephone (28%) and in-person (17%). The survey also found that consumers considered a channel indispensable when it provided convenience (50%), reliability (45%), and speed (41%).

Digging into consumer motivation, the survey found that respondents were most interested in fast response times (52%), knowledgeable and ready staff (47%), and rewards for loyalty over a length of time (42%). At the bottom of the list were automated service (8%), branded social communities (9%), and multiple touchpoints that add value to the experience (10%).

Bottom line, customers want to save money (77%), save time (49%), and make their lives easier (47%). All of those needs can be met through a variety of communication channels.

Live Chat – Instant communication allows the customer service department to immediately see and address the customer's request for help. Live chat is also the option preferred by most shoppers (92%). An effective chat option can nurture the customer relationship, reduce bounce rates, increase time on site, boost conversion rates, and all while collecting timely feedback.

Leveraging advances in AI, machine learning, and natural language processing (NLP) to replace the conventional customer service channels, chatbots have gotten better at natural-sounding conversation, such that 27% of customers were unsure whether their last customer service interaction was with a human or a bot (PWC Report). It is estimated that chatbots could save $11 billion in annual costs and 2.5 billion customer service hours by 2023.

Email – Since its beginning in the 90s, email has been a preferred and effective communication tool. For marketplaces, email provides convenience and reliability to communicate with sellers and buyers about news, issues, products, and questions. By giving customers the option to sign up for promotional emails, the marketplace customer service team can easily create value with the customer by notifying them of new products, delivering discount codes, and informing them of other promotions. Additionally, by providing an email address for direct contact with the customer service team, customers feel empowered to ask for help or air their grievances using a familiar and comfortable communication method.

Social Media – In an age when many people post personal details about their lives on social media, complaining about poor customer service on social media seems a natural step for many consumers. To get ahead of the reputation damage, marketplaces must focus a portion of their customer service resources on social media platforms.

To build a positive image on social media, begin by being an active participant and engaging customers in a dialogue in these ways:

- Be present across multiple networks, like Facebook and Instagram.

- Consistently follow up with community members to gauge response.

- Encourage the community to leave reviews.

- Use social media for promotions and special offers.

To improve customer service, use social media in these ways:

- Take feedback seriously by responding to posted messages and sharing solutions when appropriate.

- Be available and respond quickly to queries and complaints posted on social media.

- Set up a dedicated support account to keep complaints off the main account and give customers an outlet for all their questions and support concerns.

- Avoid chatbots, as a greater level of personalized service over social media will be perceived as better, more genuine interaction.

25.3 Refunds

Many customers read the refund policy before they buy, so a carefully crafted refund policy is vital, for operators, sellers, and customers alike. A good refund policy should contain the following information to ensure a quality customer experience.

Be clear and concise. When writing the return policy, use conversational language. Avoid complex, legal jargon that could confuse customers or leave room for misinterpretation.

Specify exact time limits. State clearly the number of days after purchase by which the product must be returned in order to receive a full refund. Also, specify whether the return package must be postmarked or received by the seller within that time limit.

List all return requirements. Specify requirements like packaging must be unopened, all original packaging must be present, all pieces (manuals, protective sleeves, etc.) must be included.

Clarify applicable fees. If the customer will be charged a restocking fee or is expected to pay to return shipping, this should be clearly described.

Define return condition. With the exception of defective merchandise or goods damaged in shipping, specify the expected condition of returned items and under what circumstances used goods may be returned for a refund.

Define refund methods. Clearly state whether refunds will be sent to the original payment method used for purchase, applied to store credit, or only eligible for exchange. If the refund method varies depending on the type or condition of product, these differences should also be carefully explained.

Make the policy easy to find. Post a clearly labeled link on every web page, send a printed copy inside the packaging, and include a link in the purchase confirmation email so that customers always have easy access to the policy.

25.4 Appeasement

Many a normal day has taken a sudden turn when an angry customer steps on the scene. These situations must be handled quickly and correctly to avoid losing the customer and to minimize the risk that they may turn to social media to air their grievances.

Many times, the customer is frustrated at trying to solve the problem on their own or because they feel getting help from the customer service department has been challenging. Whatever the case, it is important to remember the customer is a person who just wants helps. Following are a few steps to help navigate the process successfully.

Remain professional – A good customer service representative is patient and empathetic. In the Gallup Business Journal, William J. McEwen states that empathetic support can be three times more effective at satisfying customers and retaining their business than support that is only fast. Expressing that empathy is found to significantly calm angry customers.

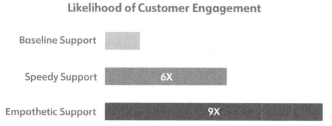

FIGURE 25.8 Customer Support

Listen to the customer – Begin by allowing the customer to explain the problem in detail. Then repeat the explanation back to the customer and ask for clarification of any missed details. This demonstrates to the customer that they have been truly heard.

Apologize and propose a solution – Some studies have shown that customers are twice as likely to be pacified by a solution when it is delivered with an apology. A simple "we are sorry for the inconvenience" is frequently enough to put the customer at ease. Next advise the customer of all available options for rectifying the situation and recommend which option would be best for the customer.

Apology vs. Compensation

Do customers prefer an apology or compensation in response to a negative experience?

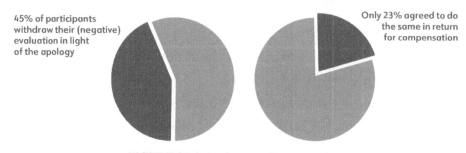

FIGURE 25.9 Apology vs Compensation

Define the return ship method – While the returns policy posted on the website and send in the original package should already clearly state the return shipping options, handling an angry customer requires special care. So clearly advise the customer of options to ship the product back or drop it off at a nearby location. Whichever option the customer chooses, ensure they have all the information and resources needed to complete the return.

Key Takeaways: Customer Service

- The primary functions of the customer service department include order status, cancellations, returns, and fraud claims.

- Customers expect marketplaces to communicate through many channels, particularly chatbots, email, and social media.

- The returns and refunds policies must be clearly explained and easy to find.

- When a customer becomes angry, remain professional and empathetic to their grievance.

Chapter 26: Advanced Technical Features

Innovation is the central issue in economic prosperity

Michael Porter, Professor at Harvard Business School

Introduction

Level 5 of the Marketplace Maturity Model is Optimizing, which includes continuous incremental improvements and major innovative transformations. Marketplaces can be optimized with advanced technical features, as described this chapter, and advanced business models, described in the next chapter.

The benefits of these advanced features include increasing revenue, improving customer experiences, decreasing costs, improving scalability, and improving control. Some features need to be implemented on the customer-facing eCommerce engine, some on the seller-facing marketplace engine, and some on both.

26.1 Internationalization

Expanding to international markets can provide exponential growth, but it is important to understand the challenges.

The following topics should be addressed when internationalizing a marketplace:

- Product title, description, and other text attributes
- Category titles used in navigating the catalog
- Currency
- Validation of addresses and other data
- Graphics (GIF, JPG, Flash, etc.) that contain text
- Site navigation
- Email content
- Page layout justification & flow (left-to-right or right-to-left)
- Weights, lengths, and other measurements (US customary v. metric)
- Reviews or other user-generated content
- Filtering for analytics and dashboards
- Formatting (dates, decimals)
- Paired characters (?! in Spanish)
- Payment processors
- Tax calculation
- Shipping options
- Top-level domains (TLD), possibly with country codes (e.g., .com.br for Brazil)
- Other data within the system (e.g., text for order status)

In addition to the technical challenges, internationalization efforts should consider new audience cultural preferences around the product catalog, images, and other content. For example, a bikini-clad Barbie doll may not be culturally acceptable in a conservative Muslim or Hindu country.

To reduce risk, a best practice is to start small by testing just one country. Partner with well-known sellers in the area to gain buyer confidence. Current sellers should be assured that this is an opportunity for them to expand globally.

Internationalization efforts must include several key steps.

Language and translation – In a survey of 8,709 global consumers in 29 countries in Europe, Asia, North America, and South America, CSA Research found that 76% of respondents indicated that seeing product information in their native language was more important than price. Beyond simply translating product information to the local language, branding must remain consistent while still capturing the cultural nuances of the target market. Hire a local marketing team to check translations and advise on culture and preferences. If the product assortment is large, it might make sense to hire in-house local translators or culture specialists.

Configuration and data – The catalog and related data structures should be designed to enable content deployment by locale. Example elements include:

- Categories, products, SKUs, and related merchandising assets (images, PDFs, etc.)

- Sites and locales

- Default language for each market

- Language stemmers for all indices to facilitate better navigation and search

- Configuration and attribute parameters

- Coupons and promotions

Product Information Management (PIM) – As the foundation of the marketplace catalog, the PIM must be able to accommodate internationalization, including information translation and local deployment. Following are some key factors to consider when evaluating PIM options.

- All product information enrichment, localization, and translation should occur in one centralized platform.

- An integrated enrichment process allows for reviews and validation to ensure the accuracy of updated data.

- Automation tools should include currency and metric conversions as well as content translation.

- Business rules and workflows simplify the management of catalogs in multiple languages by helping validate and control product information quality, enhance localized asset management, and manage locale-specific product attributes.

Single-Site vs. Multi-Site – Another very important consideration is how many sites should be built. The following table identifies potential impacts for each option, but these impacts are usually dependent on the software used.

A single international site for all target countries aggregates management responsibilities but minimizes customization. Group sites—sorted by language, currencies, or compliance—offer a bit of room for customization and increase the maintenance workload. Individual sites for each country create the most amount of work for the development team and allow for the greatest amount of cultural customization.

Options/ Parameters	Single-Site	Regional Sites	Country-Specific Sites
Number of Sites	One	The number of currencies, languages, etc.	The number of countries
Number of Catalogs	Many	The number of currency groups plus one	The number of countries plus one
Number of Prices/Product	One per currency	One per currency or locale	One per currency or locale
Customizability	Low	Medium	High
Organizational Complexity	Low	Medium	High
Navigation	One navigation	Each group has its own navigation.	Each site has its own navigation.
Search Tuning	Can be localized. Metrics are aggregated per site, but no country breakdown.	Can be localized. Metrics are aggregated per site, but no country breakdown.	Can be localized. Analytics are aggregated per site.
Merchandising	Create dynamic customer groups based on locale. Localize all campaign elements based on locale or IP address.	Create dynamic customer groups based on the locale for each group. Localize campaign elements based on locale or IP address for each group.	Independent per site. Promotions must be imported and exported to run in multiple countries.
Content	One content library	One content library per site (or group)	Each site has a local library, or all use a shared library across sites.
A/B Test	Can test all countries or target specific countries with a customer group qualifier.	By group	A/B tests are site-specific.

Table 26.1 Single Vs Multi-Site
Source: Trailhead Salesforce Module

26.2 Enhanced Seller Stores

Many marketplaces have the option for sellers to create enhanced seller stores, which provide customers an immersive and rich virtual shopping experience. Amazon offers a DIY product that helps brands to create and design multi-page stores to showcase their products and brands.

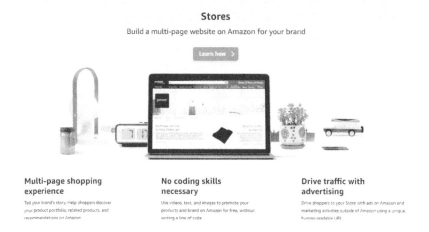

Stores

Build a multi-page website on Amazon for your brand

Learn how >

Multi-page shopping experience

Tell your brand's story. Help shoppers discover your product portfolio, related products, and recommendations on Amazon.

No coding skills necessary

Use videos, text, and images to promote your products and brand on Amazon for free, without writing a line of code.

Drive traffic with advertising

Drive shoppers to your Store with ads on Amazon and marketing activities outside of Amazon using a unique, human-readable URL.

FIGURE 26.1 Seller Stores

Walmart's enhanced content moves beyond basic product information by allowing brands and merchants to create distinctive listings with rich media, like videos and interactive product tours. Beyond simply displaying basic elements of an item page, enhanced content allows a brand to narrate a meaningful story around the product with use of multimedia and custom branded assets.

Enhanced seller stores can also include a listing of all the seller's products and navigation within this subset of marketplace products.

26.3 Alternative Payment Methods

With rapid fintech breakthroughs, many customers now want payment options outside the big three—Visa, MasterCard, and American Express. Marketplace operators should consider accommodating alternatives like gift cards, mobile payments, e-wallets, bank transfers, and financing options. Alternative payment methods are expected to account for 60% of all global eCommerce. Some of the more popular alternative payment methods include the following:

- PayPal and Venmo

- ACH, e-checks, and wire transfer

- Apple Pay and Google Wallet

- Bitcoin or other cryptocurrencies

- Amazon Pay and Alipay

- Klarna and Bill Me Later

In countries where many citizens do not have credit cards, some marketplaces offer cash-on-delivery. Another alternative for unbankable or underbanked customers is to offer payment with cash in a store or at a kiosk as part of the ordering process.

26.4 Quoting Capability

In-person negotiations often include questions around special pricing for large quantity orders. A marketplace can provide an online equivalent with a Request for Quote (RFQ) capability. This typically happens through the marketplace messaging system to minimize platform leakage. The marketplace will keep a record of the communication and ensure that billing and seller fulfillment align with the quote.

Quoting functionality can also be used to customize a product, but there are practical limits to the amount of customization that can be done through a messaging system. More advanced customization is usually done through a Configure, Price, Quote (CPQ) solution.

CPQ is frequently used in complex B2B purchases, such as machinery, electronics, or other customizable products. Consumers who have purchased a computer online are familiar with the CPQ solutions that enable selection of options for memory, disk capacity, software, etc. Sometimes advanced configuration may require a punch-out from the marketplace to the seller's systems to perform the CPQ process.

26.5 Enhanced Risk Management

Unlike a traditional eCommerce model, marketplace operators allow sellers to access the platform and sell goods directly to the customer or have orders fulfilled by the operator. In either case, the operator manages risks on both sides of the supply chain. The operator must ensure the customer receives quality goods within the promised timeframe, while at the same time protecting the interests of the seller and shielding them against fraud, chargeback, and false returns.

26.6 Customer Loyalty Programs

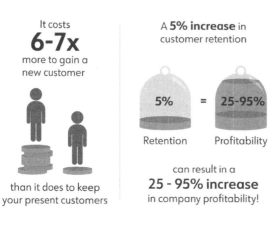

It costs
6-7x
more to gain a
new customer

than it does to keep
your present customers

A **5% increase** in
customer retention

5% = 25-95%

Retention   Profitability

can result in a
25 - 95% increase
in company profitability!

FIGURE 26.2 Customer Retention &
Profitability
Source: Bain & Company & Earl Sasser of the

Retaining customers is far less costly than acquiring new ones, so a robust loyalty program is worth the investment to reduce churn. While traditional loyalty program activities like punch cards have lost their appeal, the impact of loyalty programs remains strong and even continues to grow. To build a thriving loyalty program, keep these ideas in mind.

- A well-built mobile app should be the central point of operation for a loyalty program. Making the loyalty program easy to use ensures customers will understand its value.

- Give long-term customers rewards—extra points, free products, or early access to new features and offers—for their continued patronage.

- Provide small, immediate benefits for all purchases. Small purchases might earn a coupon toward the next purchase, while a large purchase could earn discounted products.

- Communicate clearly and frequently with loyalty members about the benefits they are receiving so that the value is clear.

26.7 Seller Advertising

Paid advertising can be a lucrative business, as demonstrated by Amazon, Walmart, Target, and eBay. Each offers an assortment of advertising options for sellers to promote their products on the marketplace.

☐ Sponsored Brand   ☐ Dynamic Display   ☐ Search Brand Amplifier   ☐ Sponsored Product

Search results on Amazon, Target and Walmart look increasingly similar as the digital commerce platforms create paid placements to capture brand spend.

FIGURE 26.3 Amazon, Walmart, and Target advertising options

When it comes to ad revenue, Amazon is king as the company's advertising business continues to outpace market trends. Amazon's ad revenue grew by 44% YoY in Q1 of 2020 while competitors Facebook and Google both saw advertisement revenue growth of 17% and 10.4% respectively.

Chapter 31 Best Practices for Sellers is devoted to a broader exploration of this topic.

26.8 Social Rewards & Gamification

Another emerging arena for marketers and brands is social rewards and gamification sites. Two of the most prominent examples are Poshmark and Tradesy.

A social commerce marketplace in the United States, Poshmark enables individuals to buy and sell new or used clothing, shoes, and accessories. More than a simple shopping destination, Poshmark is a vibrant community powered by millions of Stylists who sell their personal style and curate looks for their shoppers, creating the most connected shopping experience in the world.

HOW IT WORKS

I Am a Seller   I Am a Buyer

STEP 01

LIST IT

Take a photo and supload to your closet in less than 60 seconds-right from your phone!

STEP 02

SHARE IT

Share listings to your network for shoppers to discover! More sharing = more sales

Listing Details   Edit

STEP 03

EARN CASH

Shipping is easy with our pre-paid label, and you'll get cash in your pocket when item is delivered!

FIGURE 26.4 Social Rewards and Gamification

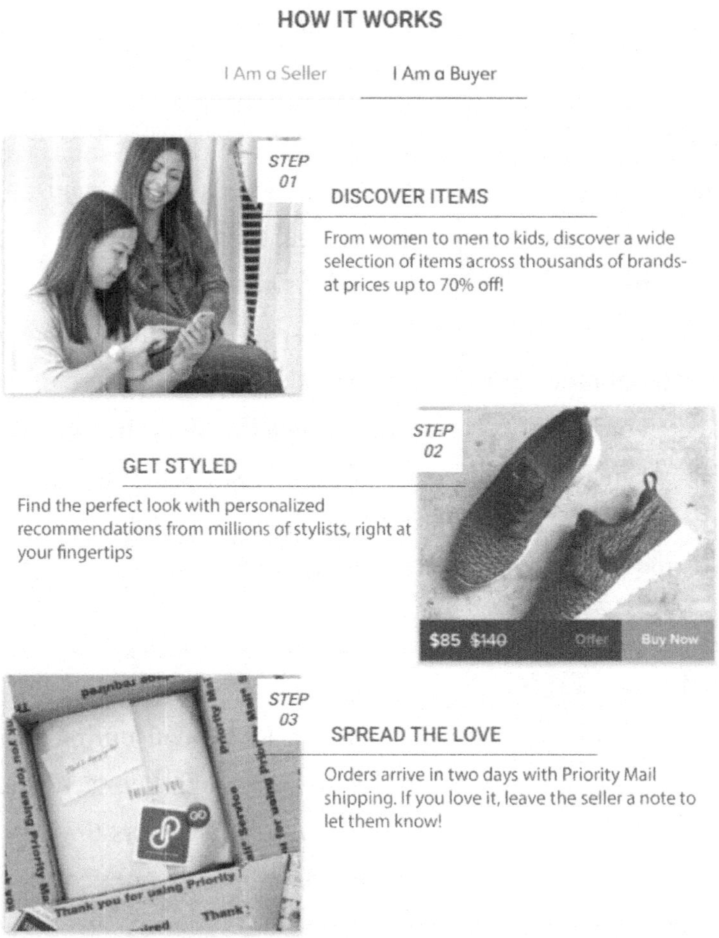

HOW IT WORKS

I Am a Seller   I Am a Buyer

STEP 01

DISCOVER ITEMS

From women to men to kids, discover a wide selection of items across thousands of brands- at prices up to 70% off!

GET STYLED

STEP 02

Find the perfect look with personalized recommendations from millions of stylists, right at your fingertips

$85 $140   Offer   Buy Now

STEP 03

SPREAD THE LOVE

Orders arrive in two days with Priority Mail shipping. If you love it, leave the seller a note to let them know!

FIGURE 26.5 Social Rewards and Gamification

Tradesy is an online peer-to-peer resale marketplace for buying and selling women's luxury and designer contemporary fashion. Through the app, sellers follow a simple process of listing and shipping and then get paid when the product is delivered. Buyers also use the app to search and purchase items. Tradesy handles all shipping and processing returns.

26.9 Automation for Marketplace

As a marketplace scales, the operator should automate as many processes as possible. This will increase efficiency, reduce human error, and enable the platform to continue to grow exponentially. The following list represents example automations for marketplace operators. Automation tools for sellers are described in chapter 31.

Automated Seller Management

When seller count grows from dozens or hundreds to thousands, manual monitoring of their performance is no longer feasible. Software rules can be configured to promote or suspend sellers based on their performance. For example, they can be automatically suspended if their rating drops below a certain number of stars, if they take more than a certain number of hours to accept orders, if they accept below a threshold percentage of orders, if they cancel a certain number of orders, if a certain number of customer returns are requested, or if they fail to meet other criteria. Likewise, sellers can automatically be promoted to premium sellers if they perform well on those same criteria.

Automated Seller Training

Onboarding and training new sellers can be a time-consuming and resource-intensive activity while trying to scale a marketplace. Automated training videos, software, and FAQs can walk new sellers through each step of the setup and launch process and remain in an online library for easy access any time a seller has a question.

Multi-channel Inventory Management Capabilities

Some sellers keep stock in multiple locations, including warehouses and retail stores with frequently changing inventory levels. They may also list their goods on multiple marketplaces. This can result in overselling, stock-outs, and poor customer experience. Automation of multi-channel management consolidates inventory, listings, orders, and fulfillment information across multiple inventory sources. With multi-channel management software, the seller can link all marketplace accounts and import data around product, inventory count, and locations.

Integrated Inventory, Order, and Shipment Updates

Every consumer appreciates up-to-date information about their order status. A seller-integrated inventory, order, and shipment tracking workflow will increase efficiency, improve customer experience, and provide an opportunity for cross-sell and upsell. Each communication to the customer provides an opportunity to include information about items that complement the customer's order, marketplace best sellers, or currently discounted items.

Automated Language Filtering in Product Descriptions, Reviews, etc.

Marketplaces publish seller-generated product information and user-generated content in the form of product descriptions, reviews, images, videos, and messages. For policy compliance of both sellers and customers, this content should be reviewed and approved. However, a manual review process is not scalable and would cost too much in time and labor. Automated language and image filtering software can monitor for restricted products, adult content, profanity, attempts to transact outside the marketplace, and any other undesirable content. An example of policy implementation could be blocking the ingestion of products where text includes the words gun, firearm, rifle, pistol, ammo, etc.

Automated Seller Payment

Paying sellers is a recurring marketplace process that can be done manually for a couple dozen sellers but becomes prohibitively labor intensive as the number of sales and orders increases. Commissions and taxes must be deducted from payments for orders completed based on the category and adjustments must be made for returns. Financial reconciliation must also be integrated with the marketplace operator's ERP or financial system. Many sellers also prefer electronic payment instead of paper checks.

Price Trackers

Price tracking tools can help research competitor pricing. Monitoring product prices on all major marketplaces ensures seller pricing is competitive enough to increase sales volume without losing money. There are many tools available, some as simple as a browser extension to track millions of products, provide price drop alerts, and chart price history.

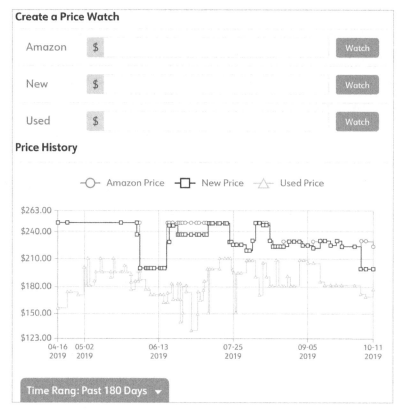

FIGURE 26.6 Price Tracking
Image Source: Penny Parrot

26.10 Omnichannel Order Fulfillment

The technological advancements expected by modern consumers are driving changes in the eCommerce world. Every participant in the supply chain, from retailers to vendors, site operators to logistics partners, is rethinking their strategy to get product to consumers faster. The chart below shows some of the recent advancements in fulfillment options that are driving customer convenience to new frontiers.

BOPIS (Buy online, pick up in-store)

In the BOPIS model, the customer begins their path to purchase by identifying the store location where they would like to pick up the merchandise. When the order is placed, the system checks inventory at the store and sends a pick request so that store employees can pick and package the merchandise before the customer arrives. This is an example of online sales driving offline traffic. Last year, over 68% of US consumers used this option while shopping online. Of those shoppers, more than 82% made additional in-store purchases while picking up the order.

BOSS (Buy online, ship-to-store)

This growing trend also begins when the customer designates their desired pickup location but does not check the store inventory. Instead, a central fulfilling warehouse picks the product and ships it to the store before the customer arrives.

ORDER	FULFILLMENT	RECEPTION	TERM
Online	Store	Pickup In-Store	**BOPIS or Click & Collect** (Buy Online, Pickup In-Store)
Online	Store	Pickup In-Store	**BORIS** (Buy Online, Return In-Store)
Online	Store	Delivery	**BOSFS** (Buy Online, Ship From Store)
Online	Warehouse	Pickup In-Store	**BOSS** (Buy Online, Ship-to-Store)

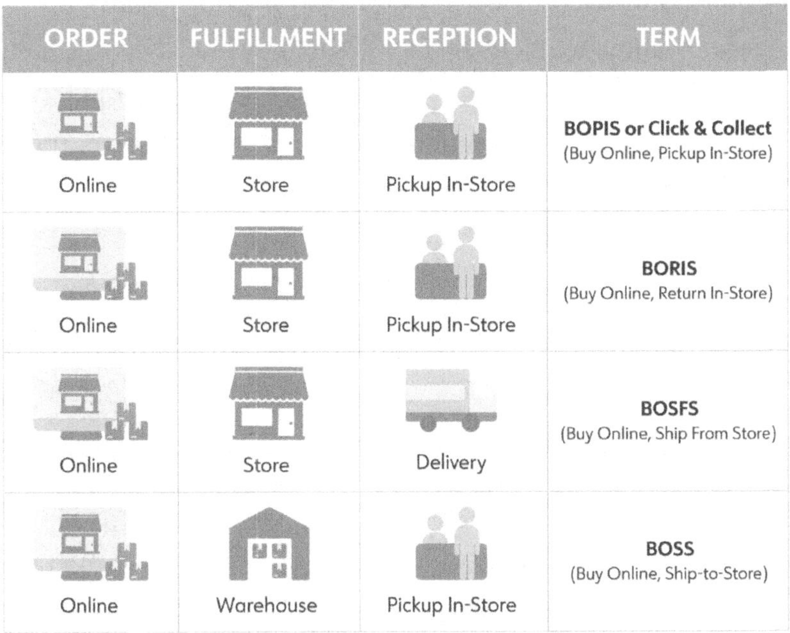

FIGURE 26.7 Omnichannel Order Fulfillment Options
Source: PredictSpring Store Order Fulfillment Methods

BORIS (Buy Online, Return In-Store)

In an effort to deliver excellent customer experience, this model allows the customer to purchase an item via the web or app and return it to the store.

Two advantages with this model are that neither party has to pay a third-party shipper and the physical store gains foot traffic and the opportunity for exchange or upsell.

BOSFS (Buy Online, Ship from Store)

This model also allows the customer to shop and pay online. A store associate then receives a notification to pick and pack the product from the store's inventory and ship it directly to the customer. By shipping from local sources, delivery is completed faster and makes use of local warehouses and store inventory to fulfill orders.

26.11 Social Media Integration

Social commerce is the process of selling and buying product over social media, a process which provides the consumer the highest level of convenience by allowing them to shop where they already are without having to navigate to an eCommerce platform. From a seller point of view, this is another channel in their multi-channel arsenal that drives traffic and has better engagement (both conversions as well as conversations) compared to other channels.

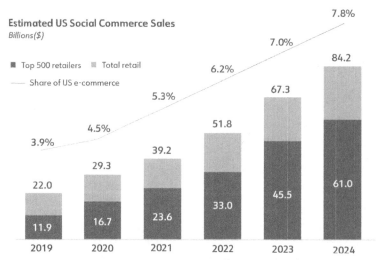

FIGURE 26.8 Estimated US Social Commerce Sales
Source: Business Insider Intelligence, US Census Bureau 2019

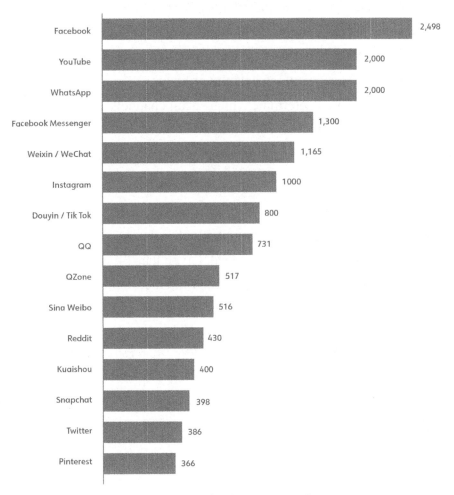

FIGURE 26.9 Most Popular Social Networks
Source: We Are Social, Hootsuite, Statista, Various Company Data

Much has changed in the way marketplaces, retailers, and brands leverage social media. No longer is it enough to have a presence and answer queries via Twitter. Modern customers want to discover new brands and products on social media, and many sellers are taking advantage of the benefits social media has to offer:

- Expand the marketplace footprint and client base and target distinct customer groups using across channels.

- Make retail locations appear more accessible.
- Improve SEO performance and lower cart abandonment rates.
- Boost traffic and conversion rates.
- Source customer reviews and recommendations for new product ideas and enhancements to existing products.
- Study analytics to determine which social channels are converting best and develop marketing strategies for each.
- Study analytics to identify **influencers** for community engagement strategies.

Facebook Social Commerce

With more than 2 billion active users globally, Facebook is the most popular social media platform in the world. Given that 140 million businesses use it daily for client and customer interaction, it is no surprise that Facebook also leads the way in social commerce.

Number of monthly active Facebook users worldwide as of 1st quarter 2020 (in millions)

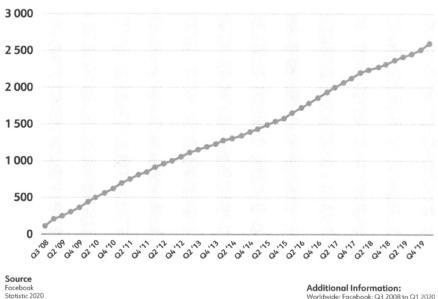

Source
Facebook
Statistic 2020

Additional Information:
Worldwide: Facebook: Q3 2008 to Q1 2020

FIGURE 26.10 Active Facebook users worldwide

One way to start with Facebook is to run product catalogs by adding item information and managing orders. Facebook Payments facilitates payment for online shopping and even peer-to-peer money transfer. Facebook ads are also helpful for brands that want to grow, as current statistics show that users are increasingly interacting with brand ads.

Instagram Social Commerce

Facebook is a great tool for advertising, but a recent survey showed 60% of Instagram users say they find new products to buy on the app and over 25% of users actually go to parent company Facebook looking for things to buy. That makes Instagram an excellent platform for new brands trying to get a foothold in the marketplace. To advertise on Instagram, a seller must first become a Facebook advertiser and then begin sharing shoppable content.

FIGURE 26.11 Instagram Social Commerce

Instagram ads function similarly to Facebook ads that appear as users scroll through their feed and stories. Additionally, Instagram sellers can tag up to five products per photo, up to 4 photos per post, so that customers can shop from brand posts as well as ads. While the checkout process previously redirected the user off the Instagram platform, Checkout on Instagram now enables customers to complete their purchase within the app.

Pinterest Social Commerce

Positioned as a source of inspirational photos across categories such as food, fashion, travel, and home décor, Pinterest is the third-largest social media network with revenue above $1 billion in 2019.

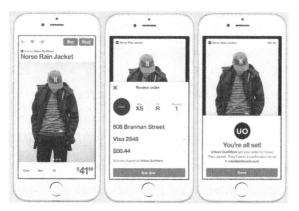

FIGURE 26.12 Pinterest Social Commerce

More than a social network, most users use the platform to search and save images on digital pinboards. Shopping is a top activity for over 48% of the users on Pinterest, and the platform provides extensive selling options for online sellers and retailers.

Some of the best features that facilitate online shopping on Pinterest are Rich Pins, Shop the Look, and "Buy It" buttons. The Rich Pins come in four categories—Product Pins, Recipe Pins, Article Pins, and App Pins— which have information about the product and redirect users to the marketplace where that item can be purchased. Shop the Look ads allows brands to tag up to 25 items in a single image. With over 459 million active users, Pinterest is continuously working with partners to support more shopping experiences on its social media platform across areas such as advertising, content marketing, measurement, creative, and shopping.

Shoppable Videos & TikTok Commerce

The rise of online shopping has forced retailers to look for new avenues to draw customers in. One of the ways they have found success combines shopping with entertainment. This is especially effective with younger generations who are looking for novel and engaging experiences while shopping.

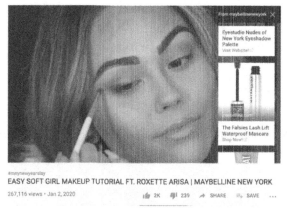

FIGURE 2.13 Video and eCommerce

Much of the growth in this space can be attributed to the rise of mobile activity, with shopping and entertainment the fastest growing segments in this space. Walmart streaming service Vudu has shoppable ads that seek to strengthen the platform's eCommerce capabilities. NBC Universal is also dialing into "shoppertainment" through shoppable ads powered by mobile-friendly QR codes.

To compete with the OTT giants and media moguls, smaller brands and sellers must amplify their video presence through other sources. TikTok is a Chinese short video-sharing platform that has shown tremendous worldwide growth in a short time. The platform currently has about 800 million active users and ranks seventh in the list of most downloaded apps of the last decade. The majority of its users are under 30 years old and content is predominantly aimed at Millennials and Gen Z.

TikTok provides a variety of ways for brands to promote themselves online. With **hashtag** challenges, brands encourage users to create content and link to the brand's hashtag, generating brand and product awareness. Creating funny videos with online items for sale engages the audience and builds brand recall. Engagement with influencers can also promote a store and the product it offers. TikTok currently offers three types of paid ads—

native ads (in-feed), brand takeovers (plays when a targeted user checks into the app), and hashtag challenges.

TikTok first-time downloads, Q2 2016 - Q4 2019

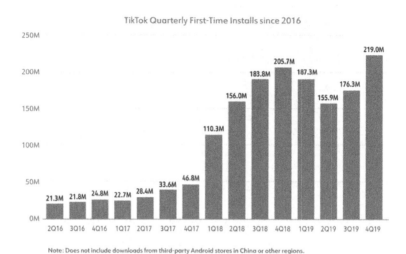

FIGURE 26.14 TikTok first time downloads
Source: Sensor Tower Store Intelligence

Retailers can also benefit from TikTok's shoppable ads which redirect users to the brand store to complete checkout. Stickers also allow users to engage with brand products in more intimate ways. Overall TikTok is a great fit for brands and sellers who want to engage younger demographics through creative and entertaining content.

FIGURE 26.15

26.12 Other Technical Features

As the platform economy develops, customers will demand the technologies they appreciate in other arenas. Operators and vendors alike can expect to adopt some form of the features below in the near future.

Augmented Reality / Virtual Reality allows the shopper to visually evaluate a product before purchase. For example, before ordering a sofa, the customer might be shown a 3D rendering of the sofa in their living room. Houzz, Wayfair, and other marketplaces already provide A/R support.

Voice Commerce is predicted to radically change the way marketplace operators and vendors function. When product information is optimized for voice navigation, fewer steps to purchase mean the customer journey will be faster than it already is.

Photo-Based Shopping, a feature already in use on Amazon and eBay, allows the customer to search for a product through a picture, even without the brand or product name.

Warehouse Robotics will maximize efficiency and cut costs and waste. Currently, there are more than 3,200 robot-enabled fulfillment centers worldwide. By 2022, spending on robotic process automation is expected to hit $3 billion.

Artificial Intelligence could one day manage a marketplace or supply chain with little to no human involvement. Worldwide, AI and process automation spend is expected to reach $15 billion by end of 2021.

Personalized Retargeting will study past behavior, search history, and geography to more accurately predict future needs and desires of each customer and provide smarter CX.

Key Takeaways: Advanced Technical Features

- Internationalization opens a marketplace to the world, but myriad considerations (language, currency, payment, tax, shipping, images, etc.) must be addressed for each locale.

- Enhanced seller stores will enable sellers to create their own destination sites to promote themselves and their products.

- Alternative payments (PayPal, e-checks, Apple Pay, Bitcoin, Bill Me Later) are gaining traction and will likely account for 60% of all global eCommerce.

- Marketplace automation tools can drive efficiency and growth of the marketplace, particularly in price tracking, repricing, seller payments, and multi-channel management.

- Omnichannel order fulfillment allows customers to receive their ordered products through BOPIS, BORIS, BOSFS, and BOSS.

- Social media will be a major driver of digital commerce in the coming years, with the potential to account for as much as 7.8% of total retail by the end of 2024.

- Some of the other major technological features that will drive the growth of digital commerce platforms include augmented reality, voice search, and artificial intelligence.

Chapter 27: Advanced Business Models

The difference between market takers and market makers
isn't product innovation, its business model innovation

Vala Afshar – SalesForce Evangelist

Introduction

Creating a "me too" copy of an existing marketplace means tough head-to-head competition with established incumbents. Often a seemingly small tweak to a business model can be a major differentiator that leads to great success.

For example, food delivery has been around for decades in the categories of pizza and Chinese food. However, adding crowd-sourced food delivery services has enabled the DoorDash marketplace to grow from nothing to a valuation of over $50 billion in just seven years. Drizly added a twist to the beverage delivery model by offering a controlled substance—alcohol. In just nine years, startup Instacart grew to a $20 billion valuation in food delivery by facilitating transactions between four parties (grocers, CPG brands, delivery gig workers, and consumers) on their food delivery marketplace.

Services marketplaces, selling controlled substances, and 3+ party marketplaces are just a few of the many advanced business models discussed in this chapter. The services marketplace business model is so transformative that Chapter 8 Services Marketplaces was dedicated entirely to that topic. While there are countless possible marketplace business models, the information here is intended to provide inspiration for exploring new variations, launching a new marketplace, or enhancing an existing marketplace as it evolves to maturity level 5: Optimizing.

27.1 Selling Both B2C and B2B

The lines between B2C and B2B eCommerce have blurred as capabilities and user experiences are extended to both individual and business customers. There is often limited cost and good ROI when expanding service from just one type of customer type to both. Although this section focuses on B2C and B2B, there are also cross-over opportunities with the C2C and C2B business models described in Chapter 3 B2C v. B2B v. C2C v. C2B.

B2B clients may require additional capabilities not offered in B2C platforms. However, if the marketplace leverages a commercial eCommerce software platform (e.g. Magento or Hybris), many of these features may be easy to implement. Example B2B features include the following:

- Multiple payment types including credit terms like net 30 invoicing
- Approval workflows with multiple requesters and/or approvers.
- Buyer organizational modeling to define roles, spending limits, etc.
- Contract pricing or discounting by buyer company
- Splitting orders into multiple ship-to locations
- Configure, Price, & Quote (CPQ) for custom products or orders.

One of the biggest challenges for B2B marketplaces adding B2C sales is channel conflict. If a wholesaler or distributor has only sold to resellers or retailers, those customers may start viewing them as a competitor. There are often approaches to minimize this conflict such as enabling the reseller to fulfill an order to an end customer and earn some margin. Another approach is punch-out capability where the shopping cart is actually transferred to the reseller. An example of a B2B punch-out is configuring a Dell computer on the Dell website but completing the transaction on a separate website.

A related business twist is how retailers and marketplaces are responding to traditional B2B brands selling direct to consumer. Retailers and marketplaces are creating more private-label brands to sell instead of branded products. The Amazon Basics brand now sells more Amazon batteries than Duracell or Energizer. The cartoon below shows this conflict from both sides.

FIGURE 27.1: The morphing of brand manufacturers (B2B) and retailers (B2C)

27.2 Digital Goods Marketplace

The Apple App store sells over $60 billion of digital goods annually with a 30% commission resulting in roughly $20 billion of gross margin. The Google Play store does about half the amount at the same commission. That is a lot of gross margin without having to ship a single physical item.

Movies, music, games, books, software, training, PDF reports, and other digital goods are all sold or rented on digital marketplaces. It is hard to find someone today who has not consumed a digital product.

This presents a tremendous opportunity for marketplaces not only in terms of the market size but also in terms of convenience of selling. Inventory is never an issue, no physical storage is required, and customers get their product instantly.

Amazon has grown a successful digital movies and music offering by bundling a basic level of service with Prime. Udemy has developed a successful marketplace for training courses developed by third-party instructors.

Offering digital assets must include structured selling and distribution agreements that clearly define the differences between licensing and ownership. Often a Digital Rights Management (DRM) tool is required to control distribution and access, including limitations by country.

Digital marketplaces are not new. A marketplace launched in 2005 offered 15 million third-party ringtones, wallpapers, and other downloads for the early cellular telephones.

27.3 Federated Marketplace

The term "federated" is similar to the relationship between the USA federal government and the 50 states. Certain autonomy is granted to each state to operate within the federal guidelines. Each state can control its local brand (flag, motto, state bird), business logic (speed limits, permits, taxes), and management (governor, mayors, laws) within the federal allowances. In the context of a marketplace, the operator enables 3P sellers to also operate and manage their own branded store on the marketplace infrastructure without any marketplace branding. A federated florist marketplace launched in 2010 enabled 10,000 florists to offer their unique products and services on the central marketplace and also operate their own branded store. For a monthly subscription fee, each florist has their own branded robust storefront on which they could sell their own products (a floral bouquet in the colors of the local college). The florist can also sell standard marketplace products (a dozen red roses, a happy birthday balloon, a box of chocolates). Sellers can also configure their own business logic like promotions or cut-off times for same-day delivery.

Some eCommerce platform vendors have an offering similar to a federated marketplace. VTEX is an eCommerce cloud vendor that enables its clients to sell products sold by other VTEX clients, with the appropriate approvals. For example, if a consumer were shopping in the branded store of a tent manufacturer, that consumer may also be able to buy hiking boots from a boot company that also has a branded store on the VTEX cloud. Since the catalogs and payment processing are all in the same cloud infrastructure, viewing the products, processing the orders, and disbursing the payment is simplified.

27.4 B2B Procurement Marketplace

Many large businesses consolidate their purchasing through procurement systems or through e-procurement platforms (also called supplier exchanges). These systems offer improved spend visibility and control and help finance officers match purchases with purchase orders, receipts, and job tickets with improved efficiency and transparency. SAP Ariba, Coupa, and Ivalua are examples of procurement platforms.

However, other corporate procurement and purchase departments still rely on interacting directly with many independent suppliers but with concerns around quality, scale, and reliability. As more millennial's lead purchase departments, they are beginning to weigh the value of buying online for the business as they already do for personal shopping.

Procurement platforms provide many advantages over classic direct supplier relations.

B2B procurement marketplaces also provide the benefit of greater transparency in product, service, supplier, pricing, and purchasing terms. Below are some of the top B2B procurement marketplace platforms.

- Amazon is the largest B2B eCommerce platform in the world and is available in 14 countries including Brazil, Canada, France, United States, Italy, India, and Mexico.

- Alibaba has been in the market since 1999 and grown tremendously growth through cross border trade and supply. The platform is known to facilitate wholesalers, entrepreneurs, small business owners, and retailers of all sizes.

- eBay Business Supply is positioned as a one-stop-shop for all business needs with offerings across automotive, technology, construction, healthcare, facilities management, manufacturing, office supply, restaurant, and retail. Currently active in twenty-four countries, a partnership with SAP Ariba in 2014 helped the platform gain a stronger foothold in the segment by adding valuable new features for corporate procurement organizations.

- Dropee is an enterprise solution that allows businesses to buy and sell in bulk and streamline operational processes to work more efficiently and effectively. The platform currently specializes in the CPG and retail spaces.

Function	Classic Procurement Channels	Procurement Platforms
Procurement Department	Leverage economies of scale to reduce supply costs	Orchestrate networks to create value for end buyers
Procurement Strategy	Reduce supply costs through standardization and economies of scale	Meet buyers' needs, creating a self-regulated supplier ecosystem
Contract management	Yes	No
Pricing	Volumes and contract negotiation led by procurement	Market-based competition between suppliers
Suppliers	Sell to procurement	Sell to end buyers
Supplier Selection Process	Suppliers selected by procurement and provided to end buyers	Authorized by procurement but selected by end buyers when buying on the platform
Supplier catalog publication and master data management	Procurement team distributes supplier catalogs, inventory internally and is in charge of master data	Each supplier is responsible for its own catalog, inventory and master data on the platform
Price	Discounts based on annual committed volumes	Constantly updated by suppliers in order to stay competitive on the platform

TABLE 27.1 Source: Mirakl & Roland Berger

B2B marketplaces present vast opportunities for business growth at global levels. In the new democratized digital world, B2B marketplace platforms will be a major driver for this goal.

27.5 Selling Restricted or Controlled Products

Many retailers and marketplaces shy away from the legal complexities and liabilities of selling controlled substances like alcohol, chemicals, weapons, and marijuana-related products. That means less competition in those markets for the companies that are willing to tackle these challenges.

Adult products	Fur	Lock-picking devices
Candles	Gambling devices	Matches
Coral	Gas masks	Medical devices
Currency	Handcuffs	Medical specimens
Damaged batteries	Helmets	Military uniforms
Dietary supplements	Human growth hormone	Night vision devices
Explosives	Jumpsuits	Pesticides
Fire extinguishers	Lab reagents	Poisonous substances
Fireworks	Lighters	Police shields
Fuels	Live plants	Radioactive products
Rough diamonds	The skin of certain reptiles	Tear gas
Seeds	Sky lanterns	Tobacco
Sharp objects	Steroids	Waste

TABLE 27.2

A myriad of licenses, permits, shipping restrictions, international regulations, plus state and local laws add complexity to these areas of business. Some items (lithium batteries, chemicals) have restrictions on shipment by air. States, counties, and cities usually have different regulations on selling liquor, wine, and beer that can vary by the day of the week or the time of day. There has been a huge rush to capitalize on the legalization of marijuana and CBD-related products and paraphernalia, but those laws also vary by state with federal regulations about shipping across state lines. Firearms, ammunition, and certain accessories like suppressors may have background-check, licensing, and shipping constraints.

In the early wild west days of eBay, there were rumors of human organs for sale. Illegal or unethical products and services are sold on dark web marketplaces. We do not advocate any such activity. There are legal and ethical ways of selling products and services which are controlled, such as wine, lithium batteries, medicines, cleaning chemicals.

Approach each product as a separate scenario which needs careful assessment before action. Some goods may not be restricted, but marketplace operators and their sellers still need authorization. Following is a list of items against which carry selling and shipping restrictions inside the US and may have similar restrictions elsewhere. Check and comply with all such restrictions before beginning operations.

Some marketplace operators have met the challenges of regulatory compliance and are finding success online.

Vivino is the world's largest online wine marketplace and most downloaded wine app. Millions of wine shoppers enjoy the unique experience of personalized wine recommendations, easy wine discovery, and home delivery.

Sovos ShipCompliant provides a full suite of cloud-based solutions to wineries, breweries, distilleries, importers, distributors, and retailers to ensure they meet all federal and state regulations for direct-to-consumer and three-tier distribution.

27.6 Multi-Party Marketplaces

Most marketplaces connect two parties: a third-party seller with a customer. However, an emerging business model is marketplaces with more than two parties. DoorDash is an example of a 3-party marketplace that connects restaurants, delivery gig workers, and consumers

All three sides of the marketplace sometimes pay or collect fees. Drivers get paid for making reliable deliveries on time, restaurants pay a commission to DoorDash on each order, and the customers pay a small delivery fee, either explicitly added to a bill or embedded in the total cost.

FIGURE 27.2 DoorDash Business Model

Instacart is an example of a 4-party marketplace that connects grocery stores, personal shoppers, consumers, and CPG brands. Via website and mobile app, the marketplace offers grocery delivery and pick-up service in 5,500 cities across the US and Canada. They partner with over 350 retailers that cumulatively operate more than 25,000 grocery stores including Albertsons, Aldi, Costco, CVS Health, Eataly, H-E-B, Kroger, Loblaw Companies, Petco, Publix, Safeway Inc., Sam's Club, Sprouts Farmers Market, Target Corporation, Total Wine & More, and Wegmans. Instacart has also been expanding into retail categories outside of grocery.

Chapter 10 Grocery Business Case Study – Instacart provides greater detail about the company's full operation.

27.7 Community Building

Community building is one of the most powerful ways to connect with an audience and develops the much more valuable fans of your brand compared to mere consumers of your brand. Vision, creativity, and time investments are needed to develop rabid fans, but they will serve as the best unpaid salespeople. Great user-generated content (UGC) is often one of the most valuable assets of communities. However, a clear vision, purpose, and value proposition is needed to encourage users to contribute that content.

Communities obviously vary based on their focus. The Etsy community is focused on vintage, craft, and handmade goods while the Farfetch community is interested in high-end luxury goods. Both are very successful marketplaces with strong communities.

Houzz is a platform and online community focused on home architecture, interior design and decorating, landscape design, and home improvement. A small community of just 20 parents started collecting images of home renovations in 2009, before the days of Pinterest and Instagram. In 2010 Houzz was formed and the user base and image collection scaled into the millions. Designers, architects, other service providers, and manufacturers also started posting photos of their work and products. Articles and discussions added to the rich user-generated content and provide even more inspiration to users. This large and passionate community of consumers and sellers provided an opportunity for Houzz to monetize connections for services, products, and advertising.

Airbnb is a brand built around a community of belonging. One of the value propositions is giving customers the chance to immerse themselves in the community they're visiting. Similarly, they allow the host community to connect with each other globally. This way both the traveler and hosts feel like part of a large community.

Some best practices around community building for marketplace include the following:

- Define the mission in a way that helps to identify the people who relate to it.

- Leverage existing communities.

- When starting a new marketplace, spend time to know and understand early members.

- Create frameworks for people to interact and facilitate conversations.

27.8 Used & Refurbished Goods Marketplace

To those with limited exposure to marketplaces, the term used good may bring visions of selling used Pez dispensers on eBay. In reality, almost all of the $2 trillion spent globally on marketplaces is for new goods. However, there is an opportunity for many marketplaces to expand their offerings with used or refurbished goods. Although used goods may not be glamorous, this market is worth $300 billion in the US.

Craigslist was one early disruptor in used goods when it took a large market share from newspaper classified ads. However, many specialty marketplaces for used goods carved vertical segments out of Craigslist. Examples of specialty used good marketplaces include 1stdibs, Chegg, Etsy, Gazelle, OfferUp, Rent the Runway, StockX, StubHub, The RealReal, Tradesy, and Vestiaire Collective. To see others, search the internet for "unbundling Craigslist. Following are a few examples of successful used goods Marketplaces.

Facebook Marketplace started in 2007 but met with limited success. Since relaunch in 2016, the new look and features, included location-based selling, 500 million people buy and sell items every month.

Letgo makes shipping options available but also allows users to find the exact location of the listing and encourages users to make in-person transactions. One nice feature is the use of video templates to upload and list items for sale.

ThredUp is a P2P marketplace platform for swapping clothes. ThredUp sends pre-paid, pre-addressed bags to users who intend to sell their used clothes, and then operator employees photograph, list, and ship the items to buyers.

OfferUp is an online mobile-first C2C marketplace with an emphasis on in-person transactions. It differentiates itself from Craigslist with a feature-rich mobile-friendly app and user profiles with ratings. One standout feature is the TruYou system that helps verify the identity of sellers and buyers through ID scan and selfie photos. Another unique aspect of OfferUp is that payment does not happen on the platform. When a seller accepts a buyer's offer, the app helps arrange a meeting time and place to close the deal including payment.

27.9 Fulfillment as a Service

Amazon has driven the customer expectation for delivery timeframes from a week to 2-days to 1-day to same-day and, perhaps soon, to 2-hour or 30 minutes with drone delivery. Small retailers and brands cannot meet those expectations on their own, but a large marketplace or a retailer with store-based fulfillment can.

Fulfillment as a service enables third-party sellers to tap into a sophisticated distributed logistics capability with no or minimal capital investments in warehouses, warehouse automation, delivery personnel, automated packaging equipment, geographic demand forecasting, etc. FBA has been a key driver of this phenomenon.

Send products to Amazon   Amazon stores products   Customers purchase   Amazon picks up products   Amazon ships products

FIGURE 27.3 Selling on Amazon FBA

Sellers send products to Amazon where they are stored in one or more of over a hundred Amazon fulfillment centers. Amazon's automated pick-and-pack robotics plus hundreds of thousands of distribution center employees efficiently store and retrieve goods. Historical data and ongoing machine learning determine the best distribution of goods across multiple distribution centers based on expected geographic demand. Shipping is handled by several carriers, including 30,000 Amazon-branded vehicles, many of which are operated by third parties. The package may even be delivered by a gig economy delivery driver from the Amazon Flex marketplace. FBA will also handle the reverse logistics of returns.

Walmart Fulfilment Services (WFS) operated under similar protocol and guarantees national 2-day delivery. WFS provides order tracking and reporting and also supports returns. Like FBA, there are restrictions on item weight and dimensions.

Micro-Fulfillment Centers are an opportunity for retailers with many stores. Stock in stores can be considered forward-deployed inventory in the delivery supply chain. Grocers like Albertsons have begun deploying small automated fulfillment robotics in many of their stores. As the pandemic reduced foot traffic in stores and increased online orders, the conversion of some retail space to local fulfillment meets changing customer expectations. Some retailers and restaurants have begun operating "dark stores" or "dark restaurants" which focus on deliveries or pick-up orders only. Dark stores or stores with micro-fulfillment centers can stock both 1P inventory and 3P inventory on consignment.

For instance, Fabric, formerly CommonSense Robotics, is a sample logistics platform that makes on-demand fulfillment possible for retailers. The company offers multi-tenant and private networks of automated micro-fulfillment centers that make on-demand fulfillment profitable by location automation physically close to end customers. These solutions enable cloud-like elasticity for retailers, enabling flexibility to build a custom solution based on inventory level, desired reach, and OPEX and CapEx requirements, expanding and flexing as needs change.

3PL services are another option for contracting with companies that provide fulfillment as a service. A marketplace can contract with one or more 3PL service providers to rapidly build a fulfillment network with no or limited capital expense, but a recurring operating expense.

Key Takeaways: Advanced Business Models

- Varying the marketplace business model can provide a substantial competitive advantage to drive rapid growth of users, revenue, profit, and company valuation.

- Some of the variations on marketplace business models include 1) selling both B2C and B2B, 2) digital goods, 3) extending a federated marketplace to third parties, 4) B2B procurement, 5) selling restricted or controlled products, 6) multi-party marketplaces, 7) building community, 8) used & refurbished goods, and 9) fulfillment as a service.

- The costs and timeframes of different business models must be evaluated as some may require substantial capital expense (e.g. fulfillment as a service).

- Constant business and technology innovation is a core aspect of attaining and maintaining Marketplace Maturity Model level 5: Optimizing.

Chapter 28: Marketplace Enablement Steps

28.1 Assessment & Planning
28.2 Business Preparation
28.3 MVP Build & Deploy
28.4 Platform Enhancement

By failing to prepare, you are preparing to fail

Benjamin Franklin – Founding Father of United States

Introduction

The Marketplace Maturity Model (MMM) covered in chapter 2 is the core definition of *what* a marketplace is by level of capability. The Marketplace Enablement Steps[SM] (MES) covered in this chapter is the core definition of *how* to launch and operate a marketplace.

Marketplace Enablement Steps are grouped by four major phases and two tracks. The four phases are assessment, minimum viable product (MVP), full deployment, and operations. The two tracks are strategy/business and technology.

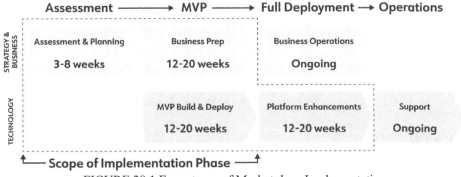

FIGURE 28.1 Four stages of Marketplace Implementation

The diagram above shows the four major phases and the two tracks. This chapter is organized into the four activities within the dashed line which highlights implementation activities. Chapter 30 "Ongoing Operations" addresses the two other activities, business operations and support.

28.1 Assessment & Planning

The assessment and planning phase defines and maps the route to marketplace success. This phase typically takes three to eight weeks, and the following table lists the core activities, the level of effort, and the parties involved.

Assessment & Planning Timeline 3-8 weeks Activities	Effort	Implementation Agency				Marketplace Operator		
		Project Manager	Strategist	Business Analyst	Tech Architect	Executive Sponsor	Business Lead	IT Architect
Strategy Formation	H	✓	✓	✓		✓	✓	
Financial Planning	M		✓			✓	✓	
Scope Definition	M		✓	✓	✓		✓	✓
Project Planning	M	✓	✓	✓	✓		✓	✓
Organizational Design	M		✓	✓			✓	
Architecture Design	M			✓	✓			✓

TABLE 28.1

Strategy Formation

British innovation researcher Max McKeown said that strategy is about shaping the future to achieve desirable ends with available means. Aspiring marketplace operators must define their desired end and their available means. In reality, marketplaces are an ongoing journey and not a single endpoint.

Although one can argue that maximizing net profit or company valuation are the ultimate objective, there are many other goals along the journey. For example, what is most helpful in maximizing profit or valuation: the largest catalog, the lowest item cost, the most customers, or depth within one niche? Sometimes the learnings from an unprofitable online marketplace can justify the investment if they dramatically improve brick and mortar operations.

Different organizations have different means, such as their customer base, access to sellers, brand value, distribution channels, technology, niche solutions, business model, content, or other assets.

Simply trying to be another Amazon, eBay, Etsy, or Uber is not a viable strategy. It is important to differentiate, and its best to do so by building upon the means unique to each operator. Examples of differentiation are described in Chapter 26 Advanced Technical Features and Chapter 27 Advanced Business Models. A thorough review of the competitive landscape helps identify potential areas of differentiation.

Markets that are currently inefficient provide an opportunity for transformation by a marketplace. For example, how efficient is it for a passenger to wait on a street corner for a taxi to randomly pass by, or for a taxi to drive randomly hoping to find a passenger on a street corner? Uber brought efficiency to the car transportation market by connecting drivers and passengers for a fee.

Key deliverables of the strategy formation work include a strategy document, competitive analysis, marketing plan, and success metrics called KPIs.

Financial Planning

Business initiatives are usually born based on a forecast of great financial returns. They are also often killed for not achieving good financial returns. Proper financial planning is key to the life and death of business initiatives.

The financial engine that drives marketplaces has a different structure than that of traditional retail or ecommerce. Revenue includes fees (commissions, subscription, listing, etc.), advertising (featured products, search headlines, display ads, etc.), and other sources (licensing data, fulfillment services, etc.).

There are also different capital expenses and operating expenses. Additional CapEx may be needed to start spinning the marketplace flywheel, but once started lower OpEx is required to keep it going. Expenses include software licensing, implementation services, marketing, staff salaries, and payment processing fees.

Financial planning activities include defining a budget and optimizing the areas of investment for maximum ROI. This exercise must be done in parallel with other activities in the assessment and planning phase. For example, the strategy, scope, organizational design, technology stack all impacts the return and the investment.

Additional details about financial planning are covered in chapter 5: Marketplace Financial Model.

Scope Definition

Clearly documenting scope is critical to managing and meeting expectations. Scope also drives cost, timeline, project plans, and technical architecture.

At a minimum, scope should include customer-facing, seller-facing, and operator-facing features and capabilities. It should also include non-visual aspects which may affect future scalability and extensibility. For example, expectations should be set about technology aspects like a microservices architecture, unit tests, and test automation.

Scope can also include other non-functional requirements (NFR) like performance, scalability, availability, recoverability, maintainability, security, etc. An example performance requirement could be supporting 100,000 page views per hour or page load times of less than 2 seconds.

It is best to take a product mindset when defining scope. Even though an aspiring marketplace operator might be a retailer, distributor, or manufacturing brand it is best to consider the digital platform as a product, much like a software development firm would. This mindset focuses on the product's purpose and minimizing the time to value by solving a business need.

A well-documented scope also serves as a baseline for change management once a project is underway. Many tools like Atlassian Jira are available for tracking scope, requirements, and change management. Chapter 29 discusses these tools.

MoSCoW Prioritization

M — **Must have:** Non-negotiable product needs that are mandatory for the team.

S — **Should have:** Important initiatives that are not vital, but add significant value.

C — **Could have:** Nice to have initiatives that will have a small impact if left out.

W — **Will not have:** Initiatives that are not a priority for this specific time frame.

FIGURE 28.2 MoSCoW Prioritization

One of the many frameworks available for scope prioritization and roadmap creation is a simple metric called MoSCoW. Scope priority is defined by whether the product must have, should have, could have, and will not have each feature.

Project Planning

A project plan involves time-bound visualization of the major project milestones and the estimated timelines and go-live dates for the same. It starts with the scope and ends when a marketplace platform is delivered with all integrations in place and final UAT done.

The project plan, or a corresponding staffing plan, also shows the number and type of resources to be engaged at each stage of the project and how they will be used through the project lifecycle.

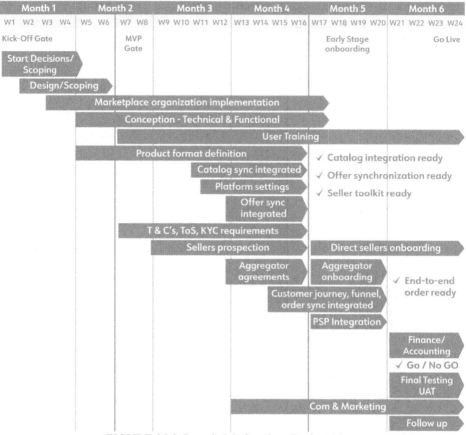

FIGURE 28.3 Sample Marketplace Project Plan

A roadmap for a project is collectively owned by the team that defines it and roles it out. Primary owners include Project Managers, Business Analysts, Business Owners, Product Owners, Technical Architects, etc.

A strategic roadmap defines a goal or desired outcome (in this case a fully functional marketplace platform) and identifies the major milestones to get there. A roadmap also serves as a communications tool, a high-level document that helps articulate strategic thinking (the why) behind both the goal and the plan.

By definition, a road map should be simple and concise enough to be understood by anyone in order to manage stakeholder expectations and communicate plans across all management teams within the company. Usually, it is the business product team and respective business analysts that help define the roadmap for the marketplace implementation project.

The process of developing a credible roadmap involves whittling down the goals and objectives that truly deserve to make the cut. This process is the result of lengthy analysis and deliberations across multiple teams. The coherence of a roadmap is enhanced when strategies and goals are set, and the team moves on to prioritizing marketplace features and enhancements based on a variety of criteria.

Organizational Design

At least some of these roles are likely to be dedicated specifically to the marketplace, especially the marketplace leader and those dealing with seller recruiting and onboarding, while others may be shared with the more traditional ecommerce operation, such as technical, marketing, finance, and customer support roles. The initial organizational structure should be able to support the build and launch phase, then revisited periodically to expand the team appropriately as the marketplace grows.

The simplified marketplace organizational design shown in Figure 28.4 below is discussed in greater detail in Chapter 20 Organization Structure.

FIGURE 28.4 Organizational Design

Architecture Design

While marketplaces have similar functionality needs, there are a variety of ways to architect such a site. An organization must determine precisely what the tech stack will look like, what technologies and software platforms will be used, and when they will be needed. The detailed architectural design in Figure 28.5 below shows the primary components and interfaces of a marketplace.

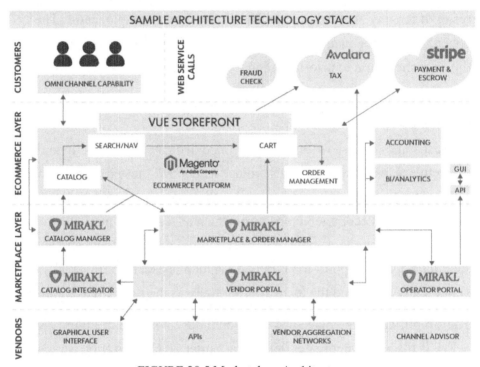

FIGURE 28.5 Marketplace Architecture

The top layer of the marketplace consists of four elements used for communication with the end users. The marketplace management configures price models and applies settlement rules and policies. Composition support is where the customer defines his request and customizes the product or service. Payment is where sellers and providers get information about financial transactions. Finally, reporting is where sellers and buyers can access information regarding services, consumption, billing, etc.

28.2 Business Preparation

Business preparation is the second stage of the marketplace implementation as shown in Figure 28.1. At this stage, many of the business activities are clearly defined, so marketplace operations can hit the ground running. A major effort of this stage focuses on sellers—category selection, terms and conditions, and recruiting and onboarding.

Business Preparation		Implementation Agency					Marketplace Operator				
Timeline 12-20 weeks / Activities	Effort	Project Manager	Strategist	Business Analyst	Tech Architect	UX Designer	Executive Sponsor	Business Lead	Merchandiser	IT Architect	Legal
Category Selection	M		✓	✓			✓	✓	✓		
Define Seller T&C's	H		✓	✓			✓	✓			✓
Seller Recruiting & Onboarding	H			✓				✓	✓		
Design UX Changes	M			✓		✓		✓	✓		
Marketing Strategy	M		✓	✓			✓	✓	✓		
Shipping Strategy	L		✓	✓				✓			
Metrics & Reporting	M		✓	✓			✓	✓	✓		
User Acceptance Test	M	✓		✓	✓			✓	✓		
Program Mgt & Governance	M	✓		✓	✓		✓	✓	✓		

TABLE 28.2

Category Selection

Deciding what product categories the marketplace will carry at launch is one of the most important early decisions. Based on an initial market opportunity study, these categories should have unmet demand and availability of high-quality sellers. One of the key deliverables of this activity is a robust category and curation strategy. Best practice dictates starting small in a niche area and growing slowly, the way Amazon started with books and became the shopping mall of the world.

Seller Terms & Conditions

Sellers should clearly understand exactly what they are signing up for, and transparency at this stage helps establish trust. Set the terms and conditions across all areas to inform sellers of marketplace operations, requirements, and rights. Some of these include:

- Privacy
- Electronic communications
- Copyrights & trademarks
- License and site access
- Fair usage of the marketplace site
- Services description
- Disclaimer of warranties and limitation of liabilities
- Applicable law & disputes
- Site policies, modification, and severability

Seller Onboarding & Recruiting

Sellers are the lifeblood of any successful marketplace, providing the breadth and depth of offerings that drive purchases and customer loyalty. Define clear internal guidelines for recruiting the right type of sellers for the marketplace. Some helpful questions include:

- Which brands or sellers are a fit for the marketplace?
- Should sellers offer products of similar type and feature or a broader selection of items?
- How many sellers should be onboarded?
- Are the sellers relevant to the global strategy (product, pricing, and quality of service)?

- What will the onboarding process look like?

Design & UX Changes

Revisit the initial designs and wireframes to look for needed UI/UX changes, incorporating time and labor estimates into the plan. The prime objective of designing a user experience that encourages customers to return is achieved by focusing on three key areas:

- Ease of navigation and a smooth path to purchase
- Appealing appearance and easy to read information
- Secure payment and transaction interface

Marketing Strategy

While the marketing plan at the assessment and planning stage is more concerned with how to spread awareness and engage buyers, the marketing plan at this stage gets into more specifics. The initial marketing budget is likely to be high as the operator seeks both sellers and buyers simultaneously. The overall marketing plan should address these points.

- Defined customer acquisition strategy
- Channel selection
- Frequency plan
- Key value proposition
- Differentiating messaging
- Growth strategy
- Communications plan for the seller audience

Shipping Strategy

The marketplace team need to decide on merchant, marketplace, 3P, or hybrid fulfillment models. Clear measurements and goals need to be defined and used to drive ongoing improvement while diagnosing and resolving issues. These could include:

- Increase conversions
- Decrease fulfillment time

- Increase average order value
- Expand market or target audience
- Decrease overall cost of shipping
- Improve operational efficiency

Metrics & Reporting

Success can only be managed if it can be measured, so determining what metrics to track in reference to sellers, buyers, and internal business operations is vital to the successful operation and growth of any marketplace. It is also important at this stage to define the frequency of reporting and who will be accountable for reviewing the data and producing actionable insights for insights.

User Acceptance Testing

User Acceptance Testing (UAT) involves testing the marketplace app, website, or other form of software to assess if it operates according to its functional requirements. UAT discovers anomalies so that they can be fixed before customers interact with the platform.

Program Management & Governance

Once new team members in place to launch and manage the new eCommerce property, team structure for ongoing marketplace management needs to be formalized. This ensures that everyone is aligned toward the project gates and timelines, marketplace vision and objectives, and target timetables for each deliverable. Various teams—steering committee, project management team, technical team, business development and operations team—create a dotted line collaboration to oversee governance.

28.3 MVP Build & Deploy

This is an important stage, where critical pieces come together. It is the third phase of the marketplace implementation as shown in Figure 28.1 and can take anywhere between twelve and twenty weeks, depending on the project complexity. MVP as a product development methodology focuses on building a workable product with minimum features for the early users who then provide feedback for future product development.

MVP Build & Deploy												
MVP Build & Deploy	**Effort**	Implementation Agency							Marketplace Operator			
Timeline 12-20 weeks / Activities		Dev Team	Project Manager	Business Analyst	UI/UX Specialist	QA Analyst	Tech Architect	DevOps	Business Team	Product Owner	IT Manager/ Lead	Tech Architect
Environment Setup, Implementation Planning	H	✓	✓					✓	✓	✓	✓	✓
Tech and Hi Level Arch	M		✓	✓			✓					✓
Taxonomy	M			✓			✓		✓	✓	✓	
Basic Integrations: tax, payments	M	✓			✓			✓		✓	✓	✓
UI Changes	M	✓		✓	✓					✓		
Seller Integrations	M	✓		✓						✓	✓	
Iterative Dev & test	H	✓			✓	✓					✓	
System Integration Testing, Load & Performance testing	M	✓			✓	✓	✓		✓			
UAT	M		✓	✓		✓			✓	✓	✓	✓
Go Live	L	✓	✓			✓	✓	✓	✓	✓	✓	✓

TABLE 28.3

Environment Setup and Implementation Planning

To test the production environment (where customers will shop), an identical testing environment is set up to uncover any environment or configuration related issues. A complete testing environment includes hardware configuration, operating system settings, software configuration, test terminals, and other support to perform the test. Careful set up of the identical testing environment is critical to ensure reliable test results.

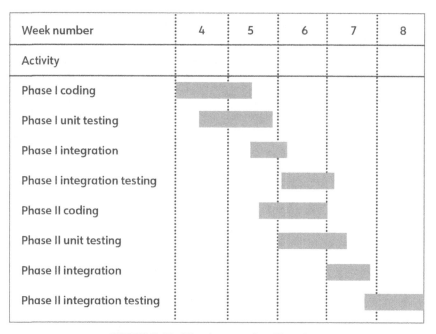

Week number	4	5	6	7	8
Activity					
Phase I coding					
Phase I unit testing					
Phase I integration					
Phase I integration testing					
Phase II coding					
Phase II unit testing					
Phase II integration					
Phase II integration testing					

FIGURE 28.6 Implementation Planning

The implementation plan, a subset of the overall project plan, moves the project plan into action. It identifies goals and objectives and lays out project tasks, roles, and responsibilities. The key components of an implementation plan are goals and objectives, scheduled milestones, resource allocation, and definition of success metrics.

Technical Architecture

Design the high-level technical architecture of the marketplace to show the various components, systems, integration, and workflows. Good technical architecture helps the operator, users, and sellers understand, negotiate, and communicate with one another and makes it easier to understand the system as a whole. Technical architecture should result in the following outcomes for the software.

- User-friendly and flexible

- Scalable and sustainable

- Intuitive and following user expectation

- Easy to add and modify functionalities.

Many organizations make the technical architecture too complex in an effort to represent too many aspects. Instead, it should be simple and primarily used for collaboration, communication, vision, and guidance across teams. It should contain significant design decisions and nothing more.

Taxonomy

To support a robust search mechanism, top-level navigation, and granular product creation, define a clear and logical product category taxonomy. Research methods for taxonomy development Tree Sort, Card Sort, Competitive Analysis, Direct Interviews with Sellers, direct interview with buyers, and Stakeholder Interviews.

Tax & Payment Integrations

Tax and payment are best handled by third-party software integrated with the ERP and marketplace platform. In this step of the MVP build and deploy, ensure that all systems work together. Many marketplace platforms have customized connectors for each of the major service providers across tax calculation and payments to make integration easier. The completion of these integrations should also facilitate the following outcomes.

- Manage tax rates locally for countries and regions where sales tax is required.
- Set prices inclusive or exclusive of tax and customize invoices.
- Connect online marketplace to third-party sales tax tool to automate tax filing.

UI Changes

The main goal of good UI is to make the user interaction efficient, simple, and intuitive. In the marketplace world, intuitive interfaces and appealing designs are an indispensable part of the user experience and can drastically impact the website performance and overall conversions.

With the UI changes identified in the initial planning and business preparation stages, examine the following:

- Input controls: Radio buttons, checkboxes, dropdown lists, dropdown buttons, text fields, and toggles.
- Navigational components: search field, breadcrumbs, image carousels, sliders, and pagination.
- Informational components: progress bars, notifications, tooltips, message boxes, and pop-ups.

One of the key outputs of the UI changes step is to ensure client specific themes and designs have been incorporated.

Seller Integration

Seller integration automates all the business processes associated with selling on the marketplace—product listing, bulk product uploads, inventory syncing—through the use of APIs. All seller integration testing is done in a sandbox setup and all sellers need to HTTPS requests.

Iterative Development & Testing

In an iterative model, a handful of processes are developed and tested. When complete, the cycle repeats with a new set of processes, thus improving the software with each iteration. This method offers rapid adaptability and turn-around while ensuring the application is functioning according to the initial set of requirements.

SIT, Performance & Load Testing

Now that all the functional testing is done, test the marketplace for integration, performance, and loads. Systems integration testing (SIT) is carried out in an integrated hardware and software environment to verify the behavior of the complete system. Modules are first tested individually and then combined to testing interaction between modules and with the system as a whole.

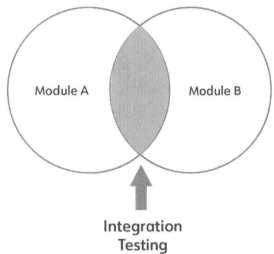

Integration Testing

FIGURE 28.7 Integration Testing

Performance testing is mainly concerned with sensitivity, reactivity, and stability under a particular workload. Speed, scalability, stability, and reliability are tested under normal load to validates the performance.

By contrast, load testing checks the performance of the system under real-world load conditions, such as multiple users accessing the application at the same time. Mostly the sustainability of the system is tested during load testing, not other parameters.

User Acceptance Testing (UAT)

UAT is key to determining if the website application and its functions are up to par and perform at a level to be successful in the market. Generally, this is when anomalies and bugs are discovered and fixed. Key elements of UAT for marketplaces are:

- Design testing
- Usability Testing
- Functional Testing
- Security Testing

For accurate UAT execution, engage professional, objective testers who have the necessary training, experiences, and unbiased perspective. For a marketplace operator, this could mean using an in-house QA testing team or a third-party, not the development team.

Go Live

Regardless of how much testing took place, the go-live moment is sure to be rocky and tense, but a go-live checklist to restructure and streamline development tasks can help mitigate some of the risks.

Set a maintenance page on the former website if migrating to a new application and update the DNS to point the domain name to the production IP address. Also ensure that monitoring is enabled, and the right people on each team are set up to receive the alerts.

Make sure SEO is in place after the right domain name is set up for the application. Check that all required redirects work as expected, review canonical links, make sure that the sitemap is referenced in robots.txt, and confirm the index follow is enabled. Care must be taken to ensure all integrations use production credentials.

28.4 Platform Enhancement

This is the last phase of the marketplace implementation as shown in Figure 28.1. After the marketplace platform has been deployed and opened to real-world users, look to carry out iterative enhancements in areas like 3P integrations, automation, SEO, and UX. Examine the data and actively seek opinions from customers and sellers, listening to the voices and digital body language of both audiences as ways to drive improvements.

Platform Enhancement

Platform Enhancement / Timeline 12-20 weeks / Activities	Effort	Implementation Agency							Marketplace Operator			
		Dev Team	Project Manager	Business Analyst	UI/UX Specialist	QA Analyst	Tech Architect	DevOps	Business Team	Product Owner	IT Manager/ Lead	Tech Architect
Advanced Integrations	H	✓	✓					✓		✓	✓	
Automations (Seller, Integrations)	H	✓	✓	✓							✓	
CX & SEO Enhancements	M	✓	✓		✓		✓		✓	✓	✓	✓
Performance Tuning	M	✓	✓			✓	✓				✓	
Advanced Reporting & BI	H	✓	✓						✓	✓	✓	
Advanced Promos & Coupons	M	✓	✓				✓		✓	✓	✓	✓
Internationali zation	M	✓	✓		✓	✓			✓	✓	✓	
Omnichannel Expansion	M	✓	✓	✓	✓	✓				✓	✓	
Social Media Integration	M	✓	✓		✓				✓	✓	✓	

TABLE 28.4

Advanced Integrations

One of the first areas for platform enhancement is eCommerce business apps, integrations that would help create a better eCommerce platform, improve sales, and provide better user experience. Third-party marketing and conversion apps provide marketing automation, customer loyalty and referral programs, conversion rate optimization, Facebook ads integration along with many other services. Shipping apps provide logistics, fulfillment, label printing, and shipping optimization. These integrations allow functionality such as automated product uploads, inventory syncing & automated route orders with dropship suppliers and give the marketplace operator a way to streamline every step of the fulfillment process, reduce handling time, and minimize errors.

Automated Seller Integrations

Key focuses of a newly launched marketplace are to onboard a large number of high-quality sellers to increase the breadth of products and services and to help sellers become successful by selling more and better on the platform. One way to get there faster is by using automation for the integration of product and order data. For example, Amazon allows many 3P platforms to integrate into Amazon Seller Central. Some of these automations help easily and accurately manage orders and track inventory in one place, without a lot of manual effort. Similarly, find ways to help sellers get better at what they are doing through the platform.

CX and SEO Enhancements

Have tools in place to identify and fix CX problems that had not been considered in the planning and building processes. Plan regular releases in the weeks after go-live to swiftly address these pain points. Along with user feedback, keep a general eye on the site design, home page, navigation, and security of the marketplace site.

SEO is mission-critical for a new marketplace, so bring in an SEO agency at the beginning. Basic on-page and technical optimization should be a standard part of all platform enhancements after launch. Investing in paid search is also a good strategy the help establish the marketplace presence.

Performance Tuning

In the way that load and performance testing are critical before launch, site performance tuning is equally important after launch. Continually check website speed and load test results to identify any bottlenecks.

Compression tools can optimize site images. Additional steps—like reducing HTTP requests by inlining JavaScript, using CSS Sprites, reducing assets like third-party plugins that make a large number of external requests—can compound to show tangible gains.

Another area to focus on is to look at the latency caused by the content delivery network (CDN). Apart from speeding up the delivery of your assets around the globe, a CDN also can significantly decrease your latency.

Advanced Reporting & BI

As more customers and sellers are added to the marketplace, the need for cutting edge business intelligence and reporting will increase so that decisions are based on data and numbers. Kissmetrics & Mixpanel provide expert level analytics for deep insights about visitor behavior and user engagement with a website or app. Baremetrics and ChartMogul provide SaaS-focused metrics like MRR, ARR, Churn, Revenue per subscription, etc. For large marketplaces, Adobe Analytics can handle large data capacity and product attributes. Also consult with marketplace strategy and technical partners for reporting options and insights. They will often have playbooks or reporting augmentations specific to growing marketplaces.

Advanced Promos & Coupons

For most consumers, discovering discounts, coupons, and other deals is an integral part of a great shopping experience. A recent survey indicated that 97% of consumers look for a deal while shopping and 92% look for promotional offers. Advanced capabilities to run coupons and promo code programs will help to boost conversions, acquisition, and customer retention.

While there are many 3P apps to accommodate advanced promotions, some best-of-breed SaaS eCommerce platforms offer dozens of promotional coupon options out-of-the-box. Using advanced promotion and discount options, sellers can run deeply customized campaigns and apply cart level discounting across product categories to grow overall sales.

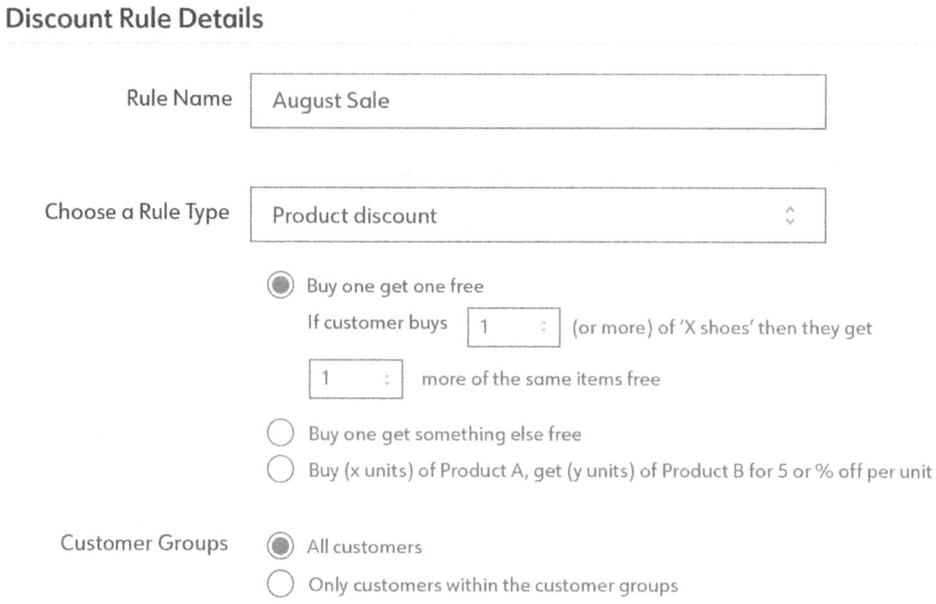

Discount Rule Details

Rule Name

| August Sale |

Choose a Rule Type

| Product discount ⌃⌄ |

◉ Buy one get one free

If customer buys | 1 ⌄ | (or more) of 'X shoes' then they get

| 1 ⌄ | more of the same items free

◯ Buy one get something else free

◯ Buy (x units) of Product A, get (y units) of Product B for 5 or % off per unit

Customer Groups ◉ All customers

◯ Only customers within the customer groups

FIGURE 28.8 Advanced Promos

Internationalization

Beyond simple language translation and cultural understanding, catering to a global audience involves technically equipping the marketplace to handle multiple languages, currencies, measurements, numbers, times, addresses, and sorting rules, and even culturally appropriate content, symbols, and images. All these should be on the radar of developers working on internationalization as part of the platform enhancement.

Omnichannel Expansion

Omnichannel shopping creates a seamless customer journey wherein the customer views all sales and marketing channels as a single entity. Focus on having quality data about the customer to create a highly personalized interaction at every channel and integrating all channel information into the backend.

Data unification can be challenging as it requires significant expertise to collect and connect data like customer behavior, purchases, and demographic data. This data needs to be collected across devices to create a single customer view. Successful omnichannel expansion enables the customer to toggle between multiple channels while completing a transaction.

Social Media Integration

Modern buyers love to share and discuss their purchases, but an increasing number are also purchasing directly through interaction with social media platforms. Social commerce is the process of buying or selling products via social media. Key enablement steps for social commerce include:

- Add a Buy button to posts to ease the process of buying items. Mostly customers are redirected to the marketplace site once they click here.

- Create shoppable galleries that allow the customer to click on the tag and redirect to the product page. Adding multiple tags on one picture allows retailers to sell multiple items within one blog or album.

- Social sharing buttons on product pages allow customers to share the store's items in their social feeds, build marketplace credibility, and create word of mouth marketing.

Key Takeaways: Marketplace Enablement Steps

- Some key elements of the Assessment and Planning stage are strategy formation, financial planning, organization, and architecture design. The role of the executive sponsor is key to this phase.

- The business preparation stage centers around seller enablement with tasks like category selection, seller terms and conditions, seller onboarding, and recruiting. The development work is less at this stage.

- The MVP build and deploy stage is where the bulk of development activity takes place, including environment set up, tech architecture, basic integrations, and UAT.

- The platform enhancement stage is heavily focused on developing enhanced capabilities around integration, automation, customer experience, and business intelligence.

Chapter 29: Implementation Methodologies & Tools

Operations keep the lights on, strategy provides a light at the end of the tunnel, but project management is the train engine that moves the organization forward.

Joy Gumz– Author

Introduction

There are various methodologies for managing the development and testing processes during the implementation phase. These methodologies have evolved over time and each comes with its own benefits and drawbacks. There is no one-size-fits-all solution for project management, so ultimately it is up to the project manager to decide which methodology is the best suited for the project at hand.

While the implementation methodologies have their own place in the grand scheme of things, equally important and indispensable are the new technologies and tools that can significantly boost the efficiency and effectiveness of project delivery. Some of the benefits of using these tools are faster collaboration, easier delegation, and accurate project tracking.

29.1 Implementation Methodologies

The Project Management Institute (PMI) defines a methodology as "a system of practices, techniques, procedures, and rules used by those who work in a discipline." There are a lot of different methodologies available in the market, so it is important to choose the best fit for the project and make minor tweaks if required.

Waterfall Methodology

This is a linear project management approach where all the requirements are identified upfront and then the implementation is executed in sequential steps. Each step has a certain deliverable that feeds the next step so there is no overlap. The number of steps may vary with the type of project, but the following steps are typical:

1. Requirements – All requirements for the entire project are identified and properly documented. Related artifacts like wireframes, visual comms, and high-level test cases are also prepared. These are signed off by the client before the project team can start on the design.

2. Technical Design – Based on the requirements, the technical architect(s) decide the technology/frameworks to be used and then develop the high-level technical design for the entire application.

3. Implementation – This is where the actual coding for the application is done. The developers write code and unit test it, while the quality analysis team carries out the functional testing against the stated requirements.

4. End to End Testing – Once all coding is complete, the entire application is tested for end-to-end scenarios and integrations with external systems. Once certified, the client teams conduct a UAT and certify the application for production deployment.

5. Operations – Once the application goes live, an operation support team is responsible to manage the day-to-day operations.

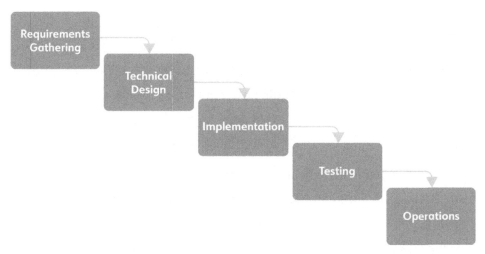

FIGURE 29.1 Waterfall Methodology

This methodology offers certain advantages like ease of use, better planning due to clearly marked stages and extensive documentation around requirements, design, and testing. However, there is are inherent risks due to sequential execution because each stage is heavily dependent on the successful completion of the previous stage. Also, the capacity to accommodate errors and change is limited as this requires going back to the beginning.

This methodology suits short and simple projects where requirements are well defined at the start and there is little chance of change at later stages. For more information on the Waterfall methodology, you may visit the following websites.

https://www.projectmanager.com/waterfall-methodology

https://www.lucidchart.com/blog/waterfall-project-management-methodology

https://www.softwaretestinghelp.com/agile-vs-waterfall/

Agile Methodology

This methodology uses short development cycles called Sprints, incremental steps that focus on continuous improvement in the development of a product or service. Iterative approaches are frequently used in software development projects to promote velocity and adaptability since the benefit of iteration is that you can adjust as you go along rather than following a linear path. One of the key objectives of the agile process is to provide benefits throughout the process rather than only at the completion. At the heart of the agile project are the core values of trust, flexibility, empowerment, and collaboration.

The project begins with a clear vision and a prioritized list of product features called the product backlog. A sprint is the set amount of time, generally one to four weeks, that the team has in order to complete the selected feature. The team then refers to the product backlog and picks another item for completion in the next sprint. This results in creation of a sprint backlog that is made up of features and tasks as part of the sprint planning meeting.

The team starts on the assigned tasks once they have committed to the Sprint backlog. It is very important that at this stage the team is free from interruptions and allowed to focus on meeting the sprint goal. Also, at this stage, no changes to the sprint backlog are entertained, though the product backlog can be edited or groomed as a run-up for the next sprint.

During the sprint process, there is a daily 15-minute stand-up meeting, called a scrum, during which members stand in a circle and each shares what they did the previous day and what they plan to today. They also discuss any challenges they might be facing. Toward the end of the sprint, the team presents the work they have accomplished as a demo to the stakeholders and collects feedback that shapes what they work on in the next sprint. The team also holds a retrospective to understand the things that need to improve the next sprint. This meeting is very critical as it focuses on three pillars of the scrum process, which are transparency, inspection, and adaptation.

Each sprint produces a deliverable that is an incremental step towards the final product. Deliverables are ideally complete in themselves and good enough to be deployed without an impact on the existing functionality.

FIGURE 29.2 Agile Methodology

Agile offers a lot of flexibility to the team in terms of planning the incremental changes that build the final product, unlike Waterfall which follows a fixed plan. Running a demo for the stakeholders at the end of the sprint and gathering their feedback helps reduce risk and aligns the development with the stakeholder expectations through course corrections. This makes agile especially suitable for creative projects where requirements are not very clear at the time of project kickoff and the sprint deliverables help define and refine the future requirements.

Not having a fixed plan may also be a drawback since resource management and project scheduling becomes harder. The success of this methodology depends on the close collaboration of the entire team, including stakeholders and sponsors. Feedback must be provided quickly, and incorporation should lead to incremental changes only, as drastic ones may set the process back by substantial time.

For more information on the Agile methodology, you may visit the following websites.

https://www.agilealliance.org/agile101/

https://www.cprime.com/resources/what-is-agile-what-is-scrum/

https://www.scrum.org/

Hybrid Methodology – This methodology is a combination of Waterfall and Agile, aiming for the best of both. It keeps a short focus on each product feature and a long focus on the overall project. Like Waterfall, requirements are gathered and analyzed upfront, and phases and sub-phases are planned based on the project duration and business priorities. Each phase gets its own backlog, but only the first one is firmly defined. The rest are defined along the way as development progresses and course corrections can be made when required.

This brings a certain amount of structure to the whole process by having defined requirements to start with but maintains the flexibility for accommodating change along the way.

Software Development Lifecycle (SDLC) – This is a systematic approach for building software that ensures the correctness and quality of the software created. The process is geared towards creating high-quality software that can meet customer expectations and complete development within stipulated time and costs. SDLC provides detailed structure around how to plan, build, and maintain the specific software. Every phase of the lifecycle consists of its own process and deliverables that become input for the next phase. The entire SDLC process is divided into a series of phases each one associated with a defined set of activities.

Forming a Strategy – Before the actual process of building begins, this important step defines the future course of the project. Based on the vision behind the application to be built, a strategy is developed for realizing that vision. All stakeholders must be part of this activity in order to ensure that the strategy fulfills the needs of each. This will take into account the desired functionality, dependencies, timelines, budgets, and constraints to come up with the best way forward.

Requirements Gathering and Analysis – This activity aims to gather all the requirements that the proposed application will address. Through a series of interactive workshops, the functional and technical experts elicit the functional requirements from all the stakeholders and domain experts in the industry. These requirements are analyzed in detail and captured in various tools. Depending upon the methodology followed, the project team may choose to capture detailed requirements at this stage or keep it high level and gather additional details as the project progresses.

Design – The requirements gathered in the previous stage form the basis for coming up with the detailed technical design for the system. The design should consider present and future needs of the client and should be in line with the strategy defined at the start. The implementation partner can also seek input from the various software and platform vendors to align the design with their platform capabilities. Third-party integration needs to be worked out in the most efficient way possible. The design must be robust since the entire code will be written on top.

Implementation – Once the design is ready, the developers are all set to start writing code. The code adheres to certain standards and guidelines that have been laid down so that it is robust and consistent. The quality analysis (QA) team is responsible for testing the code against the stated requirements. They run both functional and non-functional tests to certify the code is ready for delivery. Implementation can be executed for the entire project at once, followed by testing in a Waterfall style, or it can be in a series of iterations where incremental functionality is built and tested and released for deployment as in the case of Agile.

Testing – While the QA team carries out functional testing during the implementation phase, there are several tests required once the entire application is ready. Some of the major tests that the application is subjected to include end-to-end testing of major scenarios, system integration testing for external and third-party systems, and UAT by the client business team to certify the application is ready for go-live.

Installation/Deployment – Once the application has been cleared in UAT, it is ready to be deployed on production servers for go-live. For on-premise software, the client procured hardware has to be set up and configured for deployment by the implementation partner. For cloud-based applications, the platform vendor is responsible for deploying the approved code. Master data—customers, products, catalogs, taxonomy, prices, stocks, sellers, etc.—has to be loaded into the application(s) in preparation for go-live. Once ready, the application is subjected to some sanity testing before it is made live to the intended audience.

29.2 Tools for Implementation

Software developers and project managers use various tools that help them work more efficiently. In fact, these tools have become an indispensable part of all software development projects without which a project could not be successful.

Project Management Tools

Project management tools are aids to assist an individual or team to effectively organize work and manage projects and tasks. These tools help with communication within the team and with the client. MS Project is one of the most widely used tools for planning and managing Waterfall projects. It enables the creation of tasks and sub-tasks for the entire project upfront, assigns them to the team, tracks progress, and produces Gantt charts for projects.

 project management requires a different kind of tools which can help manage the fluid nature of the projects.

JIRA from Atlassian is a tool created for issue and bug tracking as well as project management and software and mobile development. The JIRA dashboard provides a plethora of useful functions all aimed to facilitate ease of handling a variety of issues. Some of its key features include issue types, workflows, screens, fields, and issue attributes. The JIRA dashboard allows high levels of customization to meet requirements for a variety of business types and software.

Trello is another popular software tool whose structure is based on Kanban methodology. In Trello, each project is represented by a board that contains lists. Each list contains progressive cards that can be dragged and dropped. Users associated with a project or board can be assigned to their respective cards. Trello features include providing comments, inserting attachments, checklists, notes, and due dates. It is also supported by all mobile platforms and has integration capability with third-party applications.

Wrike is one of the best tools available when it comes to integrating project management with email. It has industry-leading feature lists and can scale. It provides all the flexibility a business needs when it comes to managing multiple projects and resources in a single place. It follows the agile process and provides accurate and up-to-date information, allowing users to add and insert any important information inside the tool.

DevOps Tools

The DevOps team utilizes a wide array of tools to carry out their activities. In the agile methodology, one of the best practices that the DevOps team implements is continuous integration (CI) and continuous delivery (CD). CI/CD follows a set of operating principles and culture that allow the application development teams to deliver code changes more frequently with better accuracy and correctness.

Apache Ant, Maven, and Gradle are code compilation tools that are very useful in conjunction with automated build tools. They can be integrated with popular Integrated Development Environments (IDEs) like Eclipse, Netbeans, and IntelliJ IDEA. While Ant and Maven use XML for configuration, Gradel makes use of Groovy-based DSL for builds.

Jenkins is another popular DevOps automation tool for teams in software development. It allows for automation of different stages of the delivery pipeline as it is an open-source CI/CD server. Another reason for the popularity of Jenkins is its massive plugin ecosystem. It offers more than 1000 plugins that make it compatible with almost all of the DevOps tools.

Another tool with a similar feature set is Bamboo, Atlassian's CI/CD server solution. It offers seamless integration with other Atlassian products like Bitbucket and Jira.

Docker was launched in 2013 and has been one of the most popular container platforms ever since as it continues to improve with time. It is also regarded as one of the most important DevOps tools in the industry. Docker has made distributed development possible and automates the deployment of apps thereby making containerization popular in the tech world. It boxes applications into separate containers making them portable and secure. Its apps are also OS and platform independent. Docker containers can be used instead of a virtual machine such as VirtualBox.

Like Docker, Kubernetes is also a container orchestration platform that offers many cutting-edge features. It works well with Docker and many of its alternatives. It was created by a couple of Google engineers who were looking for a solution to manage containers at scale. Kubernetes allows for grouping of containers into logical units.

Nagios is another open-source and one of the most popular free DevOps monitoring tools by monitoring infrastructure to detect and fix issues. It also records events, outages, and failures. Its reporting provides data on trends with the help of graphs and reports to help in forecasting outages, errors, and security threats.

Source Code Management (SCM) Tools

Source code management (SCM) is used to track changes to a source code repository. SCM tracks the history of changes to a codebase. When there are updates from multiple contributors SCM helps resolve conflicts, it is also now synonymous with Version control. When it comes to complex marketplace implementation, the software project usually grows in the amount of and people writing it and add to that communication overhead. SCM software helps with keeping things in control.

GitHub is one of the popular SCM tools that help development teams to collaborate review and manage code. For developers working on Salesforce development projects, CodeScan is one of the leading static code analysis solutions. Then there is Visual Studio Code that provides a source-code editing tool for MacOS, Windows, and Linux.

Git is one of the very popular tools for DevOps with wide usage across the software industry. It is valued by remote teams and open-source contributors as it is a distributed SCM (source code management) tool.

All of these tools allow organizations to track development progress. One can save different versions of source code and return to a previous version as and when required. This tool is good for testing and experimenting as you can create separate entities and merge these features once they are ready to be rolled out.

Testing and Test Management Tools

The QA team uses a number of different tools to manage their testing process and to carry out testing of software applications.

TestRail is a popular test management tool that enables tracking of software testing efforts and organizes the QA department. It has an intuitive web-based interface that simplifies creation of test cases, handling test runs, and smoothly managing the entire testing process. Apart from creating test cases, it allows execution of testing based on created test scenarios. This tool helps to create a bug and upload it to integrated bug trackers like GitHub, YouTrack, and Jira. TestRail also allows creation of projects and informative reports, as well as customization of the system using open TestRail APIs.

JIRA is another popular test management tool that is used for writing and executing test cases, logging defects and tracking them to closure, and generating various reports. When using JIRA for agile project management, stories can be linked to test cases and defects making it easy to track each story to closure.

Selenium is a major automation testing tool for all web application testing tools. It can be executed across multiple browsers and operating systems and is compatible with all of the major programming languages and automation testing frameworks. Selenium allows you to come up with robust browser-centered automation test scripts that are scalable across multitudes of environments. One can also create scripts using this tool to help with rapid reproduction of bugs, exploratory testing, and regression testing.

Katalon Studio is one of the most comprehensive test automation tools that spans across API, Web, and mobile testing. It is known for its feature set, including recording actions, creating test cases, generating test scripts, executing tests, reporting results, and integrating with many other third-party tools throughout the lifecycle of software development. It is also extremely versatile as it can run on Linux, Mac OS, and Windows. It can also support iOS and Android apps testing as well as web applications on all major browsers and API services. It allows for integration with other testing tools like JIRA, qTest, Kobiton, Git, Slack, and more.

Knowledge Management (KM) Tools

For effective collaboration among project teams, it is very important to share knowledge between team members. KM tools provide a platform to effectively capture knowledge and share it with other team members.

Confluence is an open and shared workspace that connects people to the ideas and information they need to do their best work. It groups related pages together in a dedicated space for the work, the team, or cross-functional projects so information is easy to find. Confluence's powerful search engine and page trees ensure finding the right content at the right time.

Zendesk is a flexible and extensible knowledge base platform that facilitates creation of self-help customer service. It caters to companies of all sizes with software that supports more than 30 languages. It also can be used as a content management system to structure the information in the database and manage it in a way that best suits the project requirements.

SharePoint is a document management and collaboration tool. It securely stores and organizes information for easy access and sharing from any device. It acts as a content management and collaboration system and intranet that helps the organization work more collaboratively and gain efficiencies in operations. It comprises a multipurpose set of technologies that has tight integration with Office 365 as well as handy document management capabilities.

29.3 Project Team Roles

Fundamental to a team's ability to deliver is identifying, defining, and communicating roles and responsibilities. Clear communication allows the team members to focus on their tasks and provides guidance and structure needed for them to excel in their roles. Some of the typical software team roles include the following.

The **project sponsor** is the individual or group that provides vision, direction, and resources both financial and personnel for successful delivery of software projects. The sponsor works with the project management team assisting them with areas such as scope clarification, monitoring, progress, and exerting influence to achieve what is best for the project. The project sponsor also leads the supplier selection process for the software until it is authorized formally. For matters beyond the control of the product owner, the project sponsor acts as an escalation path. The sponsor also comes into the picture for important issues such as authorization of change in scope, phase-end reviews, and go/no-go decisions when the stakes are high.

Strategist/Subject matter expert (SME) or domain expert is a person who is a marketplace expert, ideally with industry expertise in the target vertical market. An SME possesses knowledge of a discipline, technology, product, or business process and provides information about functional and technical aspects of the software product that is being built. It is important to include SMEs very early on when the software product vision statement is being created. Feedback from the SMEs can be highly useful and can save a lot of back and forth down the line.

Product Owner is a software development role that represents the business and end users and mostly responsible for collaborating with the user's group to ascertain what features will make it in the product release. Another key area of responsibility of the Product Owner is prioritizing the backlog and maximizing the return on investment of the software project. This role is also partly responsible for documentation of user stories and requirements for the software project. In smaller projects, the product owner and the business analyst may be the same person.

The Project Manager (PM) role is one of the most important when it comes to delivery of the software project, they are mainly concerned with the who, what, where, when, and why of the software project. They are required to have a deep understanding of the stakeholder requirements and effectively communicate with each of them. Part of their responsibility includes creating and managing the project budget and schedule as well as processes like risk management, issue management, and scope management. They also oversee software testing, delivery, and formal acceptance by the customer or end user. One of the important activities the

carries out is documentation of lessons learned from the process of software development.

Scrum Master's role is to facilitate scrum in an agile methodology project. They are tasked with assessing any problems that could hinder the development team from delivering on the product goals. Scrum Master ensures that the development team is following the scrum framework and acts as a buffer between the development team and any inside or outside influences that detract from a project deliverable. Scrum master works with the product owner to help maintain product backlogs and ensure that the work required is understood and the team makes continuous progress on the software being built.

Business Analyst (BA) is a key link between the business and project team. The BA works with the Product Owner to understand the requirements for the project and helps detail them out. This person helps document these requirements by detailing out the stories for the development team to understand. The BA works closely with the development team to explain what is required to be built and get clarification wherever required. On smaller projects, the business analyst may also serve as the product owner.

Technical Architect's role is to take the business requirements and convert them into a technical solution. Hence it is required that the technical architect is brought on the project early and is involved in the planning phase to get first hand understanding of the requirements from a customer point of view. The technical architect acts as a development team leader to work closely with developers providing estimates and other technical detail for the planned solution. This becomes an information input for the project manager who uses it to create the statement of work and the work breakdown structure documents.

Software Developers work on both front end and back end and their primary role is building the deliverables and communicating the status of the software project to the technical lead or project manager. They also help in using the technical requirements from the technical lead to generate cost and timeline estimates.

Quality Analysts are responsible for testing the software being built by the software developers. They conduct functional testing on the software to ensure that it meets the requirements that have been laid down by the product owner. They also conduct system integration testing (SIT), performance testing, end-to-end testing once the system coding has been completed. QAs play an important role in ensuring that the product being delivered meets the quality standards laid down at the beginning of the project.

User Experience Designer's role is mainly concerned with grasping user needs and solving problems to make product more user friendly and intuitive to attract and retain users. They are tasked with conducting user research and testing, developing wireframes and task flows based on the user persona and user needs. They collaborate with designers and developers to create and user friendly and conversion focused marketplace platform. They are required to find creative ways to solve UX problems and communicate design ideas and prototypes to developers. They need to be brought very early into the marketplace project scope when it is being conceptualized.

User Interface (UI) Developer's role is to create digital platforms that facilitate seamless interaction between buyers and sellers. Its main goal is to improve the user experience by making web page or software interactions simple, fun, easy, and effective. This involves translating creative software design concepts and ideas into reality using front end technologies. This role needs to have a deep understanding of interface design solution both in its practical intent and creative vision to be able to convert it into engineered software/ codes. One might as well call the UI developer a bridge between the presentation layer and the backend layer. This role requires strong design skills on how the platform or program engages the user in a positive way. This role requires in-depth knowledge of user interface development tech stack and frameworks such as HTML, CSS, JavaScript, Angular, ReactJS, VueJS, Typescript, etc.

29.4 Project Implementation Approaches

The **Big Bang Approach** is used in scenarios where the stakeholders of the project are not completely certain about their requirements and they also have not analyzed all the features and characteristics they are going to have in their software product. In this model, all or most of the requirements are gathered at the beginning and put into practice while building the first prototype.

Since this approach holds no planning or analysis, it involves a tremendous amount of risk over other project implementation approaches. Though this approach is moderately simple to implement, there is still difficulty in developing a product without proper analysis. The big bang approach focuses on testing all of the modules as soon as they are built and ready for integration. These modules are then brought together and tested by running the entire product for checking and tracking any bugs within the product.

The **Minimum Viable Product (MVP)** is a methodology used for quick and quantitative market testing of a product or its feature. In theory, it is a simple, bare-bones solution that can work. It aims to bring the product in its most viable form rapidly to the market. Once the product is launched, the market response is gathered, and the product is further adapted to the needs of the customers and the market. The key objective of MVP is to figure out which features to cut so that business can adapt to a new direction and build something the market and customer actually need.

29.5 Post-Launch Support and Hypercare

The post-launch support stage refers to the period once the marketplace is launched and is often referred to as hypercare. It's a time immediately following a system Go Live where an elevated level of support is available to ensure the seamless adoption of a new platform. Hypercare support is a critical phase for smooth rollout and handover of the new digital commerce portal after it goes live. When done well Hypercare saves a lot of time and rollback of the applications. Hypercare in marketplace platform support is considered as the phase after the application goes live on production. The main aim of hypercare support service is to ensure that when hypercare support ends, the system should be stable and can be released to more end users.

At this stage, the focus is on customer support, platform stability, and data integrity. It requires collaboration between functional, technical, and security experts. Marketplace platforms are complex beasts and unexpected issues require immediate resolutions to be contained to avoid any major roadblock to a successful implementation rollout. The best practice is to have dedicated support that understands where to channel their escalations in order to receive immediate resolutions. The team for this phase should have trained experts on the new platform and technical processes; each should have the authority to quickly identify the issue, resolve the problem in the system. Some of the key services that come under the purview of hypercare are:

- Technical support services

- On-site training services

- Handling issues and queries

- Escalation plan designing

Key Takeaways:
Implementation Methodologies & Tools

- Various project implementation methodologies serve different needs and requirements. Waterfall works well when all the requirements are gathered up front and there is little chance of changes later on. Agile works better for shorter development cycles and an iterative approach.

- Software Development Lifecycle (SDLC) is a systematic approach for building software where each phase consists of its own process and deliverables that feed in as input for the next phase. The entire SDLC process is divided into a series of phases, each one associated with a defined set of activities.

- DevOps is a set of practices that combines software development and IT operations with a view to shorten the systems development life cycle. It aims to provide continuous delivery with high software quality. Several DevOps aspects came from the agile methodology and complement agile software development.

- Project implementation tools are mainly used across four key areas: project management, DevOps, testing, and knowledge management.

- The Minimum Viable Product (MVP) is a methodology used for quick and quantitative market testing of a product or its feature. In theory, it is a simple, bare-bones solution that can work.

Chapter 30: Ongoing Operations

We are what we repeatedly do. Excellence then is not an act, but a habit.

Aristotle – Greek Philosopher

Introduction

Once the marketplace is set up and running smoothly, the primary focuses should be to grow the customer base, bring in high-quality sellers, and reach a virtuous cycle. It is equally important to set up realistic goals in terms of both timelines and metrics.

Keep in mind, building a marketplace takes more time than a simple online business, as a marketplace operator needs to build both buyer and seller communities. While a traditional business model may begin to show a positive cash flow in only six to nine months, a marketplace may require several years to achieve similar earnings. For instance, Airbnb started showing results after four years.

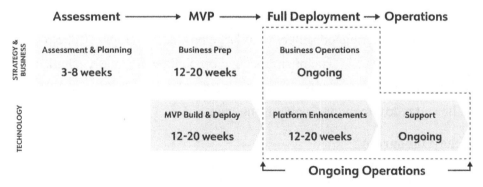

FIGURE 30.1 Typical Marketplace Project Timeline – Ongoing Operations

When first launching a marketplace, it is imperative to clearly define which teams will steer ongoing operations, what their collaborative workflow look, and what sort of cadence will govern meetings, reviews, and metrics. Such teams include the following:

- Business Development & Sales – Defines the seller recruiting and onboarding system

- Business Support – Defines the seller support and the payment processes

- Product Management – Defines product enhancements based on user feedback

- IT/Technical Support – Defines the technical system and the level of support

30.1 Daily Activities

Big-ticket items that constitute the daily operations for a marketplace are recruiting sellers, onboarding sellers, seller support, incident management, and product curation.

Recruiting Sellers

A successful marketplace offers customers a wide selection of products provided by a large number of high-quality sellers. But instead of allowing anyone to sell on the platform, the recruitment process must be frequently and carefully monitored to ensure only reliable sellers are admitted. Focusing on experienced sellers with large product catalogs will help to keep quality in check. The business development team usually handles seller recruiting, but very large marketplace operations will have a dedicated recruitment and onboarding team.

Seller Onboarding

Proper training for new sellers is critical to ensure they will properly represent the marketplace brand and find success on the marketplace.

Develop a marketplace seller guide and a seller product catalog to aid with this process. Also, survey the sellers to get feedback on the effectiveness of training materials.

Some of the metrics to be tracked include the following:

- Daily active seller rate

- Supplier growth rate

- Listings growth rate

- Best-selling suppliers based on types of goods and services

- Order defect rate per seller

- Average listing price

To measure success in the process of seller recruiting and onboarding, define a target number of sellers per core category and ideal seller profiles. Tracking these metrics will keep customer experience at the forefront as the marketplace grows.

Seller Support

It is the responsibility of the marketplace to help sellers succeed on the platform by providing easy access to support regarding their account and inventory. Seller support can come in the form of email, phone, or even chatbot and should be addressed promptly with resolutions that are easy to execute.

Some of the metrics which speak to the effectiveness and efficiency of seller support operations are number of seller issues logged per day, number of seller issues resolved per day, active time per issue, and number of first-call resolutions.

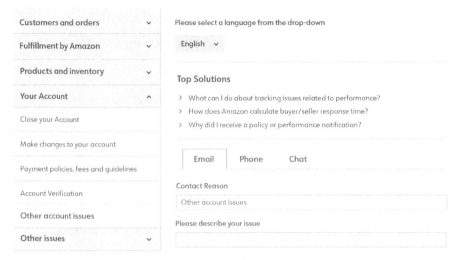

FIGURE 30.2

Incident Management

At a daily activity level, the purpose of Incident Management is to restore normal service operation as quickly as possible and ensure that marketplace maintains agreed on SLA levels. These activities include:

- Monitor service levels, identify trends, and assist in continual service improvements

- Report periodic metrics to the product, seller support, program, and business teams

- Manage expectations related to incidents

Metrics that will help to identify incident patterns are number of total incidents, major incidents, recurring incidents, and incidents resolved by L1 support.

Product Curation

It is the process of creating unique product collections that appeal to a specific audience and demographic. There are many advantages of curation that benefit both buyers and sellers. Curated collections offer an easy way to match customers with products that meet their tastes and interests. This function leverages customer segmentation, data analytics, and personalization techniques to create a unique product collection for increased engagement and sales. Customer engagement and marketplace growth will occur naturally when the products are curated on a daily basis.

Online shoppers look for more meaning and context around the products they purchase, and this can come in many forms like stories, trusted recommendations, or curated product pairings. Effective product curation takes time and creativity but, with persistence and continuous research into customer data, it can create a lasting impact on the marketplace.

30.2 Weekly Activities

Stepping up one level from the daily operations, key items that warrant weekly overview are analytics, marketing, category curation, and incident summary.

Marketing & Analytics Review

Reviewing both seller and buyer data will provide insights to attract more quality sellers and execute better-targeted campaigns to the consumer. Some seller metrics to review include the following:

- Weekly total revenue and orders
- Sales reports of total revenue and total orders by products and categories
- Best selling items by total sales and quantity of items sold
- Top viewed items.

Here are some buyer metrics, the marketplace operator should examine:

- Number of buyers
- Buyer growth rate
- Average dollar amount purchased per buyer
- Average number of orders per buyer.

Incident Summary

An incident is an event that causes a disruption or reduction in the quality of service and is said to be resolved when service resumes normal function. An example of an incident in a marketplace platform might be when a seller is able to see things beyond his access. Resolving the incident requires business support and technical teams to come together. It is important not only to resolve but also put proper checks and balances in place to ensure the incident will not occur again.

A weekly incident summary typically contains the following information:

- The total number of incidents and the average time to the first and second escalations
- Details of each incident, including the time of the incident and the device and service for which the incident was generated.

Category Curation

This process involves examining both buyer and seller data and asking questions about how to better manage inventory, what categories should be added, and how customers can be better served. From a weekly operations point of view, a marketplace operator should look at how they are enabling sellers to cross-sell, upsell, and consider new product categories. Typical weekly activities around category curation include the following:

- Notifications about best-selling items seller should consider carrying
- Notifications on what inventory is about to run out and what is the ideal level of inventory seller should be carrying
- Providing business forecast for upcoming seasonal sales so the seller is prepared
- Look at the internal site search data to identify categories of products to stock and notify sellers who might be selling similar but not exact products.

For detailed information on some of the key performance metrics, please refer to Chapter 21 of this book - Key Performance Indicators (KPI's).

30.3 Monthly Activities

In order to continue improving customer and seller experience on the marketplace, key monthly activities include internal steering committee meetings, key supplier review meetings, enhancement project status, new category evaluation, and P&L budget reviews.

Internal steering committee meetings

A smooth-running marketplace employs a project steering committee that is answerable to the top executives of the organization and may even have some leadership as members. While the executive team drives the vision and direction of the business, any initiatives or goals conceptualized at the top level are handed to the steering committee, which then breaks down these goals into practical action steps for achieving them.

The steering committee itself does not manage the project but steers the project and program managers toward the desired outcome for the marketplace project. This is achieved through deliberation, ideation, consideration, recommendation, and decision making, and it could be around the following areas:

- How to get more users and buyers
- How to increase the breadth and quality of supply
- How to improve the customer experience

The main purposes of the steering committee are as follows:

- Serving as the main advocate for marketplace initiatives undertaken
- Establishing how online marketplace project benefits are defined and measured
- Selecting the right expertise to manage the project

- Checking, approving, or rejecting any project management plans
- Monitoring progress against the project management plan

Supplier Review Meetings

A healthy marketplace is made up of sellers of varying breadth and depth. To achieve this, seller recruitment, onboarding, continuing management should be performed in the most efficient manner possible. The supplier review meeting provides a great platform to evaluate the following and course-correct if needed.

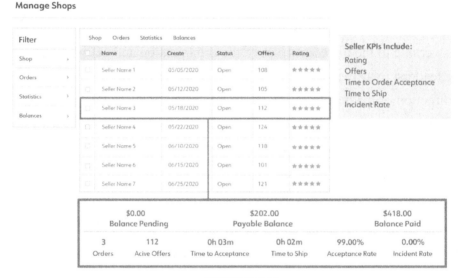

FIGURE 30.3

- Monitor and segment sellers based on performance. Some of the key seller KPIs include ratings, offers, and time to order acceptance. Tracking seller performance should be an ongoing process, even while onboarding new sellers into the system.
- Review the seller enrollment guidelines to see any changes that could better define the ISP (ideal seller profile).
- Consolidate and review seller feedback and find ways to incorporate them into the platform.
- Review any specific issue or concern raised by a seller or customer, as relates to sellers.

- Ensure there is continuous education related to catalog creation, management, and enhancement for sellers.
- Keep a check on seller malpractices such as incorrect attribute values and fake products.

Enhancement Project Reviews

Enhancement projects are designed to add incremental value to the marketplace. While a new feature adds functionality that was not previously available, an enhancement makes doing something that was possible before simpler or more powerful by adding to the existing functionality. These could be related to the existing platform and processes or even creating a new capability or area of expertise. Idea sources for enhancement may include seller feedback, buyer feedback, ideas from business support teams, or an issue or a challenge a group of individuals faced. Depending on the nature of enhancement, the steering committee will assign a team owner and a priority level.

The approach to product enhancement follows a specific well-defined methodology which involves the following:

- Understanding the existing product architecture and functionalities
- Analyzing new additions to the software.
- Creating an action plan for implementation of the additions
- Integrating product with other systems and devices

New Category Evaluation

As growth is the constant goal of any online marketplace, the operator should always be on the lookout for opportunities to introduce new product categories. This activity includes both high-level overview and deep drilling to build a detailed report of each product category. The aim of this exercise is to gain insights into customer experiences, new market trends, and market competitors. Some of the questions the category evaluation answers are as follows:

- Which product categories contribute significantly to overall sales?
- Which product categories are laggards?
- What are micro and macro trends in a category?
- Which geographic regions have more margins?

In large marketplaces, this exercise is carried out by category managers whose sole mandate is to grow their categories and evaluate new ones for growth.

P&L Budget Review

This is one of the key monthly items for review. A profit and loss budget is a financial plan of what to sell in the marketplace, what will it cost, and what possible overhead and interest will likely be incurred. The P&L budget estimates how much profit or loss a marketplace will make on a monthly basis and works as a primary financial roadmap for the marketplace operator. Forecasting models help when the marketplace is built and launched, but as the business grows, the monthly budget is based on previous financial history and growth plans for the marketplace. A healthy understanding of spending and revenue patterns is required. At the end of the month, the P&L budget is compared against actuals and the variance is tracked. A cash flow forecast, on the other hand, helps to understand when cash will move in and out of the business.

30.4 Quarterly Activities

To keep the marketplace operating smoothly and get ahead of potential bottlenecks, the operator should schedule quarterly tasks around terms and conditions reviews, legislation and tax compliance reviews, competitive landscape review, and 1P>3P or 3P>1P product migrations.

Terms and Conditions Review

Given the highly dynamic nature of doing business on a marketplace, the operator should continually review fees, pricing models, and even seller terms and conditions. For instance, Amazon regularly runs limited-period fee promotions for its seller community to motivate them to grow their business on the Amazon marketplace. Additional incentives are also given to sellers who move up on the ratings scale. On the other hand, there may be instances when commissions need to be increased, like when the cost of logistics has gone up due to external factors. Under all circumstances, the focus should be to take calculated risks that will bring long term growth and increase customer trust in the platform.

Changing legislation & tax compliance

While legislation and tax guidelines do not change often, a marketplace operator needs to be diligent about compliance, especially a large, multi-national operator. Because every country maintains a different tax structure and operating guidelines, a quarterly review of both legislation and marketplace practices will ensure compliance in all countries of operations and avoid penalties or reputation damage.

Competitive Landscape Review

As with any business sector, quarterly analysis of the competition will evaluate their strategies for strengths and weaknesses and identify ways to get ahead. In the online marketplace environment, analysis of the following parameters will provide valuable insight.

- Evaluate the customer experience of the competitor's marketplace website. Examining product photography, CTA's, product descriptions, overall site optimization, ad spend, overall traffic, etc., can highlight opportunities to exploit the weakness.

- Get an understanding of competitors positioning, look at how they are talking about their marketplace, subscribe to their newsletters, and follow them on social media.

- While Amazon has demonstrated pricing alone can be a major marketplace battleground, be sure to examine the competition's price-to-value ratio as well. Customers may not mind paying extra for better a buying experience and expedited shipping.

- Given the impact of shipping on customer experience and loyalty, check the price, timetable, and method of the competition's shipping practices.

- Customer reviews and ratings can be a valuable source of market intelligence, so follow social media to see what people are saying about the competition.

Transitioning Items from First Party to Third Party (or Vice Versa)

Hybrid marketplaces offer both first-party products (items carried in inventory) and third-party products (items fulfilled by third parties). As more intelligence is learned from operations it may make sense to transition some products from first-party to third-party, or vice versa.

As the marketplace starts getting more and more sellers to the platform, it's time to consider what items can be best fulfilled through 1P and what's best left to 3P. Usually, it is good to have products with high value, high margin, and frequent purchasing to 1P while products with lower margin and value can be sourced through third-party. This exercise should be done at least once a quarter. There are two primary considerations in this analysis.

- What's best for the business in terms of profitability
- What's best for the end consumer

As marketplace operator, one should think of both aspects while taking decisions relating to 1P vs 3P for a product or a category. Some of the big marketplaces like Amazon offer choices to sellers of either using 1P (Vendor Central) or 3P (Seller Central) or even choose a hybrid model where they can sell both ways on the marketplace. There are many advantages to this for the seller, the key one being that it gives them a chance to experience models and choose what works best for them.

Certain items may also make sense to start selling as private label or private brands. Amazon Basics includes examples of batteries, paper plates, and other commodities that are only associated with the Amazon brand.

30.5 Annual Activities

Annual reviews items have the greatest business impact as the decisions involved result in long-term consequences and benefits. Foremost among them are budgeting, strategy planning, UX redesign, and security review.

Annual Budget

Income lines for a marketplace include items like fees, commissions, and advertising, while expenses are generally items like vendor pay-outs, software licensing fees, and marketing. In the first year, the two main expenditures will be building the platform and getting the word out about the marketplace.

Strategic Planning

Marketplaces are like any business in that a solid strategy addresses questions around industry growth, key competitors, customer trends, and any macro-economic trends or new government regulations that impact the course of the product development and marketing campaigns. The annual strategy review should also include a full SWOT analysis. For a marketplace, strengths could be customer base, financial resources, and product breadth. Weaknesses may include market position, margins, or customer service. Opportunities might be found in new complementary markets or new partnerships. Threats can come from disintermediation, falling prices, and external factor like recession or changing technology.

UX Redesign

Typically UX is redesigned when customer journey targets are missed resulting in poor page value and lower conversion rates. To a layman, UX redesign seems like a minor facelift, but the process involves meticulous planning and research. The UX design team must recognize, understand,

and validate the problem at hand and create a case for the redesign. Key steps in this process are as follows:

- Check the marketplace web pages to see if the experience is satisfying and efficient.
- Ascertain if the brand goals and value proposition align with the user experience.
- Study user feedback and reviews to understand what elements users want redesigned.

Security Review

Marketplaces lose millions of dollars each year thanks to hackers and fraudulent buyers and sellers. An annual security review and proper fraud detection tools will protect a marketplace website from threats and keep online transactions safe. Here are some measures to include in the annual security review.

An annual review is a good time to check the overall security budget for the marketplace store. Even if there is a good data security program in place, it's important to ensure you're keeping up with industry changes and evolving security threats. While most operators focus mainly on fraud prevention, there should be enough room to provide measures for data protection as well.

Encryption practices are another area that requires review. While SSL certificate and encrypted transmission of payment data is a must to maintain PCI compliance, there may be other places in the business that might require encryption of data. If the data is on the cloud, then the default encryption offered may not be enough. One may require stronger encryption tools.

It is a good time to review the data collection practice and refine it further. Review the collected data and only collect what is required. Destroy completely what is no longer in use.

One often overlooked aspect is physical data security. Think about how easy or difficult it is for an employee or visitor to walk in and out of the premises with customer data on it. Restrict data access, ensure you have data segmented, customer data is separated from all the other data within the network.

Key Takeaways: Ongoing Operations

- When first launching a marketplace, it is imperative to clearly define which teams will steer ongoing operations, what their collaborative workflow look, and what sort of cadence will govern meetings, reviews, and metrics.

- Some of the big-ticket items that constitute the daily operations for a marketplace are recruiting sellers, onboarding sellers, seller support, incident management, and product curation.

- Weekly operations consist of marketing and analytics review, incident summary, and category curation.

- Monthly operation items include internal steering committee meetings, supplier review meetings, enhancement project reviews, new category evaluation, and P&L budget reviews.

- Quarterly activities include looking at First-Party vs Third-Party Product Migrations and reviewing seller terms and conditions.

Chapter 31: Best Practices for Sellers

You will get all you want in life if you help enough other people get what they want.

Zig Ziglar – American Author

Introduction

Most of this book is focused on best practices for marketplace operators. However, this chapter focuses on what marketplace sellers should do to be successful. For both new and well-established eCommerce businesses, the marketplace format should be the strategic focus for better market share and growth. Thanks to recent platform advances and the increasingly borderless business environment, entering the marketplace business model is now relatively easy. Any business can now launch quickly, leverage built-in audiences, and make use of established marketplace tools that make it significantly easier to market, sell, and fulfill products and services.

Each online marketplace has its own unique requirements, product categories, listing fees, commission structures, and audiences. A clear understanding of different selling strategies and how they affect different marketplace models will help to ensure a smooth start and steady growth. Many consumers consider marketplaces to be search engines for products. Roughly 55% of U.S. consumers start their product research on Amazon, with a 7-8% sales conversion, much higher than the average 2-3% on many brand eCommerce stores. Marketplaces have been increasing market share as eCommerce sales continue to increase annually.

According to Marketplace Pulse, "2020 was the best year for eCommerce marketplaces in over a decade." Due to the pandemic and unprecedented demand, marketplaces such as Walmart.com and Target.com have seen greater online sales increase than Amazon and taken some market share, thanks in part to their click and collect and last-mile fulfillment. However, the pandemic has forced competitors to bolster their own offerings. In the first quarter of 2020, Target saw its digital comparable sales shoot up more than 140% compared to the same period the prior year. Walmart's eCommerce sales rose 74% in the same period.

In addition to mass market marketplaces such as Amazon and Walmart, there are vertical marketplaces that target a narrower range of customer needs. Google continues to invest in Google Shopping, which includes a marketplace, and Facebook has invested in both a marketplace and social commerce, for example with Instagram. While the largest mass retail B2C marketplaces may seem similar to the consumer, the seller's role can come in a variety of forms. Third-party sellers retain ownership of their products and use the marketplace to interact with consumers. First-party vendors sell their products wholesale to the marketplace. In some cases, hybrid sellers may operate both 1P and 3P accounts. Additionally, qualifications to sell and available tools vary widely by marketplace.

31.1 Marketplaces as Sales Channels

While marketing channels influence transactions, marketplaces are sales channels where transactions happen. Aside from national retailers that have their own marketplace, third-party marketplaces make sense for most brands to include in their sales channel mix. For many brands, marketplaces are their primary sales channel. For other brands, particularly those that sell wholesale to retail stores nationally, marketplace sales may not be their primary sales channel, but a critical online sales channel. Depending on the industry, Amazon may have 60% or more market share of online U.S. sales. For brands that are well optimized on Amazon and do not have a pipeline of new products to introduce, expanding to new marketplaces often makes sense.

Even though historically market share from online sales, including marketplaces, has been relatively small for CPG brands, eCommerce and marketplaces are where most sales growth is happening. With national retailers often reluctant to take on new brands in their stores, marketplaces can be the best place to reach national audiences. In addition to marketplaces being scalable national sales channels, they also offer the opportunity for cost-efficient, national advertising reach to impact in-store sales. Though currently Walmart and Target offer geographic and store-level advertising, Amazon offers greater reach and the ability to impact more national retail store sales. For some CPG brands that sell 3P on Amazon, the impact of marketplace advertising on national store sales is the only way to be profitable. Brands with wholesale sales to national retailers that also have a marketplace presence have to implement agreements with wholesale customers and retailers to avoid channel conflict, brand denigration, price erosion, and more. Brands that sell wholesale often have agreements that give them exclusive rights to sell on marketplaces In general, Amazon turns a blind eye to MAP Pricing, so brands selling to retailers and on Amazon often have to differentiate the products they sell on marketplaces. To best prioritize opportunities, brands should plan their omnichannel sales strategies by benchmarking their instore sales with their online sales and benchmarking their online sales channels.

31.2 Launching on a Marketplace

Though from both the buyer and seller perspective marketplaces are unique in many ways, at the core they arere sales channels like others.

Therefore, in many ways, they need to be approached similarly to reflect a brand's other sales channels. Marketplaces should be part of a brand's financial planning and budgeting as are other sales channels, and resources allocated based on financial importance, and growth opportunities. Marketplace economics are different than both a brand's DTC eCommerce (where they own the customer relationship) and wholesale sales channels. Before seeking approval to sell on a marketplace, brands need to understand the economics, the competition, realistic sales, and their breakeven.

After setting up a seller account and launching an initial list of products, sellers grow on marketplaces by launching new product categories, product lines, assortments, brands. Growth continues as sellers launch into new countries, such as Amazon's seventeen marketplaces, and then new marketplaces. Each marketplace has somewhat different requirements and processes. Once a new seller is approved to sell on a new marketplace, the great majority of the account creation process begins. This process includes the following steps:

- Develop a budget, particularly for marketing and investment spending in customer acquisition and during the first few months after new product lines are introduced.

- Register trademarks and secure GS1 UPCs for each product, to be used in product catalog creation.

- Develop channel management and channel control documents and processes.

- Define policies around unauthorized 3P sellers. If the brand will compete with other sellers, financial planning should reflect competitive pricing and reduced margins.

- Create the product catalog and inventory feed and categorize the product assortment.

- Upload product feeds and inventory files according to marketplace taxonomy so that customers will be able to find the products easily.

Fulfillment will vary by marketplace, whether drop-shipping directly to the consumer, using 3P logistics, or shipping to the marketplace itself for fulfillment through existing infrastructure, such as FBA. Accounts settings that deserve careful attention include tax collection, notifications, returns handling, and international sales.

31.3 Customer Engagement & Product Strategies

Bringing customers to a marketplace website and completing a sale is only the first half of the challenge. According to one study, 54% of consumers will stop doing business with a seller if they have a bad customer experience. To ensure customers have an excellent experience and want to return for more purchases, sellers should focus on positive engagement to drive sales.

Customer Reviews

Social proof is shown to have significant impact when making decisions. Studies show that customer reviews may influence over 95% of online shopper decisions. A product or seller with many positive reviews is perceived to have higher quality or better service, while a product or seller with fewer reviews is viewed as risky. Amazon is a review-driven ecosystem where highly rated sellers are rewarded and poorly rated sellers get lost in the shuffle. Even Walmart.com considers seller feedback as one of the key criteria when accepting applications for the invitation-only marketplace.

Sellers should focus on maintaining positive reviews and ratings on every platform where they sell. Develop a framework to solicit reviews and reward customers for contributing. Combined with effective SEO and competitive pricing, positive reviews can help brands grow quickly.

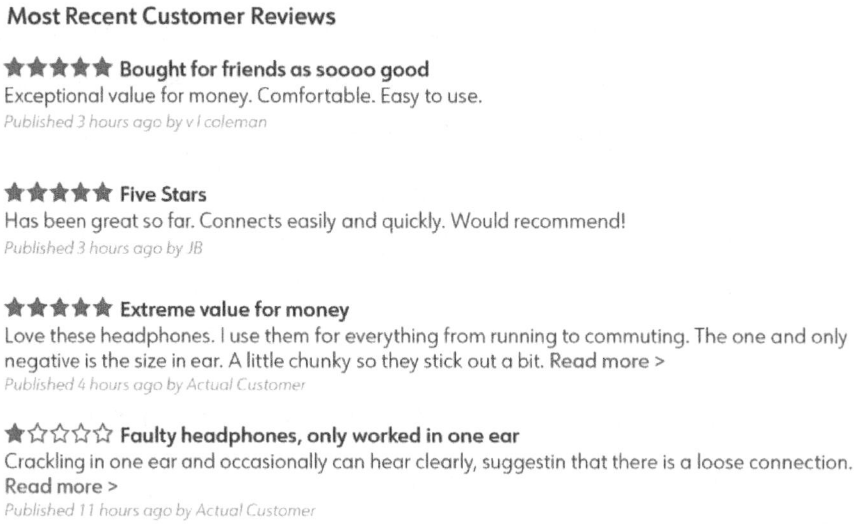

Most Recent Customer Reviews

★★★★★ **Bought for friends as soooo good**
Exceptional value for money. Comfortable. Easy to use.
Published 3 hours ago by v l coleman

★★★★★ **Five Stars**
Has been great so far. Connects easily and quickly. Would recommend!
Published 3 hours ago by JB

★★★★★ **Extreme value for money**
Love these headphones. I use them for everything from running to commuting. The one and only negative is the size in ear. A little chunky so they stick out a bit. Read more >
Published 4 hours ago by Actual Customer

★☆☆☆☆ **Faulty headphones, only worked in one ear**
Crackling in one ear and occasionally can hear clearly, suggestin that there is a loose connection. Read more >
Published 11 hours ago by Actual Customer

FIGURE 31.1

Product Page Optimization

When it comes to product pages, SEO directly affects the amount of traffic the marketplace site generates. With thousands of merchants vying for customer interest, store owners must have quality pages in order to compete with other sellers and draw relevant traffic that converts.

Keep Listing Titles Concise – The ideal length across major marketplace platforms is 50–75 characters for readability search ranking. Incorporate the following four items in any product title:

- Primary keywords
- Audience pain point
- Brand name
- Differentiating product attributes, such as size

Include Benefits Descriptions – Each buyer has a different reason for looking for the same product, so be sure to include multiple benefits in the product description. Also, aligning the primary keywords and long-tail variations with the benefits will boost search engine rankings.

Use Bullet Points – Studies have shown that information presented as a block of text is more difficult to digest than information listed with bullet points. Small headings and bulleted product features will make product descriptions easy to scan and drive conversion.

Use Quality Images – All the effort put into creating excellent titles and product descriptions will be wasted if the product pages do not include quality product images. Many consumers skip the text and browse products based on images alone. Include a minimum of four images from a variety of angles to show the various product features. When applicable, provide a photo showing product dimensions or what comes in the box. Video demonstration of the product in use and a zoom feature on the photos will also motivate consumers to purchase. High-resolution professional images with white backgrounds make the product the focal point on the page while photos shared in product reviews by customers who have purchased the product add authenticity and credibility. Here are some other guidelines for effective product images.

- Plan the image sizes, filters, thumbnails, etc.
- Shoot images with professional lighting.
- Photo editing tools will make post-production easier and deliver a better result.
- Understand the different requirements for category and product pages.
- Optimize the images for (alt tags, page load speeds).

Product Strategies

As marketplaces continue to increase sales and take market share, for CPG and other brands that historically have generated most of their sales through wholesale sales channels and retail stores, omnichannel product planning (and pricing) needs to be at the forefront of strategic and annual planning. To minimize channel conflict and maximize profitable marketplace sales, product differentiation across sales channels is sometimes required. Sellers use other strategies to minimize channel conflict, including good/better/best product strategies, branding, and packaging strategies. Specific to marketplaces, product strategies often include a hybrid account structure where some higher-margin products are sold 3P and lower margin, high unit volume products are sold 1P vendor. Other than the previous product strategies above, marketplace product strategies are generally similar to other sales channels, including new product categories development and line-filling based on competitive analysis and SKU efficiencies analysis. Over time, marketplace product catalogs may become increasingly different from the products sold in other sales channels, such as stores. Product management and marketing strategies should reflect evergreen products that are carried for multiple years and seasons.

31.4 Marketplace Advertising

The biggest challenge every seller faces on a large marketplace is how to stand out from the crowd. A seller without a solid marketing strategy may sink before having an opportunity to swim. Though marketplaces provide automation, almost all sellers integrate 3P marketing automation platforms which provide more control and autonomy. Following are some of the advertising products the major marketplaces offer to the sellers.

Sponsored Products are directly promoted on Amazon and other major marketplaces. Choose which products to advertise, assign keywords, and enter a cost-per-click bid. When a shopper searches for one of those keywords, the ad is eligible for display alongside the search results. A fee is paid only when a shopper clicks on the ad, at which point the shopper is taken to the detail page of that offer.

Sponsored Brands are ads that feature the brand logo, a custom headline, and up to three brand products. These ads appear on search results and help generate recognition for a specific seller and product portfolio. They can be an effective way to reach consumers who are browsing but do not know what they want to buy. These banner ads promote products right on top of search results to make more people aware of the items that the sponsored seller offers.

Coupons allow sellers to create compelling promotions in the form of digital coupons that show up in marketplace search results. Offer discounts appear as either a percentage or set dollar amount and target select customer segments wherever possible.

Promotions Manager has been shown to boost sales and exposure by as much as 10 % over time for sellers who use it consistently. On eBay, the Promotions Manager enables sellers to create compelling offers that not only grab the attention of buyers but also encourage them to spend more. These can be used to promote deals and offer incentives that will reward shoppers for buying more. Promotions can be used to attract more buyers, clear old stock, increase average order size, and even lower shipping costs by bundling more items per order.

Promoted Listings, shown to increase sales by as much as 30% over time, help items stand out among billions of listings and be seen by millions of active buyers. These kinds of ads follow the customer through their buying journey and are prominently placed in search results and product review pages. The advertising fee is paid only when a sale is completed making it a very cost-effective and low-risk strategy.

Performance Ads are Walmart's pay-per-click advertising option that uses an internal relevancy algorithm to determine where and when the ads appear. Unlike Google AdWords, Performance Ads do not rely on keywords but instead work like Amazon ads using product and user data to determine placement.

Native Banner Ads appear at the top of product category pages as customers browse similar products. This method works well for sellers looking to improve brand awareness and recall.

Catapult Ads promote a specific product or category by appearing at the top of the product listing page with the text "Featured Item." Instead of using the internal relevancy engine, these ads rely on product categories and are used to boost sales of a specific high- or low-selling product.

Site Search Feature Ads are meant to promote brand products on a related product page. For instance, if a user clicks on the ad of a certain seller, they go to a page that features all products offered by that seller. This enables shoppers to use filters to narrow their choices. Site Search Ads help drive individual product sales while improving brand awareness and recall.

31.5 Inventory & Order Management

Inventory management, in particular avoiding overselling, is even more important in marketplaces. If a brand is out of stock, it is much easier for a shopper to find another brand's products. Overselling keeps sellers from participating in important marketing programs like Subscribe & Save, negatively impact rank in search results, and can cost a seller the buy box. Many 3P sellers create their product catalogs using Excel inventory files, which marketplaces provide based on product categories, while others use automated product feeds.

For both 3P sellers and 1P Vendors (on Amazon), inventory planning and management can be one of the most time consuming and important seller tasks. Third-party software exists to help sellers forecast demand, prioritize, and allocate inventory. For sellers who use FBA, Amazon also offers multi-channel fulfillment where Amazon fulfills non-Amazon orders too. Most Walmart.com marketplace sellers fulfill themselves rather than using a 3PL. However, as Walmart rolls out its fulfillment service in competition with Amazon's FBA, more sellers will have to manage inventory across multiple shipping locations. Amazon's inventory management tools and reports are among its most mature and include inventory analysis to improve inventory performance and planning—but only for products fulfilled by Amazon.

Traditionally sales order management has four steps: cross-checking the order against the stock on hand, generating and printing picking-packing slips, coordinating with the shipping carrier, and communicating with the customer until the product is delivered. These processes are largely automated on the big marketplaces. A best of class order management system (OMS) centralizes all orders in a single location, making it easier to maintain up-to-the-minute information on stock levels, order status, placement, shipment, and other order related updates to help track orders. By integrating a quality OMS with the marketplace systems, all parties will have a transparent view of stock levels and the customer will have a positive experience.

31.6 Pricing Strategies

Given the ease of online shopping and price aggregator sites that provide side-by-side comparison, developing a winning pricing strategy is complex and critical. If factors like product quality, shipping costs, and delivery times are equal, customers will always purchase the lowest-priced item. Here are some common pricing strategies to stay ahead of the competition.

Cost-plus Pricing – This is one of the safest ways to price products as it ensures an ample profit margin. After adding together the direct material cost, direct labor cost, and overhead costs for a product, add a standard markup percentage. Here is an example:

a) Direct material costs = $10.00
b) Direct labor costs = $2.00
c) Allocated overhead = $2.00
d) Profit margin = 20%

Total cost a+b+c = $14.00, plus a 20% margin would make the sale price $16.80.

Value-based Pricing – Contrary to cost-plus pricing, this strategy considers the perceived value customers associate with the product. This works well for brands that have high emotional connection or where quality is the most important factor affecting the customer's decision.

Dynamic Pricing – This type of pricing requires automation and makes use of data analytics to monitor the competition and arrive at a competitive price. Automation and data intelligence help to bundle similar offers while a customer is buying a product. Although such tools require an upfront investment, the automation substantially reduces the effort spent on pricing tasks.

Competitor-based Pricing – For new sellers who are unsure of the initial value of the product or service, tracking the competition can help to determine the best price point. This strategy is particularly effective when many vendors offer the same goods and services at relatively similar price points.

Target Return Pricing – This strategy functions similarly to a cost-plus model but centers around the desired rate of return on the investment made. This formula is particularly effective if the seller wants to break even. Here the producer looks at the total investment in the development, distribution, and marketing of the product against the expected quantity to be sold to reach the desired ROI.

Target Pricing = Unit Cost + Desired Return x (Invested capital/unit sales)

The only limitation of this method is to accurately project the number of sales when changes can impact the break-even period.

31.7 Shipping & Fulfillment

To thrive and excel in the competitive marketplace, fast, reliable, and affordable fulfillment is an absolute must. Recent advancements in shipping and returns software have reduced the cost of fulfillment automation. The latest innovations are enabling the following processes:

- Intelligent or Smart Order Routing – Based on shipping speeds, delivery fees, warehouse locations, and other factors, each order is sent to the most effective fulfillment partner.

- Automated Inventory Management – This ensures stock levels are always up to date across multiple marketplace locations.

- Automated Shipment Tracking – This automatically marks packages as Shipped once a delivery is initiated and provides the buyer with current delivery information.

Shipping Options

Modern consumers have come to expect a variety of shipping methods and options. Following are several ways to give the customer value and build loyalty.

Free Shipping – Thanks to Amazon, customers now expect marketplace operators to adopt this model. And in fact, free shipping is known to create faster checkouts, better conversions, and stronger loyalty. However, as the name suggests, shipping costs are borne by the seller, a direct cost that can deeply cut the profit margin. A good strategy is to add free shipping only after an order value threshold is reached or for a particular season or sales campaign.

Flat Rate Shipping – This is the next best thing to free shipping. Regardless of the order value or delivery location, the shipping fee remains fixed and customers know what to expect.

Live Rates – Live rates cover the operator's costs and bring in a certain level of transparency for the customers, but they can vary hugely based on delivery location and item weight.

Mixed Strategies – It is not necessary to choose a single strategy without variation. Instead, mixing and matching strategies provide both sellers and operators the opportunity to find the best fit for the business.

Shipping Best Practices

To ensure a smooth customer journey and encourage repeat purchases, it is important to establish standardized shipping practices that customers can rely on.

Diversify your carrier strategy – Fast and reliable fulfillment has become a differentiating factor in the competition for online shoppers. To ensure competitive pricing and fast service, maintain contracts with multiple carriers, and make shipping decisions on an order-by-order basis.

Keep it crystal clear – Nothing beats simplicity, so define shipping and fulfillment guidelines that are easy for the buyer to read and understand. A well-written shipping policy will answer customer questions, build their trust, and boost conversion rates.

Matters of weight – Selling on a marketplace requires efficiency and accuracy. Continuous monitoring of product weights will help to maintain accurate shipping costs, provide customers incremental cost benefits, and encourage them to return for future purchases.

Get the right team – Because shipping is a critical component of the overall customer experience, build a team devoted to enhancing shipping. This team should have complete ownership of the fulfillment process, including examining the current process for efficiency, developing new tactics to improve the system, and even informing customers of shipping promotions like flat rate or free shipping.

Keep customers informed – Completing an online purchase brings excitement and anticipation as the customer anxiously waits for delivery. Sellers can maintain those positive feelings by keeping customers updated about their shipment at each stage. Begin with an email or text confirming receipt of their order, follow up with an estimated delivery date, and include the carrier's tracking number.

31.8 Marketplace Optimization

With marketplaces always evolving, and competition increasing, once launched a seller is constantly optimizing their account. Though launches usually make the most scalable impact, optimization is often quicker and, by combining opportunities, can increase topline and margins by double digits. Optimization opportunities should be quantified and prioritized using marketplace reporting tools and third-party tools.

Like other eCommerce sales channels, optimization opportunities include product, pricing, marketing, and channels, and should take advantage of unique aspects of marketplace selling, such as the Flywheel Effect. Best practices reflect not only looking at current results, but also market share and competitiveness.

For example, a seller should prioritize investment and marketing spend on growth opportunities where they do not already have a dominant market share. If the seller has 50%+ market share on a certain product or category, heavy investment in promotions of that product will only cannibalize the margin from existing customers. Whether for paid advertising, organic search rank, or product page optimization to increase sales conversion, often the place to start is looking at the 80/20s. Identify the 20% of products, categories, or advertising efforts that generate most orders, then focus on optimizing those opportunities. For some products, driving traffic to the product page will provide the greatest boost, while for certain categories increasing sales conversion should be the focus. When many sellers are offering the same products, focus on increasing buy box ownership to limit the ability of others to advertise and to boost sales conversion.

Chapter 21 Key Performance Indicators and Chapter 24 Conversion Rate Optimization provide greater discussion on these topics.

Key Takeaways: Best Practices for Sellers

- For sellers and brands that are well optimized and do not frequently introduce new products, spending more resources on marketplaces makes sense. It also offers cost-efficient, national advertising reach.

- Marketplaces should be an integral part of a brand's financial planning and budgeting, and financial resources should be allocated based on importance and growth opportunities.

- One of the key areas of customer engagement is reviews. Sellers should focus on maintaining positive reviews and ratings on every platform where they sell.

- While the major marketplaces offer the best of the breed advertising products, having 3P marketing automation will always provide more autonomy and control for the seller.

- With consumers having access to price trackers and aggregators, developing a winning pricing strategy is critical to succeeding in the marketplace game.

- Maintain contracts with multiple carriers and make shipping decisions on an order-by-order basis to ensure competitive pricing and fast service. For any optimization effort, the starting point should be the 20% of the products and advertising campaigns that generate the most orders.

Appendix A Vendor List

eCommerce Platforms	Site & Search Navigation
Magento Commerce	Oracle Endeca
VTEX	Solr
Shopify	Lucid Works
Oracle Commerce Cloud	Loop54
SAP Commerce Cloud	Google
commercetools	Nextopia
BigCommerce	Algolia
Salesforce Commerce Cloud	Swift Type

Marketplace Platforms	Order Management
Mirakl	Magento Order Manager
Webkul Marketplace	Manhattan Associates
Unirgy	Oracle Order Management Cloud
VTEX	SAP Order Management
Sharetribe	Salesforce Commerce Cloud Order Management
Arcadier	IBM Sterling
Marketplacer	NetSuite
Izberg	Webgility

Catalog & PIM	Fraud Check
Akeneo	Riskified
Riversand	Simility
Salsify	Signifyd
Stibo Step	Forter
SAP	Sift Science
Agility	Kount
Heilar	Bolt
Informatica	Sift

Tax Automation	Payment Platforms
Avalara	Google Pay
Intuit ProSeries	PayPal
TaxJar	Amazon Pay
Sovos	Apple Pay
Taxify	Venmo
Canopy	Stripe
Macola	Square
Thompson Reuters OneSource	Visa Checkout

Shipping & Fulfillment	Customer Service Platform
Magento Shipping	Magento Order Manager
ShipStation	Zendesk
ShipBob	Salesforce Service Cloud
ShippingEasy	Oracle Service Cloud
Rakuten Super Logistics	Zoho Desk
Fulfillify	FreshDesk
Sellbrite	HappyFox
Ordoro	HubSpot Service Hub

Email Marketing Automation	Digital Ad Management
Marketo	AdRoll
Oracle Marketing Cloud	Criteo
Salesforce Marketing Cloud	Marin
Dotdigital	4C
Klaviyo	Kenshoo
Campaign Monitor	MediaMath
MailChimp	Adobe Advertising Cloud
ConstantContact	Basis

Social Communication	Marketplace Vendor Aggregation
Sprout Social	ChannelAdvisor
Oracle Social Cloud	Mirakl Connect
Buffer	Salsify
Hootsuite	Solid Commerce
Sprinkl	SellerActive
Salesforce Social Cloud	Ecomdash
Falcon.io	ProductsUp
Adobe Social	Cim.bio

Web Analytics	BI & Datawarehouse
Google Analytics	Tableau
Crazy Egg	SAP Analytics
KISSmetrics	Mode Analytics
Adobe Analytics	ReportPlus
Clicky	PowerBI
Open Web Analytics	Terradata
Mint	Cloudera
Clicktale	Marklogic

Appendix A

Retargeting Tools	Web Hosting
Chango	Magento Hosting
Adroll	HostGator
Google Adwords	A2 Hosting
Criteo	Flywheel
Perfect Audience	Bluehost
Retargeter	Rackspace
Rocket Fuel	Hostinger
SiteScout RTB	WP Engine
Stock Images	Video
Unsplash	Vplayed
Pixabay	TVPage
FreePik	90 Seconds
LiquidPixels	Powtoon
ShutterStock	Animaker
Pexels	FirstData
FreeStocks.org	Braintree
Pic	Bluesnap
Product Photography	Pay over time & Subscription
Ortery	Klaviyo
GF Studio	Brex
Lens Flash	Affirm
Pencil One	Bill Me Later
Pow Product Photography	Order Groove
Pixelz	Recurly
Robert Leishman	Bold
Product Photo	PayPal Credit
Amazon Consulting	Live Chat
Toucan Advisors	Drift
FountainheadME	LiveAgent
AMZ Advisors	Intercom
Albert Scott LLC	Live Chat
Eli Commerce	Live Person
Nozani	Snap Engage
Channel Key	Acquire
Orca Pacific	Tawk.to

Appendix B Top Marketplaces & Retailers

Top 100 Marketplaces around the world based on monthly visits

#	Name	Region/ Country	Product Category	Visits/month
1	Amazon	Global	General	5.7B
2	PayPay Mall	Japan	General	2.1B
3	eBay	Global	General	1.6B
4	Mercado Libre	South America	General	661.7M
5	AliExpress	Global	General	639.1M
6	Rakuten	Global	General	621.5M
7	Taobao	China	General	545.2M
8	Walmart.com	USA	General	469.0M
9	JD.com	Global	General	318.2M
10	Etsy	Global	Arts, Crafts & Gifts	266.3M
11	Shopee	Southeast Asia	General	260.3M
12	Target.com	USA	General	258.3M
13	Flipkart	India	General	242.6M
14	Best Buy	USA, Canada, Mexico	Electronics	229.3M
15	Allegro	Poland	General	208.6M
16	Tmall	China	General	202.8M
17	Lazada	Southeast Asia	General	172.7M
18	Americanas	Brazil	General	134.6M
19	Wayfair	North America, Europe	Homewares	125.3M
20	Zalando	Europe	Fashion	119.0M
21	Wish	Global	General	111.6M
22	Coupang	South Korea	General	93.0M
23	trendyol	Turkey	General	82.7M
24	bol.com	Netherlands	General	78.0M
25	n11	Turkey	General	77.9M
26	ASOS	Global	Fashion	76.3M
27	Tokopedia	Indonesia	General	74.2M
28	Cdiscount.com	France	General	68.7M
29	Gmarket	South Korea	General	65.1M
30	Ozon	Russia	General	64.4M
31	Fnac	Europe	General	62.7M
32	OTTO	Germany	General	57.3M
33	Snapdeal	India	General	56.4M
34	Myntra	India	Fashion	48.0M
35	GittiGidiyor	Turkey	General	47.3M
36	eMAG	Eastern Europe	General	43.8M
37	Discogs	Global	Music	43.6M
38	Poshmark	USA	Fashion	41.8M
39	Marktplaats	Netherlands	General	41.8M
40	Jumia	Africa	General	36.9M

41	Casas Bahia	Brazil	General	36.4M
42	Submarino	Brazil	General	33.3M
43	Newegg	USA, Canada	Electronics	32.4M
44	Dafiti	South America	Fashion	30.5M
45	Bandcamp	Global	Music	29.7M
46	Overstock	USA	General	28.2M
47	Souq	Middle East	General	27.9M
48	ManoMano	Europe	Homewares	27.6M
49	Barnes and Noble	USA	Books	26.8M
50	Real.de	Germany	General	26.3M
51	Rue du Commerce	France	General	26.0M
52	Farfetch	Global	Fashion	23.6M
53	Darty	France	General	22.8M
54	Trade Me	New Zealand	General	19.6M
55	La Redoute	France	General	19.4M
56	Sears	USA	General	18.7M
57	Houzz	Global	Homewares	18.6M
58	Extra	Brazil	General	17.0M
59	Lamoda	Russia	Fashion	16.1M
60	Reverb	Global	Musical instruments	15.4M
61	iPrice	Southeast Asia	General	15.3M
62	Linio	South America	General	15.0M
63	Conforama	Europe	Homewares	14.7M
64	G2A.com	Global	Electronics	13.6M
65	AbeBooks	Global	Books	13.2M
66	dba	Denmark	General	11.7M
67	Worten	Europe	General	11.4M
68	Tradera	Sweden	General	11.3M
69	cdon	Scandinavia	General	10.9M
70	GunBroker	USA	Weapons	10.7M
71	Ricardo	Switzerland	General	10.6M
72	Beslist.nl	Netherlands, Belgium	General	10.5M
73	Qoo10	Southeast Asia	General	10.5M
74	Privalia	Brazil, Mexico, Italy, Spain	Fashion	9.8M
75	Zalora	Southeast Asia	Fashion	9.2M
76	Joom	Europe	General	9.1M
77	Wehkamp	Netherlands	General	8.4M
78	notonthehighstreet	UK	Arts, Crafts & Gifts	8.4M
79	Catch.com.au	Australia	General	8.3M
80	digitec	Switzerland	Electronics	8.1M

81	Spartoo	Europe	Fashion	7.9M
82	shopgoodwill.com	USA	General	7.9M
83	Kaspi	Kazakhstan	General	7.3M
84	Fruugo	Global	General	6.9M
85	TheRealReal	USA	Fashion	6.5M
86	Aukro	Czech Republic	General	6.2M
87	The Iconic	Australia, New Zealand	Fashion	6.1M
88	Grailed	USA, Canada	Fashion	6.1M
89	GAME	UK	Electronics	5.8M
90	Depop	Global	Fashion	5.8M
91	Shpock	Europe	General	5.7M
92	Bonanza	Global	General	5.4M
93	Vipshop	China	General	5.2M
94	Galeries Lafayette	France	Fashion	5.1M
95	ePRICE	Italy	General	4.8M
96	Nature & Découvertes	France	Homewares	4.7M
97	Tradesy	USA	General	4.5M
98	Rue La La	USA	Homewares	4.0M
99	BrickLink	USA	Books	3.7M
100	Tophatter	Germany	General	3.5M

Estimated monthly visits for February 2020, from SimilarWeb. Traffic to different domains for the same marketplace (e.g. amazon.com, amazon.co.uk, amazon.de etc.) has been combined.

Top Marketplaces in United States based on monthly visits

#	Name	Product Category	Visits/month
1	Amazon	General	2.3B
2	eBay	General	637.9M
3	Walmart.com	General	446.4M
4	Target.com	General	249.5M
5	Best Buy	Electronics	180.3M
6	Etsy	Arts, Crafts & Gifts	170.3M
7	Wayfair	Homewares	86.7M
8	Rakuten	General	56.7M
9	Poshmark	Fashion	38.3M
10	AliExpress	General	33.4M
11	Overstock	General	26.4M
12	Wish	General	24.8M
13	Barnes and Noble	Books	24.4M
14	Newegg	Electronics	22.8M
15	Sears	General	17.5M
16	PayPay Mall	General	13.7M
17	ASOS	Fashion	13.4M
18	Houzz	Homewares	11.5M
19	GunBroker	Weapons	10.3M
20	Taobao	General	9.7M
21	Reverb	Musical instruments	9.5M
22	Discogs	Music	7.8M
23	Bandcamp	Music	7.7M
24	shopgoodwill.com	General	7.6M
25	TheRealReal	Fashion	5.6M
26	Farfetch	Fashion	5.1M
27	Mercado Libre	General	5.0M
28	AbeBooks	Books	4.6M
29	JD.com	General	3.9M
30	Tradesy	Fashion	3.7M
31	Bonanza	General	3.7M
32	Rue La La	Fashion	3.6M
33	Grailed	Fashion	3.3M
34	Tophatter	General	2.9M
35	Flipkart	General	2.8M
36	Tmall	General	2.6M
37	1stdibs	Arts, Crafts & Gifts	2.4M
38	Shopee	General	2.4M
39	Lazada	General	2.3M
40	Jane	Fashion	2.2M
41	Depop	Fashion	2.1M
42	G2A.com	Electronics	1.9M
43	eCRATER	General	1.4M
44	Myntra	Fashion	1.4M
45	Storenvy	General	1.3M
46	Jet	General	1.2M
47	BrickLink	Toys	1.0M

Glossary

A

A/B Testing – a user experience research methodology consisting of randomized experimentation with two variants to determine which performs better

Aggregator – a software that checks various websites for regular updates and collates the content to be viewed in a unified manner in one desktop application

API – a set of protocols, instructions, and specifications that allows two or more software applications to interact and exchange data; used to integrate third-party data within marketplace systems

Average Order Value (AOV) – the average amount spent in one transaction by a shopper

B

Benchmarking – measuring the quality of a retailer, its business approach, its competitive positioning, and the performance of its brand in the market

Big Box Store – a retail outlet characterized by a large amount of floor space, massive product inventory, low prices, and high sales volume

Bounce Rate – the percentage of the overall site visits in which visitors navigate away from the website without navigating to pages beyond their initial landing page

Bundling – a marketing and selling strategy where several similar products or services are offered as a one package, often at a lower cost than the sum of the individual unit pricing

Buy Online Pickup In-Store (BOPIS) – One of the ways online stores are adding more convenience to purchase, this allows consumers to buy items online and pick it up in-store instead of having it delivered. It is also referred to as click & collect

Buy Online Return In-Store (BORIS) – a reverse logistics method which allows consumers to buy items online and return the items to a brick-and-mortar store

Buyer Persona – a semi-fictional representation or sketch of an ideal prospect which is created based on market research and real customer data

C

Call to Action (CTA) – a device to encourage webpage visitors to take a desired action, such as a buy button or an information collection form

Cart Abandonment – when consumers place items in the virtual cart for purchase but do not complete the transaction

Cascading Style Sheets (CSS) –a style sheet language used in formatting the presentation document or webpage written in the markup language; a cornerstone technology of the world wide web

Chargeback – the return of funds to a cardholder when the transaction is considered fraudulent

Churn Rate – the percentage of customers who cut ties with the company, product, or service

Consumer Packaged Goods (CPG) – products which sell quickly and at a relatively low price, such as food, beverages, clothes, toiletries, and household products

Content Management System (CMS) – a backend interface that simplifies content editing, ex. WordPress

Cost-per-click (CPC) – an advertising model in which the advertiser pays a defined cost to the publisher each time a visitor clicks on the advertisement. See also Pay-Per-Click (PPC)

Cross-Sell – to recommend to an existing customer a product or service which is related to or suited to the customer's previous purchase

Crowdsourcing – a practice of ideas, goods, services, or financing from a loosely-defined, external group of people

Curation – the process of identifying and controlling the products or services offered on a marketplace

Customer Relationship Management (CRM) – the system of managing and monitoring interactions with current, previous, and potential customers, usually through the use of software

D

Digital Rights Management (DRM) – the technologies and processes used by digital publishers and content creators to control sales and licensing of digital content and services

Direct-to-consumer (DTC) – a business model wherein the customer interacts directly with the manufacturer for ordering and fulfillment without the presence of a distributor or retailer

Disintermediation – the removal of intermediary parties, such as wholesalers or distributors, so that customers interact directly with businesses

Dropship – a streamlined logistics method wherein the seller accepts customer orders for product not held in stock; goods are shipped from the manufacturer directly to the end user

E

Endless Aisle – allowing online customers to view and order items which are not stocked in brick-and-mortar stores

Enterprise Resource Planning (ERP) – a software used to integrate and manage varying facets of the business, such as inventory, purchasing, sales, logistics, finance, and marketing

H

Hashtag – to begin a phrase with a hash character (#) in order to group together messages of specific topics

I

Influencer – an industry expert who shares reviews of products and services with their large group active social followers

J

JavaScript – an object-oriented programming language used to enable interactive web pages

K

Keyword – frequently used words or phrases entered into a search engine to find a specific product, service, or topic

L

Landing Page – the webpage to which a user is redirected after clicking a link or button

Liquidity – the reasonable expectation of being able to sell what is listed

Listing Fees – the amount a marketplace charges a seller to list products on the site

Long-tail Keywords – lengthy and specific phrases which yield narrow, precise results

M

Margin – the profit of a sale after deducting the cost of goods

Marketing automation – software platforms which automate repetitive tasks and track performance of multi-channel marketing efforts

Metadata – a descriptive label applied to digital assets to help search engines effectively identify and understand the content

Microsite – A web page or small group of pages contained within a primary website

Monetization – creating a revenue source from a previously non-revenue-generating item, such as selling advertising space on a webpage

N

Network Effect – the increased value of a product or service as the number of users increases

O

Omnichannel Retail – a strategy that seeks to improve customer relationship by providing a unified shopping experience across physical, online, and mobile locations

On-Demand – a revenue model in which customers pay only when resources or services are used, in contrast to a recurring subscription model

Open source – a type of software in which source code is released under a license which grants users the rights to use, study, change, and distribute the software to anyone and for any purpose

Order Management System (OMS) – software that administers all functions of order fulfillment, such as order entry, customer service, marketing, accounting, inventory management, purchasing, and warehouse management

P

Pageview – a metric which measures the number of visits to a webpage

Payment Gateway – a merchant service provided by an eCommerce application service provider that authorizes credit card or direct payments processing for e-businesses, online retailers, and traditional brick-and-mortar retailers

Payment Processor – a company that manages credit and debit transactions by communicating information between the customer's bank and the merchant's bank; also called Payment Service Provider (PSP)

Pay-Per-Click (PPC) – see Cost-Per-Click

PCI DSS – an information security standard for organizations that handle branded credit cards from the major card schemes

Pipeline – The traditional, linear method of conducting business where the product is designed, manufactured, distributed, and sold to the end user

Pop-up Shop – a temporary storefront opened to take advantage of a trend or seasonal demand, usually situated in the high traffic area of a mall

Product information management (PIM) – the process of managing all the information required to market and sell products through distribution channels

R

Reintermediation – the process used by platforms to reintroduce new types of intermediaries into the platform value chain

Reverse Logistics – the process of retrieving returned product from the customer to recapture value or for final disposal

S

Search Engine Marketing (SEM) –techniques used to maximize the visibility of websites in search engine results pages

Search Engine Optimization (SEO) – improving the quality and quantity of traffic to a website or web page from search engines

Service Level Agreement (SLA) –a contract that is agreed upon and signed off between a service provider and customer to define the scope of service and performance standards expected

Sharing Economy – an economic model defined as a peer-to-peer based activity of acquiring, providing, or sharing access to goods and services that is often facilitated by a community-based, online platform

Social Commerce – the process of buying or selling products via social media

Secure Sockets Layer (SSL) – a protocol used for transmitting private documents via the internet

Software as a Service (SaaS) – a software licensing and delivery model in which software is licensed on a subscription basis and is centrally hosted

U

Upsell – to encourage a customer to buy something more expensive than their current consideration

User Experience (UX) – The design, layout, and flow (customer journey) driven by the front end of a system including the practical, experiential, affective, meaningful, and valuable aspects of human and computer interaction

User-generated Content (UGC) – product- or company-related content (review, photo, video, comment) that is created by users and published on digital platforms or social media

Index

Acknowledgements

"It takes a village" is an underestimation for writing a 400+ page book on a complex and evolving topic like marketplaces. It took a global team spread across three continents over a year to complete this book.

Special thanks and kudos go to the core team of Tom Gaydos (CMO), Stephen George (Content Director), and Thiago Cruz (Design Analyst) for staying sane after meeting with me three times a week for year. Without their contributions this book would still be just an outline. For the second half of the year, professional editor Carrie Del Pizzo helped trim our original 150,000 words down to a manageable manuscript. Many a tree owes its life to Carrie.

Innumerable people from McFadyen Digital contributed content in their areas of specialty. This includes Anu Antony, Sandro Batista, Paul Becker, Sushant Chakraborty, Arun Chinnakkaruppan, Ed Coke, Gustavo Fabbro, Shylesh Kurup, Swapna Manjunath, Oommen Ninan, Sudhanshu Rawat, Vincy Sebastian, Lucas Ivan Seidenfus, Pratik Sharma, Padmaraj Subramaniam, and Juby Varghese. These professionals and others eagerly shared their wisdom in diverse domains learned over years of real-world marketplace projects.

Thanks are also due to our clients who entrusted their transformations to McFadyen Digital. Many took risks stepping into projects with new business models and/or new technology. We innovated together and this book contains many of the lessons learned on those pioneering journeys. Transformation is never without challenges, but together we worked through the unexpected and ultimately found solutions.

Ten and fifteen years ago in our early days of custom-building marketplaces, we didn't call them marketplaces, much less have documented marketplace best practices. In 2016 thought leaders Geoffrey G. Parker, Marshall Van Alstyne, and Sangeet Paul Choudary published the Platform Revolution: How Networked Markets are Transforming the Economy—And How to Make Them Work for You. That book defined the platform business model which is the foundation of marketplaces. By standing on the shoulders of these giants we've been able to see best practices for marketplaces.

And finally, this year-long journey couldn't have been undertaken without the support of my loving wife Fran and our children Zoey and Alec. They missed many evenings and weekends with me while I was writing, editing, and rewriting chapters of the book. I'm most thankful for being blessed with such a loving and understanding family.

About McFadyen

McFadyen Digital is a global strategic commerce agency that creates award-winning online marketplace and eCommerce experiences for the world's most prominent brands. Our clients seek to delight their customers with memorable online shopping experiences, and we deliver those results on-time and on budget.

With over two decades of experience with large enterprise commerce projects, our strategy, technology, design, and ongoing innovation services, delivered from our offices in the US, Brazil, and India, provide scalable and repeatable results. During 20 years of global delivery, McFadyen Digital has optimized the quality, cost, and timeframe benefits of on-shore, near-shore, and off-shore team collaboration.

McFadyen's Marketplace Enablement Services take clients from the strategy and discovery phase, through launch, to ongoing optimization and beyond. In addition to the technical implementation, this methodology contains a complete go-to-market engagement strategy that includes audience identification, vendor recruiting and engagement, consumer recruiting and engagement, pilot testing processes and communications, and go-live digital engagement campaigns.

We wrote the book on Marketplace Best Practices because it's what we live every day as we help our retail and B2B clients deliver the scalable marketplaces that their customers demand.

In addition to this book, McFadyen Digital has created thought leadership content such as the Marketplace Maturity Model, available for download at mcfadyen.com/mmm, and the industry's first online marketplace platform vendor comparison, The Marketplace Suite Spot report, available for download at marketplace-suite-spot.com. To learn more please visit us at mcfadyen.com, check out our Ecommerce + Marketplaces Blog at mcfadyen.com/blog, or email us at info@mcfadyen.com.

Made in the USA
Middletown, DE
03 October 2022

11777984R00265